The Christian Handbook of
Abuse, Addiction & Difficult Behaviour

Edited by Brendan Geary
& Jocelyn Bryan

kevin
mayhew

First published in 2008 by
KEVIN MAYHEW LTD
Buxhall, Stowmarket, Suffolk, IP14 3BW
www.kevinmayhew.com

ISBN 978 1 84867 033 4
Catalogue No. 1501111

Cover design by Rob Mortonson
Edited by Delian Bower and Katherine Laidler
Typeset by Richard Weaver

Printed and bound in Great Britain

Contents

To the formation and academic communities of
Cranmer Hall,
Ushaw College and
The Wesley Study Centre

Introduction

Jocelyn Bryan and Brendan Geary

This book is concerned with a range of social issues that any of us could have to deal with in our families, workplaces or churches. By way of illustrating the prominence of these issues, it is worth noting that in the period during which this introduction is being written many of the topics dealt with in this book have been brought to our attention by the media. There have, for example, been reports of child abuse – sexual and physical – that took place in Jersey in the 1980s,[1] as well as the disturbing and shocking story of Josef Fritzl in Austria, who sexually abused his daughter and kept her and three of their children locked in a cellar for 24 years.[2] The growing awareness of this issue and the media's interest mean that it is likely that there could be more of this by the time this book is published. There has been a report on the cost to the NHS of bullying behaviour,[3] as well as a report to the House of Lords on concerns for vulnerable adults,[4] mentioning, among other things, ways in which they are victims of abuse or bullying and harassment. The other subjects covered in this book – partner violence, addictions, workplace violence, difficult people, sexual and internet addiction – also feature regularly in newspaper and media reports.

These subjects may seem far removed from our own worlds. The growing media attention given to these issues, however, also demonstrates that it is becoming increasingly common for our lives to be touched by one or more

1. http://www.bbc.co.uk/insideout/content/articles/2008/02/28/south_west_child_abuse_s13_w2_feature.shtml
2. http://news.bbc.co.uk/1/hi/world/europe/7371959.stm
3. http://news.bbc.co.uk/1/hi/health/4992906.stm
4. http://www.publications.parliament.uk/pa/jt200708/jtselect/jtrights/40/4016.htm#a82

of these areas of concern. Some of these topics may cause a certain revulsion or instinctive negative reaction among many people. Child abuse, for example, is considered so heinous that people convicted of these crimes need to be separated from other prisoners for their own safety. Any of us who have had to deal with a relative suffering from alcohol addiction knows just how difficult and emotionally draining this can be. No matter how well disposed, it is difficult to continue to be compassionate in the face of drunken and abusive behaviour, with the devastating effects this can have on families and relationships, not the least of which is the secretiveness and deception that often accompanies this problem. Similarly, the topics of sexual addiction and the growth of internet pornography can raise alarm bells for us. There has also been concern about the amount of time employees spend online – particularly if this involves accessing pornographic websites.

This book has been written to help anyone who finds themselves having to deal with an issue that challenges their normal management or pastoral skills. This can be in the form of a behaviour which is illegal – like child abuse or harassment – or one that causes difficulties in the workplace or church – for example, people whose behaviour is disruptive or difficult in some way. Some of the subjects here require professional intervention – for example, child abuse or gambling addiction. Others require clear policies and perhaps a change in our own behaviour.

The topics have been chosen because they are difficult, and challenge us as managers, colleagues, health professionals, family members, friends or pastors. Each chapter begins by asking the question, 'What is it?' The authors of each chapter have particular expertise as therapists, psychologists, psychiatrists, lawyers, support workers or managers. This is then followed by a section which asks, 'How should it be dealt with?' The authors have drawn on their clinical or professional experience to make recommendations on how best to handle these difficult issues. In some situations therapeutic treatment can be effective, but this is not the solution in every circumstance. An important feature of this book is the third section of each chapter, where the authors were invited to offer a Christian response or theological reflection related to each subject. Accordingly, this book is designed for people who want to ask what their Christian faith might have to contribute to understanding and responding to the problems presented. The authors were asked to give case examples to illustrate the points they wish to make, and also to provide lists of 'do's' and 'don'ts' in order to make the book as practical as possible. There are references in the footnotes, and the authors have provided three book recommendations and suggested websites which can be accessed for those who want further information.

The first section of the book deals with the topics that have been selected for inclusion. In his chapter on child sexual abuse, Brendan Geary begins by providing important data on abuse and its consequences for victims. He distinguishes between different types of abuse and discusses the current approaches to therapy with sex offenders. He explores issues of relevance to the Churches and presents information about a hopeful development entitled Circles of Support and Accountability. He also looks briefly at the related topic of protection of vulnerable adults.

In her chapter on domestic abuse, Lesley Orr deals squarely with the problems of patriarchy and how some of our assumptions, traditions and social culture support abuse and violence, and do not provide adequate support for women who are vulnerable. She also challenges the Churches about the ways in which they have contributed to abuse through theology and collusion with the dominant culture, which empowers men at the expense of women. The chapter also addresses the issue of re-education. Abusive partners are not top of the priority list for therapeutic investment, and, based on the available research, results in terms of behaviour and attitude change are not encouraging. This issue is clearly a challenge to our society and our Churches.

There are three chapters dealing with addictive behaviours. In the chapter on alcohol and other addictions, Chris Cook combines his experience as a psychiatrist specialising in addictions with his training as a theologian and his vocation as a priest in the Church of England to help us to understand addictive behaviour. His chapter deals with alcohol in particular, but also pays attention to addiction to other substances. He presents current thinking on treatment and offers a theological reflection on how we understand this difficult problem.

Jim Walsh, in the second chapter related to addictions, makes use of his extensive experience of working with pathological gamblers to present information on this subject. This chapter is largely based on American research; however, this is particularly useful from the British point of view as a result of the changes to gambling legislation in the United Kingdom and the likely effects this will have. He also challenges our society from a Christian perspective as we all benefit indirectly from gambling through taxation revenues.

Mark Brouwer, a minister and therapist, and Mark Laaser, a psychologist and author, write on the disturbing area of sexual addiction and internet pornography. The internet has led to an explosion of websites related to sexual material, as well as providing the means for abusers to make contact with victims and for child pornography to be distributed. Mark Brouwer and Mark Laaser concentrate on adult pornography and the problems experienced by those whose addictive behaviour is sexual in nature.

There are three chapters dealing with a range of difficult behaviours. In the first of these Jocelyn Bryan looks at a group of people who may not break laws, threaten violence or become involved with the police or other statutory services. The focus of her chapter is on those who may be called 'difficult people' or 'troublesome personalities'. As well as describing various types of difficult people, Jocelyn takes the discussion a step further by asking what these people have in common. She suggests that all of them are dealing with aggression in maladaptive ways: by being aggressive, avoidant or passive-aggressive. She focuses on the need for a Christian response which does not mean allowing disruption and abuse of other workers or volunteers to happen in the name of being kind and compassionate.

Brendan Geary and Edmund Montgomery have written on the issue of bullying and harassment. Childhood and school bullying is now being given more time, resources and attention. This chapter, however, focuses on adult bullying in the workplace and in the Church. There is also a helpful section on the current legal position in the United Kingdom. The authors present current research finding on bullies, victims and bystanders. They avoid simplistic solutions, recognising that intervention is not a simple matter for those who are victims or witnesses.

Mike Fitzsimons is a Catholic priest and former youth and community worker, with experience of working with members of society who are prone to violent and aggressive behaviour. In the last chapter in this section he addresses the issue of violence in the workplace. This is an area of growing concern not only for police and prison officers but also for nurses, clergy, voluntary sector workers and others. He presents different ways of understanding violent behaviour and offers practical and sensible advice about how to respond in a potentially violent situation. Needless to say, it would be wise to follow this up with training, as reading a chapter will not provide all that is necessary in a difficult situation.

The second section of the book takes a more thematic approach. This section will be of interest not only to managers and religious leaders but also to people involved in courses in practical theology or ministry, where the three issues of theological reflection, use of social science research and appropriate care of self come together. Alison Moore, from her vantage point of caring for ministers and their families, offers a practical and insightful chapter on caring for self, dealing squarely with the Christian attitude of putting the needs of others first. Alison shows that we cannot care adequately for others if we are not healthy ourselves. Her chapter is practical and clear, and will be an invaluable aid to individuals and to those who train people for pressurised jobs – especially those dealing with the public – and ministry.

Alan Bartlett, a lecturer and Church of England minister, begins his chapter on theological reflection by asking the question, 'What added value is theology bringing to this conversation?' In accessible and engaging language, he invites the reader to use the lens of theology to explore the issues that have been presented in this book. He refers to the pastoral cycle of ongoing experience and reflection, to show how the process of practical theology can lead to more informed, enlightened and compassionate action.

The final chapter, by Jocelyn Bryan and Brendan Geary, endeavours to gather together some of the themes that have emerged in previous chapters from the perspective of psychology. Many of the topics relate to violence, emotion regulation, self-esteem, boundaries, sexual differences, and dysfunctional relationship patterns. Hopefully this will present an overview and a framework to understand better these patterns of behaviour.

The authors who have contributed to this book come from both sides of the Atlantic and from Catholic, Anglican, Methodist and reformed traditions. Male and female, married and celibate, ordained and lay, we hope that this range of backgrounds brings a variety of perspectives and experiences to our task. The authors have backgrounds in psychology, counselling, social work, teaching, theology and ministry to varying degrees. We hope that the result demonstrates the value of working in an ecumenical and interdisciplinary context.

This book has been a labour of love, as the authors are all passionately involved with their subjects as teachers, therapists or practitioners. We thank them for their cooperation in putting this book together. We are grateful to our colleagues and families who have put up with discussions of what one of our friends calls 'grisly topics' as we have worked to bring this to completion. We also would like to thank Delian Bower, the editor, for his patience and assistance.

Pentecost Sunday 2008

Part I

Child Sexual Abuse

——— Brendan Geary ———

Child abuse arouses fear, disgust, anger and contempt. It is a disturbing subject about which it is difficult, if not impossible, to remain dispassionate. Researchers suggest that at some point during their childhood about one in three girls and possibly one in four boys are victims of some kind of inappropriate sexual behaviour ranging from talk about sex (or sexualised talk), through inappropriate touching, to intrusive sexual acts. Violent sexual acts on children involving penetration are not the norm. It would appear that the more intrusive the violation, the younger the age, and the more frequent the abuse, the more damage that tends to be done. It has also been shown that abuse committed by trusted family members or friends tends to leave deeper psychological scars. The high prevalence rates mean that, knowingly or not, many of us will have contact with someone who, at some time during their life, has suffered from abuse.

John's story

> John was a young, personable, engaging primary school teacher. He was enthusiastic, related well with pupils, staff and parents, and was liked and appreciated by the head teacher at the Church school where he taught. John's easy manner and willingness to work outside school hours on sports and social events meant he was trusted and held in high regard. He would stay with the pupils during breaks, take them for football on Saturdays, and direct school shows. Over time he got to know the parents, who invited him to family events and gratefully accepted his offers to babysit, especially for the 10–12-year-old

> boys with whom he appeared to have a particular rapport. This impressive facade came crashing down when one of the students let it be known that John had been touching him inappropriately after school when he was 'coaching' him in maths. After the first allegation the floodgates burst; five more students began to tell their stories, and John eventually pleaded guilty to 23 cases of sexual assault.

While John's story might not make the national headlines, it is probably more familiar to people who work in the area of sexual abuse than the more lurid, high-profile cases of child rape and assault that are presented to readers in the headlines of national newspapers. The Soham murder case and the story from Newcastle upon Tyne of the abuser who lifted a 6-year-old girl from her bath, abused her and then dumped her naked in the middle of the road in the snow[1] are highly charged, but unrepresentative of the majority of cases of sexual abuse. The churches have not been exempt from this subject: the exposure of cases of paedophilia and ephebophilia, and even rape, has led to changes in the canon law of the Catholic Church,[2] the setting up of the Nolan Commission[3] in the Catholic Church in England and Wales, and an independent review to uncover historic cases of sexual abuse in the Church of England.[4]

This chapter will begin by exploring what is meant by abuse and will then describe briefly the effects of abuse on victims. There will then be sections on the different types of child abuse, with examples from clinical experience. A discussion of approaches to treatment will be offered, followed by a section on the Churches and abuse, and a reflection from a Christian perspective.

1. Hill, A. (7 July 2007). 'Constant danger', *The Observer*, pp. 20–21.
2. *On More Grave Delicts Reserved* (Vatican City, 2001).
3. Catholic Bishops' Conference of England and Wales (2001). *A Programme for Action: Final report of the independent review of child protection in the Catholic Church in England and Wales* (London).
4. Butt, R. (22 October 2007). 'Church pledges to root out decades-old child abuse cases', *The Guardian*.

What is child sexual abuse?

It is important to define what is meant by sexual abuse. The National Society for the Prevention of Cruelty to Children (NSPCC) offers the following definition:

> Sexual abuse occurs when an adult exploits their power, authority or position and uses a child sexually to gratify their own needs.[1]

A sex offender is someone who engages in sexual behaviours that are considered illegal. This is important, as laws regarding age of consent vary in different countries and may be different for boys and girls. Researchers, as a rule of thumb, will use 16 as a cut-off point, with the perpetrator being at least five years older than the victim. It is important to bear in mind that child sexual abuse involves touching and non-touching behaviours. Showing pornography to a child, exposing genitals, watching a child undress or use the bathroom, or initiating an unwelcome conversation about sexual development or adult sexual topics also constitute abuse, as they invade the private world of the child.

Statistics

Statistical data are a prerequisite of serious study in any area, particularly when it can have an effect on public policy and law. Having said that, it is particularly difficult to obtain reliable data where child abuse is concerned. Authors agree that most crimes go unreported, and victim reports, for various reasons, may not be as objective and reliable as a researcher would like. Despite their limitations, statistics can be instructive.

David Finkelhor conducted a national survey in the United States which suggested that approximately 27% in their sample of 1,481 women and 16% of their sample of 1,145 men reported an experience of sexual abuse from their childhood.[2] Until recently, it was accepted that women were

1. NSPCC (2005). *Keeping Children Safe: A child protection awareness programme.*
2. Finkelhor, D., Hotaling, G., Lewis, I.A., and Smith, C. (1990). 'Sexual abuse in a national sample of men and women: Prevalence, characteristics and risk factors', *Child Abuse and Neglect,* 14, 19–28.

perhaps three times more likely to have been victims of sexual abuse than men. However, recent research suggests that there are more male victims than was previously thought. Males are more reluctant to report abuse than females, and this may contribute to the under-reporting of these offences. The recent reports of sexual abuse in the Catholic Church in the United States, Ireland, England, and other English-speaking countries, appears mostly to have involved male victims. Given the reluctance of boys and men to report abuse, one wonders if the abuse would ever have been reported were it not for the interest of the media and the support of sympathetic media personalities and counsellors.

Freeman-Longo and Blanchard[1] offer some important and provocative statistics from the United States:

- 20% of children risk being victims of abuse before their eighteenth birthday.
- As many as 17% of men in the United States are prepared to admit to having sexually abused a child.
- 90% of sex abuse cases do not go to trial.

Statistics like these led the American Medical Association (AMA) to describe sexual assault as a 'silent-violent epidemic'.[2] The Home Office in the United Kingdom reported that in the period 2006–2007 there were 57,542 recorded sexual offences. Interestingly, this represented a decrease from the previous four years.[3] The NSPCC offers the following statistics:

- More than 25% of all rapes recorded by the police are committed against children under 16 years of age.
- 1% of children experienced sexual abuse by a parent or carer and another 3% by another relative during childhood. 11% of children experience sexual abuse by people known but unrelated

1. Freeman-Longo, R. and Blanchard, G. (1998). *Sexual Abuse in America* (Vermont: Safer Society Press).
2. American Medical Association. 'Sexual assault in America' (Press release, 6 November 1995) quoted in Freeman-Longo, R. and Blanchard, G. (1998). *Sexual Abuse in America* (Vermont: Safer Society Press).
3. http://www.homeoffice.gov.uk/rds/pdfs07/recorded-crime-2002-2007.xls

to them. 5% of children experience sexual abuse by an adult stranger or someone they have just met.

- Three-quarters of sexually abused children do not tell anyone about their abuse at the time, and around a third still have not told anyone about their experience(s) by early adulthood.[1]

It appears that the number of people convicted or cautioned for offences related to internet child pornography quadrupled between 2001 and 2003, and that the cost of child abuse, mostly dealing with the consequences rather than focusing on prevention, is in the region of one billion pounds a year.[2]

Effects of abuse

One of the consequences of media interest in sexual abuse has been an increase in the study of the effects of abuse. While some children and adults appear to be able to recover more quickly than others, not everyone shares the same psychological resiliency or capacity to recover from traumatic events in a robust way. We do know that many victims have suffered serious consequences as a result of abuse. Victims of sexual abuse often display a higher incidence of psychological problems and difficulties in social and interpersonal functioning. They can have difficulties in trusting others and often have low self-esteem, as well as feelings of powerlessness and alienation from themselves and others. One victim who was abused by her father wrote as follows about her experience:

> I was robbed of my childhood, my innocence, my ownership of my own body, and my sexuality. I withered away. Not all at once, but in one way or another, piece by piece, and finally my whole person, my body, and my soul were taken away from me.[3]

1. Key facts and figures about child abuse and the NSPCC, http://www.nspcc.org.uk (retrieved 21 November 2007).
2. http://www.politics.co.uk/issue-briefs/domestic-policy/children/child-abuse (retrieved 21 November 2007).
3. McGlone, G.J., Shrader, M, and Delgatto, L. (2003). *Creating Safe and Sacred Places: Identifying, preventing, and healing sexual abuse* (Minnesota: Saint Mary's Press), p. 44.

Two large studies from California and Canada present a convincing picture of the devastating effects of abuse on children. In the Californian study[1] it was found that victims of sexual abuse were two and a half to four times more likely to suffer mental health problems than those who had not been abused. The following problems were mentioned in the report: drug abuse or dependence, major depressive disorder and manic episodes, phobia, panic and obsessive-compulsive disorder. There appeared to be higher levels of mental illness among women than men. The study concluded that people who have experienced abuse in childhood (under 16 years of age) have significantly higher levels of mental illness than non-abused individuals.

A group of Canadian researchers[2] investigated physical and sexual abuse and reported similar findings. They also found that the men who had been sexually abused had a higher incidence of disorders than men who had been physically abused. This confirms our sense that sexual abuse is more damaging than physical abuse. It appears that a history of physical or sexual abuse increases the possibility of mental illness later in life, and this is stronger for women than for men.

Sexual abuse can also manifest itself behaviourally and can be seen in increased aggression or avoidance/dependency, substance abuse, impulsivity or delinquency. Recent research also suggests that early experiences of abuse may have permanent effects on the structure of the brain.[3]

Consequences for victims

Robert Freeman-Longo and Geral Blanchard write that 81% of sex addicts report that they had been abused as children.[4] They also report an estimate that a high percentage of men and women involved in prostitution were victims of incest, physical abuse or sexual abuse. They lament that a consequence of prostitution is often arrest and involvement in the

1. Burnam, Audrey M., Stein, Judith A., Golding, Jacqueline M., Siegal, Judith M., Sorenson, Susan B., Forsythe, Alan B., and Telles, Cynthia A. (1988). 'Sexual assault and mental disorders in a community population', *Journal of Consulting and Clinical Psychology,* 56, 843–850.
2. MacMillan, H. L., Fleming, J. E., Streiner, D. L., Lin, E., Boyle, M. H., Jamieson, E., Duku, E. K., Walsh, C. A., Wong, M. Y. Y. and Beardslee, W. R. (2001). 'Childhood abuse and lifetime psychopathology in a community sample', *American Journal of Psychiatry,* 158 (11), 1878–1883.
3. Teicher, M. H. (2002). 'The neurobiology of child abuse', *Scientific American,* March, 68–75.
4. Freeman-Longo, R. and Blanchard, G. (1998). *Sexual Abuse in America* (Vermont: Safer Society Press).

criminal system. This seldom leads to therapeutic help to deal with the abuse that led these people to prostitution in the first place, but may in fact reinforce feelings of anger, bitterness, victimisation and hopelessness. They also report statistics suggesting that many adolescent girls who become pregnant have either been abused in the past or are victims of abuse when they become pregnant.

It is also recognised that a number of men and women who sexually abuse others were victims of sexual abuse themselves. While it is noted that not every person who has been abused becomes an abuser, it would appear that up to one third of those who are abused later behave in this way themselves. Gerard McGlone, a Jesuit priest and clinical psychologist, alerts us to the need to be careful not to equate a history of abuse with becoming an abuser. In his study of sex-offending and non-offending Catholic priests, he found that 19% of priests who had not offended against children said that they had been abused in their childhood. However, when asked, they said that they did not go on to become offenders themselves.[1]

The circles of damage perpetrated by sexual abusers radiate beyond the individual victims. Many perpetrators are themselves affected by their behaviour. While they have a powerful range of ways of justifying the abuse, the fact that they are secretive, manipulative, threatening and/or cunning demonstrates clearly enough their knowledge that what they are doing is wrong. Many perpetrators express relief once they are caught and have the opportunity for treatment. One recovering abuser wrote:

> Twenty years ago I was a respected member of my community, publisher of our local paper, and a sexual abuser. Being arrested was the best thing that could have happened to me. I was lucky to get treatment . . . and it worked. I have now been back in society for nearly 10 years and have not abused again. I have been given a second chance and I will not throw that away.[2]

1. McGlone, G. J., SJ. (2001). 'Sexually offending and non-offending Roman Catholic priests: Characterization and analysis.' Unpublished doctoral dissertation, California School of Professional Psychology, Alliant University, San Diego.

2. Freeman-Longo, R. and Blanchard, G. (1998). *Sexual Abuse in America* (Vermont: Safer Society Press) p. 5.

Communities also suffer: parishes, religious communities, social and neighbourhood networks, families, schools, businesses. What is the appropriate response when a former trusted employee has been charged, arrested and/or found guilty of child abuse? How should you respond if an employee has been using a work computer to download child pornography? It is easy to understand how a concerned employer, priest or co-worker might want to terminate the contract of an employee in order to protect children as well as the good name of the school, parish or business. However, the problems of unemployment will only exacerbate the stress related to discovery and involvement in the legal and criminal justice systems. There are no easy answers. The number of victims of sexual abuse extends far beyond the individual who is assaulted.

Sexual abuse and the abusers

It may be instructive to take a moment to think about what kind of person comes to mind when the phrase 'child abuser' is used. It would be surprising if our mental image was not influenced by media reports of socially inept, unattractive, devious, unhappy, aggressive, predatory, manipulative white men. Many people still have the 'stranger-danger' rhyme ringing in their heads. The reality is somewhat more complex. The most surprising thing about sex offenders is how ordinary they are. Men and women from all social classes and walks of life are found among sex offenders. While offenders are mostly men, there is a growing awareness of women who also abuse. In the autumn of 2007 a 44-year-old female probation officer pleaded guilty to two charges of engaging with sexual activity with a child (15-year-old boy),[1] and a female tennis coach was convicted of sexual activity with a 13-year-old girl.[2]

These two cases illustrate the fact that child molesters tend to be family members or people in positions of responsibility or trust (priests, teachers, probation officers, clergy). They seldom use force or aggression. It has been noted that they often use what are known as 'cognitive distortions' to

1. Ahmed, M. (30 October 2007). 'Truant officer "broke one of last taboos" by having sex with errant pupil', *The Times*, p. 15.
2. Heffernan, C. (3 November 2007). 'Tennis coach jailed for sex acts with "infatuated" girl', *The Guardian*, p. 13.

justify their behaviour. Cognitive distortions are distorted ways of thinking that help child molesters to excuse, minimise, rationalise or deny their abusive behaviour. The following examples will help to illustrate this kind of distorted thinking:

- I was showing the child affection.
- The child came on to me. I didn't initiate this.
- He never told me to stop.
- I was not given any sex education and I did not want this child to grow up ignorant like me.
- She knows I did this because I love her.

These 'cognitions' (ways of thinking) enable the offenders to commit the offence without experiencing the anxiety, shame or guilt that would normally accompany these actions. One of the problems with presenting information about child molesters is that almost all of our information comes from people who have been involved in the criminal justice system. We know little about people who are attracted to children but who have never acted on their desires.

Libby Purves presents a sympathetic portrait of this kind of person in her novel *More Lives Than One*. The novel focuses on Kit Milcourt, an inspirational teacher who is falsely accused of sexual abuse of a female pupil while on a school trip to Venice. Before he is told that the girl has retracted her accusation, Kit tells his wife that he could not have been guilty of abuse of a girl as he was attracted to boys. The story continues with Kit saying:

> If the human creature you instinctively desire is a boy of eleven, you do not deserve to live. Anybody can tell you that. I agree . . . I don't deserve to live. But here I am. A paedophile, what they call a fixated preferential paedophile, and not even a sensible one. Sensible ones jump off high buildings or drive into trees as soon as they understand what they are.[1]

1. Purves, L. (1998). *More Lives Than One* (London: Hodder & Stoughton), p. 183.

Libby Purves captures the anguish, self-hatred and fear of men who find themselves attracted to children but who manage never to act on their desires. Kit's wife Anna searches her local library for information to help her to understand. She finds plenty on criminology, psychology and approaches to treatment, but, Libby Purves continues:

> Through tears of fear and indignation she eventually concluded there was no way through this jungle which could lead her to the Kit she knew. Why did nobody write about non-offenders? Why was there no literature about the contained, the reluctant, the horrified paedophile? What the modern age needed, she thought savagely as she put the last book back, was a really good textbook on 'How to be repressed.'[1]

Libby Purves' novel is a salutary reminder that not every person with paedophilic desires necessarily acts on them, and that these people deserve understanding and help. How do you ask for help if your sexual desires are both abhorrent to society and, by definition, criminal?

There are a number of issues to bear in mind when trying to understand child molesters:

- Is the person attracted to boys, girls or both?
- What age range is the molester attracted to/involved with?
- Has violence or aggression been a part of the abusive behaviour?
- Does the abuser have an interest in adult sexual relations or is he/she only interested in children?
- Is the abuse restricted to family members or is the focus of desire and abuse children who are not related to the abuser?

Bearing in mind what has been written above, it is possible to consider three broad types of offenders: paedophiles, familial offenders and ephebophiles. It is important to note, however, that no system of categorisation

1. Purves, L. (1998). *More Lives Than One* (London: Hodder & Stoughton), p. 214.

adequately accounts for the extraordinary range of deviant sexual interests and behaviour. This categorisation is broadly useful but also limited.

Paedophilia

Mental Health professionals make use of the *Diagnostic and Statistical Manual of Mental Disorders,* currently in its fourth edition, which is commonly known as the DSM-IV.[1] This provides criteria for a range of psychiatric disorders, and is often a useful starting point for discussion of a mental health problem. The criteria for paedophilia are as follows:

- Over at least six months, recurrent, intense sexually arousing fantasies, sexual urges, or behaviours involving sexual activity with a prepubescent child or children (generally 13 years or younger).
- The fantasies, sexual urges, or behaviours cause clinically significant distress or impairment in social, occupational, or other areas of functioning.

While these criteria are useful they are not without difficulties when it comes to providing a clinical diagnosis. It is also evident that the word paedophile is often used incorrectly in the media, as it is frequently used to describe any sexual behaviour involving an under-age child or adolescent. The word paedophilia comes from the Greek words for 'child' and 'love'. In some ways it is a misnomer, as the behaviour we are describing is not about love, but about abuse, power and control. Bill Marshall prefers to use the term 'child molester'. This focuses on the behaviour and does not depend on strict adherence to the criteria described above. The term 'paedophilia' will continue to be used for the moment in order to distinguish this group (who are sexually interested in prepubescent children to whom they are not related) from other groups.

Some paedophiles are attracted only to children. These are called 'exclusive type'. Others are attracted to adult men or women as well as children. These are known as 'non-exclusive type'. The key feature for a diagnosis of

1. American Psychiatric Association (1994). *Diagnostic and Statistical Manual of Mental Disorders* (4th edition) (Washington, DC: Author).

paedophilia is an attraction to children who do not have the visible characteristics related to puberty. In reality, this often involves children who are 14 years of age and younger. 'Exclusive type' paedophiles are often attracted to children in a specific age range – for example, 10–12, as was the case with John, whose story was presented at the beginning of this chapter. It appears that those attracted to females are often attracted to 8–10-year-olds, and that those attracted to males are attracted to slightly older children.[1] Some paedophiles, like John, have a preferential erotic attraction to children, which is 'fixated' – that is, it is as if this attraction is hard-wired into the brain. There are other child abusers who are deemed to have 'regressed' from a normal interest in adult partners. The word 'regressed' in this context suggests that the person is functioning emotionally and sexually at an age range that is less than his or her biological age – for example, a 30-year-old who is relating emotionally as a child or adolescent. Those who are fixated can have very high numbers of victims, often more than 100. John J. Geoghan, the former priest whose exposure as a child molester led to the sex abuse crisis in Boston in 2002 which then spread throughout the United States, was accused of abusing an estimated 200 children.[2]

Those who are regressed tend to have fewer victims, as their sexual behaviour is often related to experiences of stress, and depends on situation or opportunity, whereas the fixated offender will often seek out opportunities and groom their victims over a period of time. This can be seen, for example, in the film *The Woodsman*, where both the main character (played by Kevin Bacon) and a subsidiary character are seen to groom potential victims by gradually getting to know them, building confidence, and showing interest, generosity and affection. It is also evident that they have a knack of choosing children who need or are starved of affection, or who have low self-esteem.

John, who was described at the beginning of this chapter, was given the clinical diagnosis of paedophilia. He had an older brother, a younger sister

1. American Psychiatric Association (1994). *Diagnostic and Statistical Manual of Mental Disorders* (4th edition) (Washington, DC: Author).
2. Boston Globe Investigative Staff (2002). *Betrayal: The crisis in the Catholic Church* (Boston: Little, Brown and Company).

and, after his mother's second marriage, a younger stepbrother. His father was in the armed forces and his family split up while his father was serving in Northern Ireland. His older brother, Phil, who is married with two children, was also convicted of sex abuse with a young girl. John admitted that when he was an adolescent he abused his own younger stepbrother, who was 6 at the time. In attempting to understand the factors that may have contributed to his deviant interest, John mentioned that during his childhood his father would sometimes rent a cottage in the country for himself and his brother. They often slept in one room, his father in a double bed and John and his brother in bunk beds. It was quite common for them to be naked together, which John found embarrassing. His father would share his pornographic magazines with his sons. This began when John was about 8 years of age and his brother a little older.

It is difficult to be exact in explaining the reasons for someone's deviant sexual interest; however, the fact that his brother also abused a child suggests the possibility of a genetic influence. A number of psychologists have also observed that if a child is exposed to inappropriate sexual activity or material, this can affect normal sexual development, especially around 8 years of age. Sex offenders often come from a disturbed family background, and difficulties in early attachment have been shown to be a feature of child molesters. John's family was disrupted due to his father's service in the army, so this could have been a contributing factor.

John reported that he felt like a child among adults and was more secure in the company of children. While he was outgoing and socially attractive, he felt like an imposter and inept with adults, had low self-esteem and had never attempted to have a girlfriend. While he did not complain of loneliness, this is often a feature of child molesters. He genuinely believed that the boys he molested were his friends, and, after his arrest, was shocked when the victim statements were read to him and he became aware of the pain he had inflicted on these children.

Familial sexual abuse

A useful (but not absolutely clear) distinction can be made between those who abuse children outside their own families and those who abuse family members. Within this category it is important to distinguish between blood relatives (fathers, brothers, uncles, aunts) and relatives by marriage (stepfathers, uncles, aunts). While the word incest is commonly used, 'familial offenders' is a more accurate descriptor. In situations where fathers abuse their own daughters, it has been suggested that this may be as a result of the mother/wife losing interest in sexual relations with her husband, who then turns to his adolescent daughter to have his sexual needs met. The daughter may remind the father of his wife when she was younger. In other situations, the perpetrator may be experiencing stress, and the combination of loneliness, attractiveness of the victim, power imbalance in the relationship and poor self-esteem may combine and lead to sexual abuse. It is not uncommon for alcohol to be a contributory factor as it leads to people losing the inhibitions that normally put constraints on behaviour that they know to be wrong or could lead to personal embarrassment.

It should be made absolutely clear that offering an explanation for familial abuse does not mean it is being condoned. Men who experience difficulties in their sexual relationships with their partners have no right to abuse or impose on their daughters or stepdaughters in order to attempt to have their own needs met. The following examples give some idea of the range of situations that fall into this category.

- Mike was a hard-working construction contractor who was divorced and recently remarried to a woman who had a daughter from a previous marriage. Mike was often under stress. He drank heavily and had been unfaithful to his second wife. Mike woke up one day with a heavy hangover and was confronted by his stepdaughter who accused him of coming into her room the previous night and touching her inappropriately. This had happened on two occasions. Mike claimed to have no memory of the event.

- David had five children, the eldest of whom was his 15-year-old daughter. His wife had died and he was left to bring up the children himself. Dave had had an abusive childhood. He was often beaten by his father, belittled, deprived of food and appropriate clothing, and kept away from school. He could not read and write. He was brought up on a farm, was isolated from other children, and was often locked out at night and had to sleep in the barn. He had a profound lack of self-esteem and little self-confidence. After his wife died he relied on his daughter not only for practicalities but also for bringing up the younger children. At some point she became his sexual partner.

- Darryl was introduced to sex by his aunt when he was 12. It was not a positive experience, but he was not able to resist, and felt both ashamed and afraid to tell his mother. As an adult, he abused his own daughter.

It is difficult to find common threads in these stories: some had been abused in their own childhoods, others not; some used alcohol, others did not; some had poor self-esteem, others did not; some had adult sexual partners available, others did not. In so far as anything is common to this group, it appears that they have significantly fewer victims than men diagnosed as paedophiles. It should be said that there are some men who are paedophiles who marry in order to come closer to victims, while others may have paedophilic interest and take advantage of family members to fulfil their desires. This may have been the case with John, who abused his own stepbrother.

Ephebophiles

The word 'ephebophile' comes from the two Greek words, 'Ephebos' meaning adolescent, and 'philia' meaning love. This is not a diagnostic term, but is used to describe adults who become sexually involved with adolescents in the 14–18 age range. As with paedophiles, they fall into two categories: those who are fixated and those who are regressed. The following two examples may help to illustrate the difference:

- Joe was a heating engineer in his mid-40s. He was shy, physically awkward, not particularly attractive, lacked social skills and had limited interests. He was arrested with a group of other men for making pornographic videos with adolescent boys. It was then discovered that he had visited countries in South East Asia on holiday where he spent time with adolescent boy prostitutes. While able to be sexually aroused by adult men, his preference was for adolescent males.

- Frank is an Anglican priest in his mid-30s. He is enthusiastic, generous, pastorally sensitive, reliable. He runs a young adult group in his parish which attracts young people in mid to late adolescence. One young man became close to him and began to talk about his difficult family situation. On one occasion he stayed behind after a meeting at Frank's house. He was clearly distressed and Frank gave him a hug. Somewhere in the embrace the hug became stimulating and led to a sexual encounter.

These two examples are very different. Joe was predatory and exploited vulnerable young men for his own sexual gratification. Frank is probably psychosexually immature, and possibly has never come to terms with his own homosexuality. The combination of affection, dependence and attraction led to a sexual relationship. Frank's sexual awakening occurred in a situation where boundaries were not respected and a young man's trust was abused. As many as 80% of Catholic priest offenders may fall into this second category, although this has been questioned in recent reviews, with one author suggesting a figure of 57%.[1] From a psychological perspective they tend to have significantly fewer victims and are less fixated than paedophiles.[2]

It is not uncommon to hear stories of high-school teachers (male and female) who become sexually involved with adolescents whom they are teaching. Whether or not the victim is under the age of consent, the behaviour constitutes a breach of trust and abuse where there is an

1. McGlone, G.J. (2003). 'Prevalence and incidence of Roman Catholic clerical sex offenders', *Sexual Addiction & Compulsivity*, 10, 2–3, 111–121.
2. Songy, D.G. (2003). 'Psychological and spiritual treatment of Roman Catholic clerical sex offenders', *Sexual Addiction & Compulsivity*, 10, 2–3, 123–138.

imbalance of power in the relationship. Problems can also occur in other situations as a result of relationships formed over the internet. Without excusing them, there are men who have found themselves involved in relationships with adolescents who might never have done so before the availability of internet chat rooms. The young people themselves, of course, are often victims of exploitation and deception in these relationships.

As mentioned earlier, the age of consent varies from country to country. Carol Sarler, a journalist, commenting on the suggestion of Terry Grange, Chief Constable of Dyfed-Powys in Wales, that we need greater clarity in the labelling of sex offenders, wrote:

> We cannot agree between one border and the next at what age a boy or girl is emotionally developed enough to give consent: Malta and The Netherlands think 12, Canada and Italy weigh in at 14, cautious Greece holds out for 15 and the good burghers of Iceland go as high as 17 . . . Quite why it is 16 in the United Kingdom is not clear.[1]

It is not abnormal to find a physically mature adolescent attractive, as advertisers who make use of models who look younger than their age know only too well. Our society, however, makes a judgement about the ability of young people to make an emotionally mature decision regarding their readiness for sexual relations. We also know that many adolescents start having sex at a relatively young age. However, there is a difference between sexual experimentation with someone of the same age, and becoming involved with a person who is more than five years older (speaking of adolescents). Sexual involvement of an adult with an adolescent is considered sexual abuse as our society concludes that young people under 16 (or whatever the age of consent is) still need the protection of the law.

1. *The Times* (20 November 2006).

How should it be dealt with?

Can it be treated?

Society's main interest in the treatment of sex offenders is in creating a safer society to protect past and potential victims. Research has focused on what factors, if any, are amenable to treatment. Researchers and those involved in the treatment of offenders consider static and dynamic risk factors separately. Static factors, as the word suggests, are those that cannot be changed – for example, age, type of victim, number of offences, any non-sexual offences, use of violence in criminal/sexual activities. Dynamic factors are those that, it is hoped, are amenable to treatment and can be changed. These include psychological factors such as submissiveness, aggressiveness, self-esteem, rumination of anger, empathy, locus of control, emotional congruence with children, attitude to women or children, loneliness, coping skills, and intimacy deficits. There has been considerable research on how these factors contribute to offending behaviour, how, and to what extent, they can be changed, and which, when changed, demonstrably contribute to lower risk of re-offence.

A range of factors has been considered when trying to understand the origins of offending behaviour of child molesters: empathy, self-esteem, coping, loneliness and intimacy deficits, cognitive factors (distorted ways of thinking) and personality factors. Child abusers, writing about their experience, suggest that personal distress contributes to their offending behaviour. Negative emotional states can be related to poor decision-making for anyone, and they are often at the root of a range of addictive or self-defeating behaviours – for example, gambling, alcohol and drug abuse, over-spending and over-eating.

Offenders themselves are aware that they are more likely to act out (abuse children) when they are experiencing negative mood states. Their adherence to treatment and capacity to learn are also likely to be enhanced if they are feeling good about themselves. Lastly, an approach to treatment that attempts to enhance the quality of life of offenders, and that supports alternative goals and values offering satisfying rewards, is more likely to be effective if the offender feels good about himself and feels that his life is getting better. This suggests that therapists, without losing sight of the primary goal of keeping children safe, should intentionally aim to enhance offenders' feelings of safety, esteem and well-being.

Approaches to treatment

There are three main approaches to the treatment of sex offenders: psychotherapy, cognitive-behavioural group therapy (CBT) and medication. Individual psychotherapy relies on a process of motivation to change and insight to lead the patient from a situation of anxiety and pain to one of greater psychological health, inner freedom and internal congruence. Berlin (1985) writes that it is impossible to work out why we have certain attractions and not others simply by a process of self-reflection and insight. Even with a motivated patient, it is unlikely that this process can lead to the change that is considered desirable. Berlin writes, 'There is little convincing evidence to show that the traditional psychotherapies alone are invariably effective means for treating paedophilia.'[1]

Sex offender treatment is now typically conducted in groups, where the offender can experience both the support and challenge necessary to bring about behavioural change. The group process is particularly effective in helping offenders to deal with their feelings of shame and vulnerability. They can also benefit from the experience of others who have spent a longer time in therapy.

John, who was mentioned at the beginning of this chapter, was actively engaged in both individual and group therapy. A significant breakthrough happened for him when he was present at a group presentation about a young man who had been abused by his teacher. The young man was the same age as his own victims, and the similarity of the circumstances meant he could no longer minimise or deny his behaviour. Over the next few months he confronted his feelings of shame and self-loathing. This eventually led to greater self-acceptance and peace. Interestingly, just after this he began to form a relationship with a woman who was slightly

1. Berlin, Fred S. (1985). 'Paedophilia', *Psychiatry*, 19, 79-92.

younger than he was. This became an adult sexual relationship over time. His paedophilic desire did not disappear, but he was helped to manage this desire with medication. He was able to inform his girlfriend of his past, and she decided to remain with him despite his history.

Reviews of recent research suggest that there are grounds for optimism regarding the value of CBT programmes, which are based on social learning theory. This theory suggests that our behaviours (and thought patterns) are learned through experience, and that subsequent rewarding experiences reinforce these behaviours and ways of thinking (cognitions). CBT programmes tend to focus on the abusive behaviour and seek to target the specific features of the abuser that are in need of change. They focus on the recognition and correction of cognitive distortions, relapse prevention (which consists of identifying the patterns of thinking and behaving that lead to abuse, and putting in place strategies to prevent further abuse), and training in empathy and other interpersonal and social skills (emotional coping, anger management, self-esteem).

This chapter began with a range of statistics related to sexual abuse. Some of these are well known, and when they are quoted, they tend to cause shock and anger. Bill Marshall, however, notes that less than one in five sex offenders will re-offend, and that for those who complete CBT programmes the re-offence rate is reduced to one in ten. He writes that 'Long-term evaluation of these programmes has demonstrated that the rate of re-offending among treated offenders is substantially lower than among similar untreated offenders.'[1] This is borne out by the fact that in the 17 years of the Wolvercote Clinic's existence (a specialist clinic in England dealing with sex offenders which has since been closed) only a handful of the 305 men who completed the programme re-offended.[2]

It is worth noting in this context that 45% of calls to the Stop it Now! helpline in the period 2002–2005 were from abusers or potential abusers concerned about their feelings or behaviour toward children. Donald Findlater, the manager of Stop it Now! was quoted in *The Times* report:

1. Marshall, W. L. (1992). 'The social value of treatment for sexual offenders', *The Canadian Journal of Human Sexuality*, 1 (3), 109–114.
2. Stacey, J. 'Making our world a better place' (Part 1), CCPAS website, http://www.ccpas.co.uk/articles/Making%20our%20world.htm (retrieved 29 February 2008).

> What our analysis shows is that there are people out there, unknown to police and social services, who are troubled by what they have done or are about to do. Our job is to agree with them the different options they can take today. The challenge for us is, can we help before a child gets hurt?[1]

These data may help dispel the myth that child molesters are untreatable or not motivated to change.

The third approach to treatment is what is commonly called 'chemical castration'. This does not, of course, involve castration, but the use of antiandrogenic (i.e. 'reducing maleness') medications that can lower testosterone, which is related to sexual arousal and performance. The medication does not work in every case, and it appears to be related to the level of motivation of the client and avoidance of alcohol and other drugs. Programmes which combine these medications with group and/or individual therapy appear to have good levels of success in preventing recidivism.

We can conclude, then, that treatment can make a difference to child abusers, although the nature of the treatment needs to be tailored to the individual. Individual therapy on its own is seldom enough, although it can be effective when combined with group therapy using CBT principles. Antiandrogenic medications have been shown to be helpful for paedophiles and other sex offenders with deviant interests. Finally, there have been a number of studies that have shown that where clients cooperate with treatment, recidivism can be significantly reduced.

Sexual abuse and the Churches

The topic of child sexual abuse is not new for the Church. Canon 71 of the Council of Elvira, AD 309, specifically penalises sexual contact with boys.[2] In the Middle Ages the Church condemned sexual involvement with boys,[3] and a number of religious orders have had to deal with sexual abuse

1. McVeigh, K. (15 May 2007). 'Worried paedophiles make most calls to child abuse line', *The Times*, p. 16.
2. http://faculty.cua.edu/pennington/Canon%20Law/ElviraCanons.htm
3. Richards, R. (1990). *Sex, Dissidence and Damnation: Minority groups in the Middle Ages* (New York: Barnes & Noble).

of members at various stages of their history. The topic has been given significant attention in the last 20 years as a result of media exposure of abuse in the Catholic Church in particular, although other Churches have also had to deal with this issue.

As a result of clergy sexual abuse scandals, the Catholic Church in England and Wales appointed a Commission under the chairmanship of Lord Nolan to 'examine and review arrangements made for child protection and the prevention of abuse within the Catholic Church in England and Wales, and to make recommendations.' This resulted in the report entitled 'A Programme for Action' (2001).[1] Similar commissions were established in other English-speaking countries. As a result of the report, the Catholic hierarchy established the Catholic Office for the Protection of Children and Vulnerable Adults (COPCA), and Eileen Shearer was appointed as its Director. The recent Cumberlege Commission (2007),[2] which was set up to review the implementation of 'A Programme for Action', notes the considerable progress made in child protection as a result of the work of COPCA, but made some observations and further recommendations.

Perhaps the most significant point to emerge from the report is the need for a change of culture in the Church. The report mentions 'an over-dependence on volunteers, the erosion of trust between priests and bishops, and a continuing resistance to change among bishops.'[3] COPCA made extraordinary progress in highlighting the issue of child abuse and promoting the 'paramountcy principle' – that the welfare and safety of children must have priority in the Church – in creating systems of reporting and in checking and training volunteers and church personnel. The Cumberlege Report makes it clear that the Church is now a safer place for children. Changing the Church's culture is a much bigger task. As with bullying and partner violence, it is the culture which supports abuse that needs to be tackled and changed. This is a far more difficult

1. Catholic Bishops' Conference of England and Wales (2001). *A Programme for Action: Final report of the independent review of child protection in the Catholic Church in England and Wales* (London).
2. The Cumberlege Commission Report (2007). *Safeguarding with Confidence: Keeping children and vulnerable adults safe in the Catholic Church.* www.cumberlegecommission.org.uk
3. *The Tablet* (21 July 2007) p. 6.

enterprise, requiring as it does transparency, accountability and delegation of powers from institutions (the churches) which often developed in a secretive, hierarchical way, with few structures of accountability.

The Catholic Church is not the only religious organisation that has had to deal with this issue. Over the past few months there have been newspaper reports of cases of child abuse involving the Anglican[1] and Methodist churches, as well as the Jehovah's Witnesses.[2] There was also a recent newspaper article in *The Sunday Herald* which presented information about abuse within the Muslim community. The newspaper report suggests that the institutional denial, moving of perpetrators, disbelief and marginalising of victims that happened in Christian Churches is also happening in the Muslim community.[3]

The Church of England's policies on child protection are outlined in the report entitled 'Protecting All God's Children', which was published in 2004. The stated aim is to create a 'culture of informed vigilance'.[4] As well as policies and procedures for dealing with allegations of abuse, there is a section on ministering to those who might pose a risk to children and a helpful list of resources and websites.

The Methodist Church of Great Britain issued a report in 2006 entitled, 'Tracing Rainbows through the Rain', which is a follow-up to the report 'Time for Action: sexual abuse, the Churches and a new dawn for survivors', published by Churches Together in Britain and Ireland (CTBI).[5] 'Tracing Rainbows through the Rain' emphasises the importance of listening to survivors of abuse and provides resources for ministry and preaching. The Methodist Church, which was one of the first Churches to produce a report on sex offenders in the Church,[6] also has a 'Safe-guarding' policy which is designed to prevent the abuse of young people

1. Butt, R. (22 October 2007). 'Church pledges to root out decades-old child abuse cases', *The Guardian.*
2. Morris, S. (24 August 2007). 'Paedophile who abused baby walks free', *The Guardian,* p. 6.
3. http://www.sundayherald.com/news/heraldnews/display.var.1628124.0.child_abuse_in_mosques_lifting_the_veil_of_secrecy.php
4. Church of England (2004). *Protecting All God's Children: The child protection policy for the Church of England* (3rd edition), p. 6. Available at http://www.cofe.anglican.org/info/papers/protectingchildren.pdf
5. Churches Together in Britain and Ireland (2002). *Time for Action: sexual abuse, the Churches and a new dawn for survivors* (CTBI, 31 Great Smith Street, London SW1P 3BN.
6. http://www.methodist.org.uk/static/news/papers/church_and_sex_offenders.htm

and to promote their welfare.[1] A range of resources is available to support churches and groups in understanding and implementing child protection policies.

Policies and reports of the Church of Scotland can be accessed at their website.[2] The Church of Scotland also issues a newsletter with helpful information, for example, on the implementation of the Protection of Vulnerable Groups (Scotland) Act, 2007.[3]

Bill Marshall, in a paper entitled 'A proposal for the prevention and treatment of child molestation by Catholic clergy', shares an experience from a visit to Taiwan, where he was told that high incidences of abuse of boys in Buddhist monasteries had recently been uncovered. He comments that 'When men are placed in positions of authority over children . . . some of them will take advantage of the situation to sexually molest'.[4] This appears to be true no matter what the religion, culture, country or organisation. It is particularly heinous when it happens in churches or other organisations like the Scouts, which are dedicated to the welfare and development of children, or by football coaches.[5]

Vulnerable adults

The focus of this chapter has been on child sexual abuse. However, it is important to give some attention to the related issue of the abuse of vulnerable adults. The authors of the Nolan Report noted that they had received several comments on their first report suggesting that arrangements for children should be extended to vulnerable adults. They mentioned people with learning difficulties, although the disabled and elderly should also be considered in this context. It was noted that other organisations had a single set of policies to cover children and vulnerable adults, and this approach was commended to the bishops.

1. https://secure2.cyberware.co.uk/~cb537/acatalog/Catalogue_Children_and_Young_People_39.html
2. http:/www.churchofscotland.org.uk/councils/safeguarding
3. http://www.churchofscotland.org.uk/councils/safeguarding/safeguardingnews.htm
4. Marshall, W. L. (in press). 'A proposal for the prevention and treatment of child molestation by Catholic clergy', submitted to *Seminary Journal*.
5. Bentham, M. (18 September 2005). 'Child abusers who shame British football', *The Observer*, News, pp. 8, 9.

What is meant by abuse in this context? In section 2.6 of a report entitled 'No Secrets', issued by the Department of Health, abuse is defined as follows:

> Abuse may consist of a single act or repeated acts. It may be physical, verbal or psychological, it may be an act of neglect or an omission to act, or it may occur when a vulnerable person is persuaded to enter into a financial or sexual transaction to which he or she has not consented, or cannot consent. Abuse can occur in any relationship and may result in significant harm to, or exploitation of, the person subjected to it.[1]

Abuse can come in many guises. Those with physical and learning disabilities and the elderly, particularly those belonging to minority communities, may not have the ability to ask for help or report their abuse. Many, of course, live in fear of their abusers, who may be their principal carers. Gary Fitzgerald, Chief Executive of Action on Elder Abuse, writes that between 2.4% and 4% of adults are victims of elder abuse.[2] The three main categories appear to be psychological, physical and financial abuse.[3] There is also sexual abuse of vulnerable adults, which often generates disbelief and, understandably, distaste.[4]

Between the publication of the Nolan Report and the Cumberlege Report, which reviewed the progress that had been made in the first five years of implementation of the recommendations of Nolan, there were changes to the law in the United Kingdom in this area. The Safeguarding Vulnerable Groups Act of 2006 (due for implementation from Autumn 2008) introduced a new vetting scheme for those working with children and vulnerable adults. The Cumberlege Report noted these changes in the law and the developing awareness of issues related to protection of

1. http://www.dh.gov.uk/prod_consum_dh/groups/dh_digitalassets/@dh/@en/documents/digitalasset/dh_4074540.pdf
2. http://www.elderabuse.org.uk/documents/Key%20issues%20relating%20to%20the%20Prevalence%20Study.doc
3. http://www.prap.group.shef.ac.uk/comcare.pdf
4. http://www.elderabuse.org.uk/documents/Key%20issues%20relating%20to%20the%20Prevalence%20Study.doc

vulnerable adults.[1] It highlighted the need for the Catholic Church to make changes in order to avoid falling behind the rest of society in this area. The same, no doubt, can be said of other Churches.

The Cumberlege Report also noted the access that Catholic priests, chaplains, religious and lay workers have to the homes of many vulnerable people through visitation, Eucharistic Ministry, groups such as the St Vincent de Paul Society and organisations that serve the needs of those with physical or learning disabilities. It is important that due care is taken of these groups, and that policies and procedures are put in place to extend protection to them. The Cumberlege Report recommended that Child Protection Commissions be changed to Safeguarding Commissions, with the dual responsibility of child and vulnerable adult protection. This makes organisational and pastoral sense, and it is hoped that it will be noted by other Churches and faith groups.

The Church of England has taken this a stage further by issuing a separate report on the topic of protection of vulnerable adults entitled 'Promoting a Safer Church'.[2] As well as articulating principles underlying this issue – such as the need to treat people with respect and dignity, and to enable people to lead as independent a life as possible – the report offers advice to pastors on how to implement good practice in worship and pastoral care. There are also sections on the care of adult survivors of abuse and procedures if an allegation is made against a church worker or member of the clergy.

1. www.cumberlegecommission.org.uk

2. Church of England (2006). *Promoting a Safer Church: Policies for safeguarding adults in the Church of England.*

A Christian response

The combination of the Christian teaching that sexual relations should be confined to the marital relationship and Jesus' attitude of respect for children, using them as a model of those who would enter the kingdom of God (Mark 10:13-16), has significantly influenced attitudes to children over the centuries. The whole thrust of the Judaeo-Christian tradition to protect the weak has also been a factor in creating a moral context where exploitation and abuse of children is considered unacceptable.

Care for victims is also supported by the central tenet of Christianity which sees Jesus as the sacrificial victim whose suffering is redemptive for humanity. Within the Christian tradition, victims have a certain status and are entitled to sympathy, assistance, rescue from suffering, and recompense for deprivation of freedom, important rights or opportunities. This may help to explain the compensation culture which has gripped the United States and is finding its way into other English-speaking countries.

While it is true that Jesus showed respect and care for children, the line in Matthew's Gospel regarding the feeding of the five thousand – which, of course, refers to five thousand *men* – should also be borne in mind: 'Those who ate numbered about five thousand men, to say nothing of women and children' (Matthew 14:21). The shadow side of the Judaeo-Christian tradition is that in many ways it continued to accept the prevailing attitudes which marginalised women and children. In the case of children, the biblical injunction to 'spare the rod and spoil the child' (Proverbs 13:24) was often used to justify physical violence and harsh punishments which would not be tolerated today. One of the achievements of the women's movement and the various liberation movements of the 1960s and '70s was that of giving voice to women and to other victims of violence, oppression or abuse – especially children.

As has already been said, victims enjoy a certain status in Christianity. Tragically, the victims of abuse have not always been heard, and in fact were often disbelieved or punished if they dared to speak up. There has been a change in recent years as educational programmes are taking the issue of sexual abuse more seriously. Organisations like ChildLine in the UK[1] and Stop it Now![2] have made a significant difference to the lives of many children and adults, as have the recent attempts of dioceses and religious Orders to provide counselling and compensation for victims of clerical abuse.

While care for the victims is paramount, care for offenders is also important from a Christian perspective. The principle of 'Love the sinner but hate the sin' still has value, especially when dealing with child molesters who are unquestionably at the bottom of the heap as far as society is concerned. Even in prisons, they need special protection as other prisoners show their contempt and anger if they are in mixed accommodation. John J. Geoghan, the former priest who abused children in Boston Archdiocese, was murdered in prison not long after his conviction.[3] There are also cases of offenders being attacked in British and Irish prisons.

Professor Fred Berlin, Director of the National Institute for the Study, Prevention and Treatment of Sexual Trauma, wrote the following:

> Almost two thousand years ago, as an outraged crowd attempted to stone to death a woman whose sexual behaviour they considered offensive, one man stepped forward to stop the retribution, speaking of revenge while espousing values such as compassion, understanding, forgiveness and reformation. He asked that persons be judged not simply by their behaviour, but with some appreciation for their humanity.[4]

As Winston Churchill said in the House of Commons in 1910, the hallmark of a civilised society is how it treats those whom it imprisons.[5] The Christian tradition challenges us to be inclusive of those whom we

1. http://www.childline.org.uk. Tel: 0800 1111
2. http://www.stopitnow.org.uk Tel: 0800 1000 900
3. http://www.nationalcatholicreporter.org/todaystake/tt082703.htm
4. Berlin, Fred S. (2000). 'The etiology and treatment of sexual offending', in Fishbein, D. H. (Ed.), *The Science, Treatment and Prevention of Antisocial Behaviors* (Kingston, NJ: Civic Research Institute), pp. 21:1–15.
5. James, R. R. (1974). *Winston S. Churchill: His complete speeches, 1897-1963* (New York: Chelsea House Publishers).

would seek to exclude from the community. Organisations like Sanctuary UK work to help churches and other groups to support sex offenders. In Sanctuary's Winter 2006 Newsletter, readers are reminded that the Probation Service started as Police Court Missionaries, and that many Church organisations are active in this area.[1]

A key challenge to Christians is in the area of forgiveness. Should victims forgive – or be expected to forgive – their abusers? Can abusers be forgiven? Should they seek self-forgiveness? This is a complex issue. In the first place it would be wrong to expect or put any pressure on a victim to forgive an abuser – or parents or others who showed disbelief or sided with the abuser, as has often happened especially if the abuser was a trusted friend or family member. Forgiveness is a difficult and demanding process, although ultimately rewarding. Each person has to undertake this journey when they feel ready, with appropriate support.

It is clear from recent research that the process of forgiveness has significant psychological benefits in the area of personal well-being and mental health, but this is a choice that has to be made by the victim in their own time. Secondly it has to be said that there is no cheap grace in this area. Mark Yantzi, a Canadian Mennonite pastor who has worked with victims and abusers, makes it clear that before forgiveness can be extended, the abuser must face their behaviours squarely and not use Christian faith as a way of avoiding the hard, searching, emotionally demanding work of therapy. He describes premature forgiveness as 'religious window dressing', and understands the fears of survivors that granting forgiveness can leave an offender feeling that he has been let off the hook.[2]

Sex offenders are often churchgoers. While this may be alarming, given the relatively high number of young children who attend churches, it can also be an asset, as many offenders return to the practice of faith or develop spiritual lives as part of their recovery. It is important to be cautious in this area and suspicious of offenders trying to create a good impression or avoiding the hard work of personal therapy and confronting

1. Sanctuary (Winter 2006). *News and Prayer Letter.* www.sanctuaryuk.com
2. Yantzi, M. (1998). *Sexual Offending and Restoration* (Ontario: Herald Press).

past abusive behaviour. However, it is at least likely that religious faith and spirituality have the potential to help sex offenders in their recovery.[1] Religious faith offers a clear set of moral guidelines, and spirituality involves a relationship with God, Jesus or a higher power. These can provide comfort, security and support. They can also be a source of challenge to inappropriate thinking and behaviours. Church communities can provide a certain amount of individual support and accountability. These should not be underestimated when trying to help a child molester change behaviour and become reintegrated into society.

The Church of England addresses this difficulty in its report 'All God's Children'. In the section entitled 'Our Theological approach', the authors write:

> Because redemption and forgiveness are so central to the gospel, the Church is not only well-equipped to assist in the rehabilitation of offenders, but is also particularly challenged by them. Our congregations can be a refuge for those who have perpetrated abuse but are seeking help in maintaining a non-abusive way of life. Other abusers may see church membership as an opportunity to be close to children in order to continue their abusive pattern of behaviour . . . The genuine penitent will accept the need for careful arrangements for their return to church fellowship. This is in line with the Church's realistic understanding of sin and its effects.[2]

This reflects an attempt to hold in balance the Christian values of the Church as a community of reconciliation and forgiveness, and a realistic appraisal of the difficulties involved in offering support to an abuser.

One of the most striking and significant initiatives in recent years has been the Circles of Support and Accountability that began in the Mennonite Church in Hamilton, Canada. Pastor Harry Nigh was asked to find accommodation for a repeat sex offender who was being released into

1. Geary, B., Ciarrocchi, J. W. and Scheers, N. J. (2006). 'Sex offenders, spirituality, and recovery', *Counselling and Spirituality,* 25 (1) 47–71.
2. Church of England (2004). *Protecting All God's Children: The child protection policy for the Church of England (3rd Edition)* 1.2, p. 3. Available at: http://www.cofe.anglican.org/info/papers/protectingchildren.pdf

the community. He was understandably uncomfortable with this request, having young children himself. However, he rose to the challenge and out of his generosity and Christian vision the Circles of Support and Accountability were born. The idea is fairly simple. Groups of six volunteers form a group around a released offender. They give up some of their time each week to have coffee together, have a chat, check up on progress with job hunting, meetings with counsellors, probation officers, doctors, etc. Once a week the whole group gathers to spend time together, have a meal, and to celebrate another week which is free of crimes against children.[1]

Gordon Stuckless, who admitted over 500 sexual acts against children while working for the Toronto Maple Leafs ice hockey team, left jail in 1998 and is a member of a circle. David Wilson, a British criminologist, interviewed him. Stuckless said:

> The worst thing would be to come home to nothing. No support. You just sit there and watch TV. Crazy ideas come into your head and you say, 'To hell with it.' You throw up your hands and that's when another victim happens. But if you have your Circle to talk to, well there you go.[2]

According to Wilson, Britain's Prison Service sex offender treatment programme, based on the principles of treatment outlined above, claims a reduction in offending of around 10–15%. The Circles of Support and Accountability programme has been shown to cut re-offending rates by 70%. This programme has now been introduced into the United Kingdom at a number of places, under the guidance of the Home Office. Not all of the groups in the UK are run by Christian groups or by Christians alone. Nevertheless, in its origins and its values, it clearly demonstrates the place for a Christian response to sexual abuse of children. It also shows that this is not simply the misguided care of Christian liberals, but a sound programme that shows compassion for offenders and cuts re-offence rates.

1. Wilson, D. (18 November 2004). 'Quality time with paedophiles', available at http://www.guardian.co.uk/comment/story/0,,1353545,00.html
2. http://www.guardian.co.uk/comment/story/0,,1353545,00.html

This chapter began with John's story prior to being arrested for molesting children. During the process of discovery, arrest and sentencing, John was befriended by the minister in his church. His family was also supported by this faith community. Speaking of his church minister, John said, 'Her non-judgemental care, compassion for me and my family, and simple presence during the toughest times, convinced me that there was something in religion for me.'

Do's and don'ts

- Do take a child seriously if they tell you that something inappropriate has been done to them.
- Don't rush to interfere. Do contact Social Services, ChildLine, the NSPCC helpline or Stop it Now! for advice and information.
- Do follow the child protection proceedings of your own organisation.
- Do provide supportive counselling or help for relatives, work colleagues or others who are affected.
- As an employer or priest/minister, contact a lawyer before making any decisions regarding employees who have been accused or found guilty of sexual abuse.
- Do advise families to report any crime that has been committed.
- Do not ask unnecessary questions of victims or abusers, but offer support as long as it is necessary.
- Do not promise to keep information a secret if it involves a child who is being sexually abused.
- Do not ostracise the perpetrator if you previously had a relationship with them. People who are guilty of abuse need as much support and contact as possible as they go through the stages of discovery, trial, treatment, probation and rebuilding their lives. Personal support does not mean you condone their actions.

Conclusion

In this chapter an attempt has been made to explain the nature of child abuse, especially outlining the devastating effects on children and the widening circle of people who become affected by this behaviour. Three different types of child abuser have been described: paedophiles, familial (incest) offenders and ephebophiles. It has been suggested that these different types of offender have different problems and represent different levels of danger to the public or to organisations. Issues related to treatment and recidivism were explored. The good news is that many offenders do not want to re-offend. Those who actively participate in treatment offer a good prognosis for changed behaviour. Christian teaching demands that we care for children and victims, but a mature Christian vision also challenges us to find room for offenders in society and (with appropriate protection and safeguards for children and victims) in our churches. The recent development of Circles of Support and Accountability demonstrates how friendship, support, compassion and faith can significantly improve the lives of offenders and make society a safer place for children.

Recommended reading

- Hanson, R. K., Pfäfflin, F. and Lütz, M. (2003). *Sexual Abuse in the Catholic Church: Scientific and legal perspectives* (Libreria Editrice Vaticana).
- McGlone, G. J., Shrader, M. and Delgatto, L. (2003). *Creating Safe and Sacred Places: Identifying, preventing, and healing sexual abuse* (Minnesota: Saint Mary's Press).
- Yantzi, M. (1998). *Sexual Offending and Restoration* (Ontario: Herald Press).

Websites

www.childline.org.uk – ChildLine

www.stopitnow.org.uk – Stop it Now!

www.elderabuse.org.uk – Action on Elder Abuse

www.dh.gov.uk – The Department of Health

Church reports

The Church of England: Child Protection and Protection of Vulnerable Adults
http://www.cofe.anglican.org/info/papers/protectingchildren.pdf
http://www.cofe.anglican.org/info/papers/promotingasafechurch.pdf

The Methodist Church: Child Protection
http://www.methodist.org.uk/downloads/Conf06_Safeguarding_pcfull.doc

The Catholic Church: Child Protection and Protection of Vulnerable Adults
www.cumberlegecommission.org.uk

The Church of Scotland
http://www.churchofscotland.org.uk/councils/safeguarding/index.htm

Domestic Abuse

Lesley Orr

Domestic abuse is prevalent throughout the world – part of the continuum of gender and sexual violence which has been an enduring reality in human history. In the UK, millions of women and their children live with the daily threat and reality of abuse and assault in and around their homes. Research evidence over the past 30 years shows clearly that domestic abuse cuts across class, age, religion and ethnicity, although women in particular groups or circumstances experience factors which increase their vulnerability. It happens in cities and towns, in tower blocks and rural communities, in salubrious villas and in the midst of poverty, to professional women and those living with disability and discrimination. It happens to Christians. It is committed by Christians. The statistical probability is that there are both perpetrators and those who experience abuse in every large organisation and in every congregation of every Christian denomination and in other faith traditions. We live in a society where fundamental human rights are daily violated on an alarming scale, with devastating personal, social, economic and spiritual consequences. Society and the Churches are challenged to respond with clear-minded awareness and analysis, with theological reflection, with compassion and justice, with practical support and with self-critical examination of our own historical complicity in all that has conspired to make domestic abuse hidden, 'normal' or 'justifiable'.

Statistics from the UK and around the world paint a horrifying picture of the social consequences of abuse. Domestic assault is the major cause of disability and death for women between 16 and 44 years, and has been declared a public health emergency by the Council of Europe. A World Bank analysis of 35 recent studies from industrialised and developing countries around the world indicates that between one quarter and one half of all women have suffered significant physical, sexual or emotional abuse by a partner.

Some groups of women face extra risk and barriers to help. Black and ethnic minority women, those with uncertain immigration status or problems with language, and disabled women (possibly dependent on an abuser who is also their carer) all confront additional costs, fears and obstacles. The danger of stalking, severe assault and death at the hands of a coercive partner is likely to increase during attempts to end the relationship and after separation.

Let's listen to the words of Anna, a Christian woman living in Britain.

> I was thrown into the cupboard under the stairs. Blood was pouring from wounds gouged deep into my breast by a screwdriver, and the awful insults were still ringing in my ears. I heard the key turn in the lock and I knew I would be enduring another long dark night of pain and shame, with no food or clothes. The next morning, he let me out and told me to clean myself up before ironing his shirt. Then we set out together for church. It was Easter Sunday, and that morning, as I listened to the story of Jesus alive in the garden, asking Mary to share the good news of resurrection, I realised finally that I had to break free, for the sake of my children; for the sake of the person God wanted me to be. For too long I had accepted the humiliation and the degradation. I kept thinking about the marriage service: surely if vows had been blessed by God, I should have been helped through this? It hadn't occurred to me that a Christian marriage could be abusive, and that added to the sense of failure and isolation. I was shamed into silence. My life was so compartmentalised. I was in the women's group and the choir and attended worship, but it was all separate from the hell at home. Everyone else in our respectable suburban congregation – they seemed to live such nice, safe lives, all playing 'happy

> families'. Maybe some of them were living with abuse too, but I never knew. Those issues were never raised and church seemed almost the last place for honest sharing of pain and vulnerability. I really didn't think the people in church would believe what was going on. In fact I knew they wouldn't, because my husband was so well thought of and a pillar of the church. Years later I met someone from that congregation who said, 'I remember one time I saw you in a state and listened to your explanation for the bruises and bandages – now I know you were covering up for him. If only I'd thought that he might have battered you, or had simply asked if there was any problem, but it didn't even occur to me.' . . . We all lived under that tyranny of respectability. Violence against any person is destructive and isolating, and it's essential for the health of the church – and to support those who suffer – that we should find ways of breaking the silence. The violence is IN the silence . . . I long to find a church where I would be able to take a hurting friend in good faith, to find comfort and prayer and peace . . . a sea of welcoming faces and outstretched arms.
>
> Living in an abusive relationship was fearful – like being kept in a dark, dismal, suffocating tomb. It's been traumatic, but I do believe that I am coming out of the shadows, into the light of new life.[1]

For over 20 years her husband – a professional man and prominent church member – chose to use escalating and increasingly frequent physical brutality and sexual degradation against her, as part of a strategy of coercive and controlling behaviour which included habitual verbal, mental and emotional abuse. Their three children were silent and terrorised witnesses. Finally she girded her courage and fled the home in which she had invested so much love and care.

1. The personal accounts and comments of women who have experienced domestic abuse, which appear throughout this chapter, come from a research project conducted under the auspices of Edinburgh University Centre for Theology and Public Issues (CTPI). See Orr, L. (2000). *Out of the Shadows: Christianity and violence against women in Scotland.* Available from CTPI.

Anna and her children found safety and support in a Women's Aid refuge, but struggled with poverty, dislocation and continuing ill health as they endeavoured to rebuild their shattered lives. The terror was not over, for this seemingly good Christian man continued obsessively to pursue and threaten his ex-wife until eventually he formed a new relationship and was remarried in their home church. He has never been apprehended or sanctioned for his criminal behaviour. During the years of abuse, the whole family were involved in their local church, but that Christian community did not seem equipped or encouraged to recognise or confront the situation, to support the woman whose rights were violated, or to offer appropriate support either to the woman and her children, or to the man who perpetrated the abuse. Their experience is by no means unique.

What is domestic abuse?

> It was like a hostage situation – trapped, physically and emotionally. I never knew what would happen from day to day, or even from hour to hour. And to live with that level of terror and anticipation of damage and pain and fear, while trying to protect three small children, is obviously an impossible task. I don't know why I thought I could sustain it, but there was a desperation to try.

All human beings ought to have the opportunity to live full and dignified lives, to develop their capacities and gifts, to explore and share their personhood. All persons deserve freedom from fear, harm, degradation and constraint. Political and economic systems of oppression violate these human rights around the world. But women like Anna are denied these rights in their homes and personal lives; they experience entrapment at the hands of their intimate partners. Understanding this reality is the key to understanding domestic abuse.

For over 30 years, since grassroots groups of women in the UK highlighted the problem of 'battered wives' and created the Women's Aid movement to respond, activists, researchers, policy-makers and service providers have debated this phenomenon, and the language which is used to define it. From 'battered wives' to 'domestic violence', from 'intimate terrorism' to 'coercive control', the terminology, stereotypes and media representations often serve to confuse rather than to clarify. But definitions are a vital tool to outline the scope and characteristics of the problem, and to help us respond effectively. Different research methods and perspectives produce radically different and competing frameworks for understanding and intervention. Key points of debate have been:

- whether to talk about *'domestic violence'* or *'domestic abuse'*.
- whether to include only abuse committed by *adult intimate partners*, or all forms of *family violence*.

- whether to focus on *acts/events*, or on *patterns of behaviour*.
- whether the problem is gender-based or gender-neutral.

If we look at the definitions currently used by the UK Government Home Office, and by the Scottish Government, the significance of these choices becomes evident.

The Home Office definition of *domestic violence:*

> Any incident of threatening behaviour, violence or abuse (psychological, physical, sexual, financial or emotional) between adults who are or have been intimate partners or family members, regardless of gender or sexuality.

This uses the language of violence (which in everyday talk refers to physical assault, force, coercion or aggression), while recognising that other actions (or threats) may be also abusive. It speaks of *incidents* between adults, gives no context, and suggests that the incidents are somehow free-floating, with no notion of power imbalance or ongoing conduct by one person against another. The definition incorporates the idea that incidents of domestic violence, as defined, happen between partners or other adult family members, with no qualifications about the significance of gender or sexuality.

The Scottish Government definition of *domestic abuse:*

> Domestic abuse (as gender-based abuse) can be perpetrated by partners or ex-partners and can include physical abuse (assault and physical attack involving a range of behaviour), sexual abuse (acts which degrade or humiliate women and are perpetrated against their will, including rape) and mental and emotional abuse (such as threats, verbal abuse, withholding money and other types of controlling behaviour such as isolation from family or friends).

This definition is careful to focus not on particular *acts* or *incidents* but rather on the *intent* and the *impact* of conduct perpetrated by partners or ex-partners. It therefore excludes other kinds of family violence. It recognises that physical, sexual, mental and emotional forms of abuse are included in a range of tactics and behaviours which function to exercise coercive control over the partner. Physical aggression and threats are among the strategies available to intimidate, humiliate, isolate, exhaust, disable, punish and reward. This characteristic pattern of behaviour has been described by leading researchers in the field as a 'constellation of abuse'[1] and as 'intimate terrorism'.[2] The harmful and often severely traumatising psychological consequences for those who are victimised are likewise similar to other victims of terror.[3]

Although incidents of physical assault may be the most readily identified as criminal behaviour, it is not helpful to measure or assess such incidents without taking into account the *context* in which they have been committed. Considerable confusion has arisen, both in academic debate and also in the domains of public policy and opinion, when acts of physical aggression and force have been tallied and taken in isolation to constitute 'domestic violence'. (The British Crime Survey,[4] for example, in common with other large-scale random samples of populations, focuses on incidents of physical threats and force.)

Some misconceptions about domestic abuse

Domestic abuse only happens in poor and deprived families.
Abusive individuals come from all walks of life and social circumstances.

Alcohol and drugs cause abusive behaviour.
Alcohol and drug use can be factors in abusive behaviour. Some men abuse their partners when they have been drinking, some only do so when they are sober, and some use violence and abuse whether drunk or sober. Drinking can provide an easy excuse, but is more of a trigger than a root cause of the choice to act violently.

1. Dobash, R. E. and Dobash, R. P. (2004). 'Women's violence to men in intimate relationships: Working on a puzzle', *British Journal of Criminology*, 44 (3).
2. Johnson, M. P. (2006). 'Conflict and control: Gender symmetry and a symmetry in domestic violence', *Violence against Women*, 12 (11).
3. Herman, J. (1992). *Trauma and Recovery* (New York: Basic Books).
4. http://www.homeoffice.gov.uk/rds/bcs1.html

Domestic abuse happens because men fly into a rage and momentarily lose control.

Some abusive men use violence indiscriminately in different situations, against men, women and children. Many more only ever use threats and violence against their partners, and do so because it seems an effective way to dominate them. Once a man has started to abuse his partner, it is likely to happen again, and to get progressively worse. It seems to provide rewards without effective sanctions to inhibit such behaviour.

Some women just 'ask for it': their actions, appearance or attitudes provoke and deserve a violent response.

A recent survey of young people revealed that 20% of teenage boys (and a significant percentage of girls) think that there are times when it's OK to beat or have coerced sex with women and girls – especially in relationships. Coercive control is often exercised through rules, restrictions and surveillance based on the man's sense of entitlement or jealousy, while those who are on the receiving end make strenuous and fruitless efforts to avoid or allay the violence. No one deserves to be abused, and it is always a violation of human dignity.

Coercion and control

Evan Stark builds on the experiences of survivors and those who support them, as well as a substantial research literature, to argue that the key to understanding domestic abuse is not physical assault, but coercion and control of intimate partners or ex-partners, which 'jeopardises individual liberty and autonomy as well as safety', and is centred on 'the micro-regulation of women's default roles as wife, mother, homemaker and sexual partner'.[1] He maintains that this strategy has been adopted by many men in liberal Western societies (like the UK) where the traditional norms and regulations which institutionalised female inequality for centuries are under challenge by changing laws and moves towards formal equality.

In other societies where women's lives are socially circumscribed by religious, cultural, political and economic inequality, individual men who

1. Stark, E. (2007). *Coercive Control: How men entrap women in personal life* (Oxford University Press).

seek domination have less need to regulate their wife's behaviour and access to resources, because male privilege and entitlement, and restrictions on women, are enshrined and supported beyond the interpersonal domain. (This does not mean that men in more traditional societies always refrain from using physical, sexual or emotional abuse, which remain potent expressions of legitimised male power.) Stark's conclusion is that domestic abuse as coercive control is primarily a liberty crime rather than a crime of assault, because it results in gender-specific infringements – appropriation of resources, subversion of rights to self-respect and autonomy – and prevents women from freely exercising their social, economic and political agency.

Domestic abuse is a gendered issue

Research to explore the complex experiences and meanings of violence used by men and women provides some helpful information. Dobash and Dobash[1] studied 95 couples in Scotland with men and women reporting separately on violence in their relationship. They conclude that women's use of violence differs in nature, frequency, intention, intensity, injury and emotional impact. Men mostly reported women's violence as 'inconsequential', which did not affect their well-being or safety and did not make them adapt their behaviour. Swan's research into violent women[2] found that moderate physical violence and emotional abuse were comparable between men and women, but that severe physical violence, injury, sexual coercion and other controlling behaviours were mostly committed by men. Most female violence was reactive and driven by defensive motives. When women were arrested as domestic violence offenders, they were often trying to get away from a violent partner, or were trying to avoid further abuse, especially where they thought their children were in danger. Swan concludes that women's violence against men is usually preceded by violence of the man towards the woman, and that in order to challenge both male and female violence, traditional gender attitudes and roles must be targeted.

1. Dobash, R. E. and Dobash, R. P. (2004). 'Women's violence to men in intimate relatrelationships': Working on a puzzle', *British Journal of Criminology*, 44 (3).
2. Swan, S. C. and Snow, D. L. (2006). 'The development of a theory of women's use of violence in intimate relationships', *Violence Against Women*, 12.

Compared with women, men are overwhelmingly involved in all types of violence. It is mostly men who commit acts of personal violence – against women and girls, as well as towards other men and boys. Men own guns and weapons more than women, and are imprisoned and murdered more than women. Violence as a means of problem solving and control for men is culturally sanctioned, both implicitly and explicitly, in different ways throughout the world.[1]

Domestic abuse is not inevitable. While evolutionary psychologists are able to offer theories which may help to explain why men are more given to aggression and violence than women, men are not biologically 'hard-wired' for violence and coercive controlling behaviour, and, as we have seen, women can also be aggressive and abusive. But we must examine links between the individual behaviour of some men, the norms of 'masculinity' into which they are socialised, and prevailing structures and values in our society – including religious ones. It is as gendered human beings – that is, masculine and feminine – that we develop our sense of self and our knowledge of the world. Social and institutional power structures at all levels, from the interpersonal to the international, support the right of some groups to exercise control over others, and the use of violence as part of that control. These unequal power relations traditionally privilege men over women, and domestic abuse both reflects and reinforces that inequality. In a fluid and changing world, personal relationships may not always conform to conventional power relations, but even when a woman exercises dominance and abuses her power in a relationship, she does so in a wider social and cultural context which affects the likelihood of that behaviour being effective. Gender norms still influence the direct experience of, and the community or institutional responses to, domestic abuse.

Understanding men's domestic abuse

Men's domestic abuse is a complex phenomenon, influenced by a number of interrelated factors. The historical context is of particular importance in

1. Garcia Moreno, C. (1999). *Violence Against Women, Gender and Health Equity,* Harvard Center for Population and Development Studies, Working Paper Series 99.15;
Lang, J. (2002). Keynote paper given at the International Conference on Eradicating Violence against Women and Girls, Berlin.

understanding violence against women in general and domestic abuse in particular as socially accepted and even encouraged. Legal changes over the centuries were not directed towards eliminating men's abuse, but rather to putting legal limits on how far a man could go, reflecting the belief that a husband had authority over his wife and was given the legal and moral obligation to manage and control her behaviour. The use of physical coercion was simply one of the 'legitimate' means traditionally used to achieve such control. In 1915, following an established precedent, a London magistrate ruled that a man could beat his wife so long as the stick he used was no thicker than a man's thumb. Marital rape was not illegal until 1991.

How do we explain domestic abuse of women?

Many theories have been proposed to explain why some (but not all) men use violence and coercion against their female partners. Some have focused on individual pathology, arguing that domestic abuse is the behaviour of deviant or psychologically disturbed men; others on attachment theory, social learning, or 'stress' factors leading to loss of control or disinhibition caused by alcohol or substance misuse. A widespread assumption, much contested in the literature, is that there is a 'cycle of violence' transmitted from one generation to the next.

At the level of popular misconception and debate, simplistic attempts to create categories or 'types' of men who abuse as somehow different from 'normal' men are profoundly unhelpful. They ignore the underlying pervasiveness of gender inequality which is embedded in the everyday experiences of women and girls, and which is supported by widespread functional violence. They also serve to separate and demonise individual men who perpetrate abuse, while failing to analyse the values, institutions and structures which so deeply shape dominant models of masculinity based on status, competition, fear of weakness, or emotional detachment. Too often they are used to excuse or minimise accountability. Many of the explanations are inadequate when gender is ignored, or are based on an unexamined assumption that male violence is somehow innate, natural or uncontrollable. However, the current welcome trend among researchers and practitioners is an endeavour to integrate valid insights from various perspectives, recognising the complexity and multi-dimensional nature of domestic abuse. Domestic abuse is multi-determined; that is to say, it is the result of many influences. The criteria for evaluating these should reflect our desire for outcomes which seek equality, empowerment, justice, dignity and well-being for all.

Battered men

But how does this view tally with the gender-neutral definition of domestic violence and the oft-heard question, 'What about the battered men'? The simple answer may be that the different definitions describe different phenomena within interpersonal relations. Surveys and statistics (and there are many) which seem to show that women are as likely, if not more inclined, to use violence against their partners, focus only on discrete acts of force and do not measure or evaluate the context, impact and 'constellation of abuse'. However, qualitative research based on crime, safety, health and service provision, regardless of the severity of physical violence, consistently tells a story of 'intimate terrorism' which entraps women and rarely men.[1] Women do use violence and aggression, can be abusive, and do hurt their partners (both male and female). It serves nobody's interests to deny or ignore the fact that there are women who are abusive towards their male partners. But without taking account of the social context, purpose and impact of the different ways women and men use force and aggression in relationships, we are ill-equipped to respond to individual need, or to campaign for the social and cultural transformation required to end abuse.

Abuse within same-sex relationships

Domestic abuse occurs in same-sex relationships, with some research suggesting it is as prevalent as that experienced by women in heterosexual relationships. It is, however, an issue that has often been overlooked, made

1. See Johnson, M. P. and his forthcoming (2008) *A Typology of Domestic Violence* (North Eastern University Press)

invisible. Gay men and lesbians can face discrimination and fear dismissal by police and social services, or find a lack of support from their peers who would rather keep quiet about the problem in order not to attract negative attention towards the gay communities. HIV status or AIDS can also play a role in keeping partners together, if one partner provides health care for the other, or if there are concerns about disclosing status. Threat of outing can be used as a weapon, and lack of dedicated, safe and knowledgeable support services may add to the isolation and confusion.

Because heterosexual intimate relationships are the socially acceptable norm, they shape our common understanding of what constitutes an 'ideal' relationship, and means that those beyond what is considered normal may be depicted as sick, deviant, comic or sinful. Homophobia increases vulnerability and compounds the abuse experienced from the partner, but it also intersects with gender inequality in ways which can be exploited differently by male or female partners. Treating same-sex and heterosexual abuse as two facets of a single phenomenon does not help our understanding of the complexities, or provision of appropriate responses. The primary focus of this chapter is on men's coercive control of women in marriage or other heterosexual partnerships, but it is vital that Church and society recognise the reality of same-sex domestic abuse, and are aware that homophobia is one of the key social mechanisms which keeps that reality hidden.

Possible indicators of domestic abuse

The most reliable indicator is a woman saying she is experiencing abuse. All women are unique and will react to their particular circumstances in their own way. The following do not always indicate abuse, but should be considered when looking at the overall picture: we cannot rely solely on signs and indicators. But it is important to be aware and sensitive to the possibility of domestic abuse. A key issue to consider is how to create the right conditions for disclosure and to offer appropriate support. Listening receptively is the key, not providing simplistic or inappropriate solutions. Referral to Women's Aid or other services providing informed advocacy is much better than offering the wrong advice.

Signs of control

> He would never allow me to visit my family on my own. And very quickly, the only friends we saw were his friends. He wrote lists of all my domestic chores, down to how I folded the towels or organised the cupboards, and went round checking obsessively when he came home. Sometimes he would take a hair from his head and leave it somewhere in the house. If it was still there when he got home, I would get hell. He really did control every aspect of my life – decided what I was doing and when; what I wore, who I talked to, whether I could spend any money.

- Partner accompanies the woman, insists on staying close, and answers questions addressed to her.
- Reluctance of the woman to speak or disagree in front of her partner.
- Verbal insults and put-downs.
- He restricts her access to family and friends.
- She is prevented from working or studying.
- Intense jealousy or possessiveness expressed by the partner or reported by the woman.
- Lack of independent transportation, access to finances and ability to communicate freely by phone.
- Harm, or threats, to pets, significant objects, children.
- Mobile phone is used to track and monitor her movements and contacts.

Indicators (behavioural, physical, psychological)

> I wanted to get over the anger, which I thought wasn't the proper Christian way to feel. I had always tried to sustain myself by praying, taking sleeping pills, blocking out what was happening to me, and pushing away the sense that things were

very, very wrong. I wanted to cry; I was so full of the pain inside. But I just pushed it all down and carried on and tried to deny it. That was the way I coped with it and hoped that God would make it go away. I was confused because I had been brought up to believe that God would look after me if I was good. So the only conclusion I could accept for years was that I was bad.

- Inability to concentrate.
- Frequent use of prescription tranquillisers and pain medication.
- Sleep and appetite disturbances.
- Damaging coping strategies – heavy smoking, substance misuse.
- Denial or minimisation of abuse to block out the reality, and to survive from day to day.
- Seeming frightened, nervous, ashamed, evasive or embarrassed.
- Unexplained physical injuries, recurring or chronic poor health.
- Abdominal and gastrointestinal complaints.
- Chronic headaches.
- Depression, anger, frustration.
- Withdrawal.
- Fear.
- Panic attacks.
- Low self-esteem and confidence.
- Exaggerated sense of personal responsibility for the relationship, which includes self-blame.

The costs of domestic abuse

The effects and consequences of abuse are profound and extend into all aspects of victims' health, well-being and sense of self. They include some or all of the following:

- Violations of personal safety, dignity, bodily functions and space for action.
- Bruises, broken bones, disability, injuries, illness, disease (including STDs and HIV/AIDS), death.
- Depression and chronic anxiety.
- Complex post-traumatic stress disorder (PTSD) and psychosomatic complaints.
- Self-harming and suicide attempts.
- Betrayal of trust and integrity.
- Use of alcohol, drugs, etc., as coping strategy.
- Undermining of self-esteem and worth.
- Shaming, dishonour and disgrace across cultural contexts.
- Impacts on earning power, educational opportunities, achievements and place in society.
- Spiritual devastation, loss of faith and/or faith community.
- Some women who are victimised may themselves become perpetrators of abuse.

There are also economic costs in lost productivity and the impact on police, social and health services. Although only a small percentage of all assaulted women make use of hospital or police services, they still constitute a sizeable proportion of the entire hospital or police client population.[1] Recent research put the estimated cost of domestic violence to the UK economy at £2.7 billion a year in decreased productivity, lost wages and sick pay.[2] A report in the *International Herald Tribune* suggested that in the US 20% of all full-time employed adults are or have been victims of domestic violence.[3] Women, the most common victims,

1. Dutton, D. G. (1995). *The Domestic Assault of Women* (Vancouver: UBC Press).
2. Pattinson, G. (2006). 'Tackling domestic violence at work'. Available at http://news.bbc.co.uk/1/hi/uk/4581808.stm
3. Holland, K. (30 October 2007). 'Reaching out to victims of domestic violence', *International Herald Tribune*, p. 11.

lose nearly eight million days at work annually because they have been threatened, stalked or physically assaulted by current or former partners or spouses.

Statistics[1]

○ Lost economic output	£2.7 billion
○ NHS for physical injuries	£1.2 billion
○ Criminal justice system	£1 billion
○ Civil legal services	£300 million
○ Social services (mainly for children)	£250 million
○ Mental care	£176 million
○ Emergency housing	£160 million

The cost to men and boys

Michael Kaufman,[2] founder of the White Ribbon Campaign, argues that men and boys have been damaged by learned behaviour - historical and contemporary social constructions of 'what it means to be a man', associated with violence and aggression in sports, among friends and at schools and work, and ensuing power relations: 'We need to reach out, to mobilise men, to make them understand that violence against women is their issue. We need, as men, to work as partners with women.'

The costs of men not changing

Rory MacRae, senior social worker with the Edinburgh Domestic Violence Probation Project and the 'Working with Men' project, has said, 'Most abusing men on some level are unhappy with their behaviour and would like to change. To start the process, one needs to look at the motivation men have for using violence; what is their understanding of why they were

1. Source: Home Office Women and Equality Unit, September 2004.
2. Kaufman, M. (2001). Presentation to *Womankind* seminar, Edinburgh. A selection of his articles, and further information about the White Ribbon Campaign for men working to end violence against women, may be found on http://www.michaelkaufman.com/index.php

violent, and what 'benefits' do they think result from continuing to abuse? It is intentional and functional. We believe that men *can* change, and that the costs of them not changing are huge.'[1]

The impact on children

> No one thinks of the kids – thinks what effect it has on them. It doesn't just affect the mother – it's the kids . . . Because they're the ones that have got to see it, and hear it.

Most children are aware of the abuse their mothers experience, and often witness or hear incidents. Many such children are also direct victims of physical or sexual abuse. In one study, 55% of mothers whose children were on the child protection register were themselves also being abused. There is a strong association between domestic violence and fatal child abuse. There have been several recent incidents of men who kill not only their partner/ex-partner but also their children. Leading experts have identified that children suffer far-reaching negative impacts on their behaviour and emotional well-being, and on their cognitive abilities and attitudes, but that they can also demonstrate remarkable resilience and coping strategies, especially when they are able to find appropriate supports in their families and communities. This complex interplay of risk and protective factors reinforces the need to shift from blaming women for their 'failure to protect', to exploring strengths, the potential to create places of safety and support for survivors, and challenges to domestic abuse offenders. It is vitally important to secure realistic and adequate safe contact arrangements. Although most women who separate from abusive partners want their children to remain in touch with their father, research indicates that many men continue to intimidate and abuse. Handover of children from one parent to the other has been identified as a 'hot spot' for repeat violence to women, and also a more generalised continuing danger of direct and indirect abuse of children.

1. MacRae, R. (2001). *Womankind* seminar, Edinburgh.

How should it be dealt with?

Programmes for men who perpetrate domestic abuse

The research into effectiveness of re-education or 'treatment' programmes is inconclusive. A comparative study of four different programmes looked at new arrests after a follow-up period of nearly five years and found no significant differences between cognitive behavioural, humanistic, pro-feminist and eclectic programmes in the light of this outcome.[1] In general, abusive men who re-offended had the same lifestyle problems as those associated with general offenders, namely frequent moves, substance abuse and prior convictions. They were young, with unstable lifestyles, negative attitudes and low verbal intelligence. This highlights the complexity of factors contributing to the behaviour of abusive men. However, there are some well-evaluated programmes in the UK, conducted by members of Respect (the National Association for Domestic Violence Perpetrator Programmes and Associated Support Services) which promotes effective, safe and ethical interventions, based on national service standards and principles. Work with offending men, and support services for their partners, must be part of an integrated, well-funded and coordinated community response to domestic abuse.

It's everybody's business . . .

Local authorities, public sector agencies, voluntary organisations, private companies and trade unions all have a vital role to develop appropriate levels of knowledge, understanding and skills, to ensure that the best possible response and service is provided to anyone affected by domestic abuse.[2] An excellent example is the Corporate Alliance Against Domestic Violence (CAADV) – members include prominent British companies including the BBC, The Body Shop, KPMG, AOL and Vodafone – who came together to ensure that employers and staff who need support receive the

1. Hanson, R. K. and Wallace-Capretta, S. (2000). 'Predicting recidivism among male batterers', Department of the Solicitor General of Canada, available at www.sgc.gc.ca
2. A very helpful short guide, *Domestic Violence Good Practice Indicators*, is available to download from http://www2.warwick.ac.uk/fac/soc/shss/swell/dv_gpi_booklet.pdf

best possible advice. KPMG has policies, training and services which seek to create a safe environment, where people feel able to ask for help. A CAADV executive member was helped by her employer, a major bank. Her manager 'got Human Resources involved, and they talked it through with me and helped me. They offered me the chance to relocate, gave me time off to see solicitors and covered my tracks.' CAADV members recognise the moral case, but also the business case for providing appropriate support. Commending this work, Baroness Scotland QC, Home Office Minister, has said, 'The impact of domestic violence goes much wider than the victim, with a cost of approximately £3 billion per year for UK employers due to lost economic output. It is shocking that one in four women will be affected by domestic violence in their lifetime and one woman is killed every two to three days. These findings strengthen the case we are making for domestic violence to be on the agenda of every statutory agency and private business, affecting as it does their customers and employees. Domestic violence is completely unacceptable and all of us should take responsibility to challenge and root out abuse among our friends, our colleagues and our communities at large.' [1]

. . . Including the Churches'

The Churches have a responsibility and a unique opportunity to contribute to this community response. The human and material resources of the Christian Church are available in every community and corner of the British Isles, no matter how isolated. In recent years several of the main denominations have published national reports, research, policies and guidelines which have broken the silence of violence, and accepted the urgent need to respond to domestic abuse, within churches as well as in wider society. The Baptist Union of Great Britain has produced a pack of leaflets and resources, for churches, victims and survivors, and pastoral workers.[2] The introduction to *Breaking the Silence* says, 'The Baptist Union is committed to learning what it means to follow Jesus in a violent world. In partnership with others, we want to help break

1. More information from http://www.corporateallianceuk.com
2. Available to download from http://www.baptist.org.uk/resources/resource_downloads/318.pdf

the silence surrounding domestic violence.' The Church of Scotland, Church of England, Methodist Church and others have also addressed the issue, in common with Christians and other faith communities around the world.[1] At local level, imaginative initiatives have happened. For example, in 1999 the Anglican Diocese of Chester came together with the Church Mission Society to establish the Parish Refuge Project. Three experienced women from different parts of the world were placed with three parishes, each with a women's refuge in their boundary. The women acted as catalysts to promote effective relationships between parish and refuge. They offered support and befriending to women and children, and also promoted the project aims at every level of church life. Parish volunteers worked at the refuges, and churches offered other kinds of support. The project challenged attitudes and ignorance, and raised awareness and understanding of the issue in a holistic way. Ecumenical groups around Britain are taking the lead in promoting charters for discussion and action against the sin of domestic abuse. In Scotland, an ecumenical planning group, representing the major Christian Churches and organisations in Scotland, ran a very successful conference on domestic abuse called 'No Exceptions . . . A faith perspective on the myths and realities of domestic abuse – it's time to face the facts and speak the truth.' Subsequently, the group ran a study day on the same theme. Based on this experience, in November 2003 the group produced an information/training pack for organisers of conferences or study days raising awareness on issues of abuse. The pack, which may be freely photocopied, can be downloaded from http://www.nationalcommissionforsocialcare.org/news/Domestic_Abuse.htm.

These and other stories of good practice are signs of hope after centuries of silence.[2]

1. Church of Scotland, *Church and Nation Committee Report 2003*; Methodist Church research, *The Way Forward* (2002) and subsequent report (2005) which includes policy and good practice guidelines; The Church of England, *Responding to Domestic Abuse: Guidelines for those with pastoral responsibility* (2006). All these materials available online from websites. www.churchofscotland.org.uk, www.methodist.org.uk, www. cofe.anglican.org

2. A WCC dossier (2005) '*Streams of Grace*' gives practical and inspiring examples from around the world of Churches' work to address violence against women.

Learning from the experts

> Fear is the most dominating emotion, because everything else is subject to it. I was almost paralysed by fear, and only a determination to protect my children released some energy to drag myself out of that total erosion of personhood . . . When you begin to claim your life back, of course you feel absolutely betrayed. It's as if you have been sold something romantic and beautifully wrapped, but when you open it up it's hideous and dangerous. Once I expected the Church to have answers to all my questions. But now, I think I have answers to some of the questions the Church should be asking about domestic abuse. And I know that may sound rather arrogant, but I've changed from being a victim and now I'm a survivor. I think my story – *our* story, all of us who have experienced violation and abuse – is a resource for the Church.

For too long, public perceptions of domestic abuse – not least in the Churches – have been plagued by a kind of thinking one writer describes as DIM:

Denial of the reality or extent of the problem.

Ignorance about the character, causes, dynamics and impact of domestic abuse as coercive control.

Minimisation of the harm done – to women, to children, to men; of the costs to communities and society.

DIM thinking has often focused on the behaviour or pathology of women who are victimised, and has denied, ignored or minimised the responsibility of the perpetrators of abuse. 'She must have done something to provoke him . . . she's crazy . . . she's vindictive . . .' These attitudes often rely on the assumption that there are appropriate and expected female roles and behaviours – especially in the domain of marriage and personal relationships – and that when women fail to perform in that domain, they might even 'deserve' to be brought in line or chastised by their husbands. These traditional and commonplace assumptions, rooted in notions of gender inequality and male entitlement, were for centuries enshrined in Church teaching and authority – even if severe beatings and cruelty might have been considered excessive assertions of patriarchal authority.

Christianity and domestic abuse

> I was made to feel guilty and responsible for leaving my husband. The shame around this subject makes it very difficult to acknowledge in a community that values marriage vows and faithful commitment and uncomplaining behaviour . . . There's still a surprising amount of stigma attached to being a divorced woman. Somehow, the institutional Church makes you feel that you've failed, regardless of the reasons for the break-up.

The history of all religions, including Christianity, is in part the history of legitimising and colluding with the abuse of women. Sacred writings, theologies, structures and cultural traditions have been widely misused to claim that male dominance and female submission is part of God's plan for humankind. John Calvin's advice concerning abused wives in sixteenth-century Geneva reflects an attitude which prevailed in Protestant and Catholic churches alike:

> Except where her life is in danger, she must bear with patience the cross which God has seen fit to place upon her, and meanwhile not to deviate from the duty which she has before God to please her husband, but to be faithful whatever happens.[1]

This counsel to patience, duty, obedience and fidelity has been repeated down the centuries by theologians, pastors and others (of all church traditions and theological persuasion) who have concluded that a measure of violence and control might be acceptable or even desirable in order to

1. Letter from Calvin to Mme de Grammont, 28 October 1559, quoted in Watt, J. (1993). 'Women and the Consistory in Calvin's Geneva', *Sixteenth Century Journal*, 24 (2); also in Livezey, L. G. (28 October 1987). 'Sexual and family violence: A growing issue for the Churches', *Christian Century*, p. 938 http://www.religion-online.org/showarticle.asp?title=1068

guard the morality of family and church. As courageous Christian voices of survivors from around the world began to break the silence of violence, they repeated a depressing litany of ignorant, inappropriate and dangerous pastoral responses to abused women: of ministers and priests who did not believe, or who blamed women for provoking their husbands; of attitudes to marriage which implied that the permanence of the institution was its highest value, even when that compromised the safety, health and well-being of women and children.

In the Old Testament of the Christian Scriptures, there are many problematic accounts of men's violence against women, described as 'texts of terror' by the biblical scholar Phyllis Trible.[1] In these stories, women are treated instrumentally, to be used, abused, discarded, forgotten or killed. But the legitimate marriage relationship, as described in the law and history of the Jewish people, exhibited many of the same features. Men 'took' wives as part of their economic wealth. Adultery was essentially a crime against another man's property. Wives had no rights of possession over their own physical or sexual integrity. This pattern has been, and remains in many places, a widespread cross-cultural reality.

Women from traditional religious backgrounds may internalise an instrumental rather than intrinsic sense of personal identity and worth, and associate their own value almost entirely with the satisfaction of others' requirements and desires. Their sense of what it means to be a 'good wife' depends on supporting, advancing and protecting their husband's public standing and reputation, even when his private behaviour is reprehensible.

> In my experience, there's a kind of collusion between church and culture that says, 'Och well, that's just what men are like'. As if that makes it all right, or as if they have to be treated like slightly wayward children. It devalues men too; it deprives them of the maturity of accepting responsibility for their choices and behaviour. I find the whole 'buddiness' rather degrading . . . Boys will be boys – 'you know he didn't mean it because he was

1. Trible, P. (1984). *Texts of Terror* (Philadelphia: Fortress).

> crying to me the next day'. I don't want men to behave like that. I don't want women to be obliged to parent their partner. And I do think that the Church can be part of that. It hasn't really said, 'Men, you should have more respect for yourselves, and you should NOT treat your wives that way.' That has to be faced openly. You know, I have never, ever heard a sermon that addresses the relationship between men and women realistically. I have never heard anyone talk about prevailing attitudes to male violence.

Domestic abuse, like all forms of gender violence, is not simply a 'women's issue': it must be a deep and central concern for all who believe that each human being is created in the image of a loving God, and who long for wholeness and justice – in relationships and communities. Most men in the church abhor and neither condone nor practise domestic abuse. They have a particular calling to stand alongside their sisters in solidarity, and to challenge any notion that it is either acceptable or particularly 'masculine' to exercise coercive control (which need not be manifested in physical violence) against women and children. The Church has been deeply involved in shaping and sustaining the values, attitudes to sex and relationships, and customs of society in this country. And the Christian Church, present in the midst of every community, has both a responsibility and an opportunity to understand, resist and seek to prevent this behaviour which distorts individual and corporate life. We are also custodians and representatives of good news: the way things are is not the way things are meant to be. The way that Jesus related to women, and his interaction with the woman caught in adultery (John 8:1-11) and the men who wished to stone her, shows that he challenged radically the prevailing ways of thinking about men and women and their responsibility for sexual behaviour.

Positive sanctions to transform behaviour can be most effective when they emerge from a community which is actively committed to counter-cultural, transforming understandings of what it means for men and women, girls and boys to be truly human. As Christians, we require imaginative efforts to develop models of human relationship and community, based on self-worth, equality, mutuality, respect, hospitality and inclusiveness. Jesus offers a challenging example of a man struggling to transcend conventions and stereotypes of male and female behaviour; he publicly confronted religious leaders, challenging their hypocrisy, and he took risks for the sake of those on the margins. He did not choose to coerce, control or dominate, or use people carelessly. He allowed the voices of the oppressed to be heard, affirming their right to space, dignity and worth. And he encouraged them to take responsibility for their own choices.

A Christian response

Action for change: A gospel imperative

> The deaconess from the local church came to see me when I was at my lowest ebb. She said, 'There's a place for you in the church any time, but only when it feels right for you.' She was there when I needed her, and kept me company when I felt really alone. She stuck with me and gave me courage. That woman was my companion through the wilderness. She helped restore my faith in my whole self, in the Church, and in God.

In recent years, there has been an outpouring of literature and action as Christian theologians, pastors and lay people (many of them survivors of violence and abuse) grapple with the hard questions raised by the reality of domestic abuse afflicting the Body of Christ in the Church as well as in the world. Some of the most searching questions are about the nature of the Church as human community and sign of God's loving purpose. How can the Church fulfil its pastoral and prophetic task to resist and overcome malevolence and injustice? How can it be a source of empowerment, hope and new life? How do we act, in faith, for change?

Two key factors required to tackle, reduce and prevent domestic abuse are *sanctions* and *sanctuary.*

> Church needs to be a place where women are respected, listened to, reassured they have nothing to be ashamed of. The priest might not always be the best person to speak to, but it's so important to preserve the confidence and safety of someone living with abuse. Don't feel compelled to give advice or solve the problem. Just be there on the journey, which can be long and frustrating for all concerned. And don't tell us we need marriage counselling! That just gives him another opportunity for crocodile tears and excuses and bullying, and to get the world on his side. I felt so alone until a couple in the church understood and were on MY side.

Sanctuary has theological resonance, meaning a place of divine presence, and, in Jewish tradition, places of sanctuary often offered refuge and protection in the midst of a worshipping community which accepted responsibility for naming a wrong, confronting it and administering justice. Many women and children affected by domestic abuse have encountered the love of God in the midst of oppression, because they have found, in the open, non-judgemental, clear-minded compassion of others, that safe and secure space (which can be physical, emotional, spiritual) offering prolonged support for refuge and encouragement. Sanctuary also has a broader quality – an intentional and public effort to stand up to domination, give it a name and a face; work with local allies to nurture the support networks which can break through the web of social entrapment.

> The Church is always good at asking victims to forgive, but not so good at challenging perpetrators to ask for forgiveness, to change their behaviour, to offer some kind of compensation for ruined lives. Until I see some evidence that justice can be done, I won't meet a God of compassion in the Church.

Compassion arises from involvement. It begins with creating the conditions for speaking out (but only when it feels OK) with listening. This is hard work. It requires an open heart, a clear mind and endurance. The experience of hearing, touching, feeling and responding to pain and suffering is the key to change. The Hebrew word for compassion means 'womb love'. The mercy of God is like that – committed, passionate, protective and nourishing; yet making space to grow and mature. Sometimes it has to take risks, to be fierce and angry. And from such engaged compassion flows the justice of true sanctuary.

> When your self-esteem is rock bottom, and your pain is raw, it is very difficult to knock on the door if you have no idea who, or what, will be on the other side. You need constant, ongoing acceptance and support . . . it has to be said, loud and clear, WE'RE HERE, WE CARE, THIS IS A SAFE PLACE, ABUSE IS NOT GOD'S WILL FOR YOU, YOU ARE NOT ALONE.

Practical recommendations

Action for change is a corporate responsibility. As individuals, citizens, congregations, clergy, church employees, and at every level of the Church's structures, there are many practical and creative ways to respond. Practical suggestions must be understood and implemented in full awareness of the underlying dynamics of power and privilege which are embedded in church structures and cultures. Honest critique and structural changes must happen at every level to lay the groundwork which will ensure some measure of safety and security for those who have kept silent because they have had well-founded fears of the dangers of speaking out in a compromised institution. The burden of risk cannot be placed, by well-intentioned church leaders or members, on those we want to 'help' or 'include'. We dare not ignore the need to address some fundamental questions about religious oppression and complicity, which have contributed to the exclusion and shaming of people suffering abuse.

Do's and don'ts

Making our churches safe places

Do

- Display posters, leaflets and information about services such as Women's Aid, Rape Crisis and police domestic abuse units in church premises, and invite speakers from local groups to raise awareness or suggest practical action.
- Acknowledge domestic abuse and other forms of gender violence in the context of regular worship – in prayers of confession and intercession, in preaching, in the use of new hymns or liturgies, in symbol and action for healing and justice.
- Be sensitive and careful in use of language and image in worship. Consider the impact or effect (both helpful and hurtful) many religious words, hymns or symbols might have on those affected by abuse.
- Encourage individuals or designated groups within the congregation to be specially informed and aware of the issues, so they can be a trustworthy point of contact and referral. They might also take the lead in any church participation in local initiatives (for example, multi-agency partnership on domestic abuse).
- Draw up a charter outlining the church's position on domestic and sexual abuse, and how it will work towards *protection, provision and prevention* in the local community. Use this as an awareness-raising exercise, perhaps to be shared with ecumenical partners.

Such initiatives not only raise the level of awareness and concern among church members but contribute to the perception that this congregation/church will be a safe place where victims and survivors might share their stories and their pain, and find solidarity in their search for justice.

Advice to those with pastoral or managerial responsibility, or who want to help a friend

Research indicates that women experiencing abuse usually appreciate being invited to disclose, if it feels safe and the listener is non-judgemental. They may turn to someone they trust, whether or not that person has an official role.

Do

- Try to find a quiet and private space to talk.
- Take time to listen and believe – don't push or force disclosure. Acknowledge the strength and courage they have shown.
- Make it clear that their safety is the first priority, and perhaps help them to make a safety plan (whether they choose to stay or leave). Women's Aid will give guidance and information to help clarify options.
- Ask what they want from you, or the church, and in the relationship with their partner.
- Ask about children, if there are any, and do everything possible to ensure that children are kept informed and involved, where appropriate.
- Take a note of what you are told, the date, the context, and other factual information, as a record.

Don't

- Judge or dismiss what you are told.
- Make decisions or assumptions on their behalf, or else you simply reflect the controlling behaviour of the abuser.
- Ever tell a woman she just needs to pray harder, or forgive, or reconcile.
- Offer to mediate or to confront the abusing partner; or put the woman, children or yourself in danger.

The kinds of question which might help to bring coercive control to light include:

- Is someone/your partner making you afraid?
- Are they making you do something/s of which you are ashamed?
- Are they controlling your movement and contacts?
- Do you feel trapped or constrained by someone's behaviour towards you?
- Have you been hurt or harmed by your partner?

Conclusion

After centuries of collusion and silence, it is time for our society to say NO to domestic abuse. Governments, local authorities, businesses and not-for-profit sector organisations are challenged to be part of the solution, not part of the problem. There have been significant changes in social attitudes and understanding, and in developing coordinated multi-agency and community responses; but we have a long way to go. It is good news indeed that churches also are beginning to listen and respond to those affected by domestic abuse. There are signs of goodwill and informed love in action. In 1994, an ecumenical consultation on violence against women in Europe issued a call to the Christian community to be a real source of encouragement and empowerment: by listening and learning from women; by acknowledging our complicity in personal and structural inequality; and by acting in solidarity with all who suffer the consequences of abuse. Let us honestly reflect on these questions and rise to their challenge. Has the Church addressed gender as a justice issue? Have we named domestic abuse in our prayers? Do we preach about the equality, dignity and worth of women in the image of God? Have we campaigned for legal and social changes? Do we work with our local partners to make churches and communities safe places? How can we be a sanctuary of God's presence, if we do not recognise and honour that presence in the bodies and lives of those who suffer abuse?

Recommended reading

- Hague, G. and Malos, E. (3rd ed 2005). *Domestic Violence: Action for change* (New Clarion Press).
- Herman, J. (1997). *Trauma and Recovery: from domestic abuse to political terror* (New York: Basic Books).
- Stark, E. (2007). *Coercive Control: How men entrap women in personal life* (Oxford University Press).

Websites

www.womensaid.org.uk – Women's Aid Federation of England
www.scottishwomensaid.org.uk – Scottish Women's Aid
www.endviolenceagainstwomen.org.uk – End Violence Against Women
www.cwasu.org – Child and Woman Abuse Studies Unit, London Metropolitan University
www.faithtrustinstitute.org – Faith Trust Institute is an international, multifaith organisation working to end sexual and domestic violence
www.respect.uk.net – Respect is the UK membership association for domestic violence perpetrator programmes and associated support services
www.womenandequalityunit.gov.uk/domestic_violence
www.scotland.gov.uk/Topics/People/Equality/violence-women

Alcohol and Other Addictions

Christopher C. H. Cook

Addictive disorders are encountered in contemporary life in a variety of forms. Few people can be unaware that Western society faces a serious problem with illicit drugs such as heroin, cocaine or amphetamine, even though most members of the population will never use these drugs. Popular debate continues about whether drugs like cannabis are really as dangerous as they are said to be, and whether or not they are truly 'addictive', and the use of cannabis is widespread amongst young people in large sections of society. Addiction to the drug nicotine, in ordinary cigarettes, is already a massive and widespread problem, which contributes significantly to ill health and mortality, as well as to the economic costs carried by our health services. Alcohol, which is said to be 'our favourite drug', is consumed legally by most members of the adult population, and alcohol misuse is widely condemned, but the borderland between alcohol addiction and heavy drinking is nothing like as clear cut as most people imagine. So, we find that drug addiction involves not just young, and not just marginalised sections of our society, but virtually all of us.

Of course, addiction is concerned not only with drugs and drug use, but also with other behaviours that show similar qualities of impaired self-control and harmfulness. Thus, many people are aware that gambling or various kinds of gaming can be addictive, and there is popular and journalistic interest in so-called 'shopaholism'. It is also suggested that various kinds of eating disorder, relationships and patterns of sexual behaviour also show addictive qualities. If the concept of addiction is extended in this way, it becomes easy either to trivialise it or to conclude that we are all addicted. Even if the harm generated by some of these behaviour patterns prevents us from dismissing the idea of addiction altogether, it is still easy to become confused about exactly what addiction is, and difficult to know when it is, or is not, actually encountered.

If addiction were only confusing, perhaps it would not be worthy of inclusion in this book. However, as has already been intimated, it is in fact a very serious social problem, with a huge impact upon our society. Furthermore, it presents a significant pastoral challenge to our churches – not only because many young people in our churches have been offered drugs, or have even tried them,[1] and not only because lust and greed begin to sound like problems which involve all of us, but also because addiction is a serious social ill which should be a focus of concern for the mission of the Church. When Jesus summarises his mission in the synagogue at Nazareth, at the very beginning of Luke's Gospel, he does so in the reading of words from the prophet Isaiah which speak of setting captives free:

> The Spirit of the Lord is upon me, because he has anointed me to bring good news to the poor. He has sent me to proclaim release to the captives and recovery of sight to the blind, to let the oppressed go free, to proclaim the year of the Lord's favour. (Luke 4:18-19)

If addiction is a form of captivity or oppression, which impoverishes those who are afflicted by it, then surely we must ask ourselves, 'How can we today continue the mission of Jesus to bring good news to the poor, proclaim release to the captives and set the oppressed free?'

Description of the problem

As we have already seen, addiction is concerned with a wide range of different drugs, including legally available drugs such as alcohol and nicotine,

1. Cook, C. C. H., Goddard, D. and Westall, R. (1997). 'Knowledge and experience of drug use amongst church affiliated young people', *Drug and Alcohol Dependence*, 46, 9–17.

as well as illicit drugs such as heroin and cocaine. It quite possibly also takes in a range of other behaviours which don't involve any kind of drug use. However, let's take alcohol first as an example.

Alcohol as an example of the problem

Figure 1: Standard (UK) units of alcohol[1]

The amount of alcohol that people consume is most easily measured in standard 'units' (see Figure 1). A UK unit of alcohol represents a single glass of wine, a single measure of spirits, or a half-pint of standard-strength beer. Each of these contains about 8g of pure alcohol. However, much beer and wine exceeds these amounts, and wine is often sold in larger glasses, so it is important to be careful when calculating the number of units consumed.

Current recommendations by the Royal Colleges of General Practitioners, Physicians, and Psychiatrists, as well as by the British Medical Association, are that men should not consume more than 21 units per week, and women not more than 14 units per week.[2] Department of Health guidelines are that men 'should not regularly drink more than 3–4 units of alcohol a day' and that women 'should not regularly drink more than 2–3 units of alcohol a day'.[3]

In England, about 35% of men and 20% of women exceed the recommended 'sensible' limits for alcohol consumption.[4] Young people, in the

1. Institute of Alcohol Studies (2004). *IAS Fact Sheets: Alcohol and you* (London: Institute of Alcohol Studies).
2. British Medical Association (1995). *Alcohol: Guidelines on sensible drinking* (London: British Medical Association).
3. Department of Health, Home Office, Department for Education and Skills, and Department for Culture, Media and Sport (2007). *Safe. Sensible. Social. The next steps in the National Alcohol Strategy* (London: Department of Health).
4. These, and other statistics in this section, are taken from the recent Government publication *Safe. Sensible. Social. The next steps in the National Alcohol Strategy* (London: Department of Health).

age range 16–24 years, are more likely than others to consume alcohol in excess of the recommended limits; 30% of men in this age group and 22% of women have drunk more than twice the recommended amount during the course of the last week.

Research shows that alcohol-related harm correlates with the amount of alcohol consumed. The more an individual drinks, the greater the risk that that person will sustain or cause alcohol-related harm. Thus, amongst 10–15-year-olds, being drunk once or more over the last year increases the risk of offending. Amongst young people, aged 18–24 years, those who binge drink are much more likely to commit criminal offences whilst drinking, or soon after. Men (all age-groups combined) who drink more than 8 units per day increase their risk of hypertension four-fold, they have double the risk of suffering a stroke, and 13 times the risk of liver disease. Alcohol-related deaths have doubled since 1979, and excessive alcohol consumption is associated with 15,000 to 22,000 premature deaths each year.

Quite apart from the human misery and suffering, the cost of all of this to the economy is considerable. It is estimated that the health and social costs of alcohol misuse, including loss of productivity in industry, amount to £20 billion per year in England and Wales.

But what does all of this have to do with alcohol addiction? Isn't heavy drinking, or alcohol 'misuse', a completely different kind of problem? Surely, the very idea of addiction suggests some kind of inability to manage without alcohol – a medical problem, perhaps – which is in a completely different category to ordinary drinking? Well, in fact, this view of things is not upheld by research. It is impossible to distinguish solely on the basis of the amount of alcohol consumed between the heavy drinker and the alcohol addict. Heavy drinking simply merges into addictive drinking, without any clear cut-off between the two. As the amount of alcohol consumed increases, the risk of harm also gradually increases, and the risk of alcohol dependence (or addiction) increases but, again, there is no clear boundary between heavy drinking and harmful drinking or alcohol dependence.

There is also something of a paradox – especially with regard to alcohol. The risk of harm increases with greater levels of consumption. Thus, the person who drinks more than twice the recommended limit is at greater risk (for example) of sustaining a drink-driving accident than the person who drinks moderately. However, there are many more people who drink moderately. Thus, across the population as a whole, some forms of harm are associated mainly with moderate drinking and not with very heavy drinking – simply because there are many more moderate drinkers. Taking a population view of things therefore requires that account be taken of the 'prevention paradox'. In order to completely eliminate alcohol-related harm, attention has to be given not only to those who drink heavily but also to those who drink moderately – in fact, to everyone. Alcohol policy research also suggests that measures which focus only on education about moderate drinking tend not to be effective.[1] Policy measures with the greatest research support take into account the drinking of the whole population – as, for example, with taxation, which reduces both the overall consumption of the population and, thus, the associated burden of harm.

1. For a review of the evidence for different forms of alcohol policy, the reader may wish to see the World Health Organisation's report *Alcohol: No ordinary commodity* (Babor, T., Caetano, R., Casswell, S., Edwards, G., Giesbrecht, N., Graham, K., Grube, J. W., Grunewald, P., Hill, L. and Holder, H. D., 2003)

What is addiction?

Professor Jim Orford[1] has shown that similar patterns and findings apply to gambling, drug-taking, eating and sexual behaviour as to alcohol, all of which he considers to be examples of 'excessive appetitive behaviours'. In each case, the behaviour can become excessive, and this is associated with harm and with features of 'addiction', but in each case it is also difficult to find any clear boundary between what is 'normal' and what is abnormal. Thus, we cannot completely separate normal drinking from alcoholism; we can only estimate how much people drink, how much harm alcohol is causing, or how addicted they are.

Up until now, the word 'addiction' has been used rather loosely and without definition. In fact, it is used relatively little now in scientific circles, as it has proved to be rather difficult to define, or at least it has meant different things to different people. If a definition were to be offered, that suggested by Professor Robert West would appear to be a good one; that is, addiction is:

> behaviour over which an individual has impaired control, with harmful consequences.[2]

However, this is a general definition and we have seen that it is not necessary to be addicted in order to sustain harm. It is also difficult to measure exactly what 'impaired control' is. If I eat rather more of a very tempting dessert than I think I should, knowing that I need to lose weight, does that make me addicted?

The dependence syndrome

A big step forward in understanding addictive behaviour was made in the late 1970s with the introduction of the concept of the 'dependence syndrome'.[3] This employs the concept of the medical 'syndrome', as a

1. Orford, J. (2001). 'Addiction as excessive appetite', *Addiction, 96*, pp. 15–31.
2. West, R. (2001). 'Theories of addiction', *Addiction*, 96, p. 3.
3. Edwards, G. and Gross, M. (1976). 'Alcohol dependence: Provisional description of a clinical syndrome', *British Medical Journal*, 1, 1058–1061.

collection of signs and symptoms that seem to occur consistently together, as a better way of talking about what it means to be addicted. The dependence syndrome, originally described in relation to alcohol, but later in relation to other drugs and behaviours, also reflects the biological, psychological and social aspects of what it means to be addicted, and it is something that can be measured, so we can make an estimate of just how addicted someone is. It has become the basis of both the internationally employed systems of definition and classification of mental disorder, those of the World Health Organisation (ICD-10) and the American Psychiatric Association (DSM-IV).[1]

The seven elements of the alcohol dependence syndrome are as follows:

- Narrowing of drinking repertoire.
- Salience of alcohol-seeking behaviour.
- Increased tolerance of alcohol.
- Repeated withdrawal symptoms.
- Relief or avoidance of withdrawal symptoms by further drinking.
- Subjective compulsion to drink alcohol.
- Reinstatement of dependence after abstinence.

Not all of these elements have to be present, and each can be present in varying degree. It will be helpful now, briefly, to consider each in turn.

Narrowing of drinking repertoire

Most people who drink alcohol have a 'repertoire' of drinking behaviours. One day they may drink beer in a pub after work with colleagues, another day they may have wine with a family meal at home, and another day they may attend a cocktail party with friends. One day they may have several drinks, another day they may have only one, and on other days they do not drink at all. However, as dependence progresses, this repertoire becomes narrower: drinking on one day is increasingly similar to drinking on any other day in quantity, type and pattern.

1. Respectively, World Health Organisation, 1992). *International Classification of Diseases* (10th Revision); American Psychiatric Association (1994). *Diagnostic and Statistical Manual of Mental Disorders* (4th edition) (Washington, DC: Author).

Salience of alcohol-seeking behaviour

Usually, drinking is subsidiary to other priorities in life. Thus, we don't drink when driving because we know that this puts ourselves and others at risk. If drinking causes us harm and, for example, a doctor advises us to cut down the amount that we drink, we take that advice because we value our health and wish to avoid harm. However, as dependence progresses drinking becomes increasingly harmful and yet it takes priority over other areas of life – it becomes the 'salient' concern. As salience increases, marriage, work, health, morality and other concerns are all sacrificed as necessary to the priority of drinking, and daily life begins to revolve increasingly around the priority of drinking.

Increased tolerance of alcohol

'Tolerance', in this context, is a pharmacological concept. The effect of most drugs is dependent upon the dose administered or consumed. The relation between dose and effect, at least for a given individual, is usually predictable. However, regular use often results in diminished effect. Thus, in order to achieve the same effect, an increased dose is required. For the drinker, this means that the amount of alcohol consumed tends to increase, so that the desired subjective experience of intoxication is maintained. Eventually, when liver damage is severe and the body is unable to break down alcohol effectively any more, a reverse tolerance may occur and small amounts of alcohol can have a disproportionately large effect.

Repeated withdrawal symptoms

After prolonged regular consumption of alcohol, physiological adaptation to the presence of alcohol in the bloodstream and other tissues takes place. Once this has happened, a falling level of alcohol (for example, as a result of an admission to hospital or during a night's sleep) results in a physiological imbalance. This is manifested in a so-called 'withdrawal syndrome', the symptoms of which are specific to the type of drug concerned. In the case of alcohol, this characteristically includes nausea, sweating and tremor. In more severe cases there may be vomiting and severe anxiety. The alcohol-withdrawal syndrome may also be complicated by fits, or by 'delirium tremens' (commonly known as 'DTs'), a potentially life-threatening confusional state associated with disorientation, delusions and hallucinations.

Relief or avoidance of withdrawal symptoms by further drinking

Withdrawal symptoms are relieved by resumed alcohol consumption and most alcohol-dependent individuals therefore learn that the discomfort of withdrawal is easily treated by having another drink. This can lead, for example, to early morning drinking in order to relieve the discomfort of withdrawal that has begun whilst asleep the night before.

Subjective compulsion to drink alcohol

The subjective experience of being dependent upon alcohol – or other drugs and behaviours – is that of feeling a strong inner drive to engage, and re-engage, with drinking (or drug use). This can be experienced as 'craving' – a strong desire for alcohol – or impaired control of drinking, such that it exceeds pre-determined limits. Most dependent individuals can stop drinking for a time without too much trouble. Remaining abstinent for the longer term is much more difficult.

Reinstatement of dependence after abstinence

The establishment of dependent drinking usually takes a number of years. Typically, it takes place gradually over a period of time. However, re-establishment, or 're-instatement', of the dependent pattern of drinking is typically much more rapid. Furthermore, it can occur many years later. Thus, someone who imagines that they have overcome their alcohol dependence, as a result of several years of complete abstinence from alcohol, may start drinking again, imagining that there will be no further problem. In these circumstances, a dependent pattern of drinking can be resumed very quickly – from within a few hours, to a few days, weeks or months. So striking is this phenomenon that it appears to be exceedingly unusual for anyone once they became severely dependent, ever to be able to return to a moderate pattern of social drinking.

The causes of dependence

What are the causes of dependence? On the one hand it is clear that there are genetically determined biological differences between people which render some of us more vulnerable than the rest to dependence upon one drug or another. On the other hand it is also clear that the environment in which we live is also hugely important. People do not use drugs that are not available to them and, even if a particular drug is available, the decision whether or not to use it will also be influenced by the attitudes of others – or the 'acceptability' of drug use within that culture or community. In addition to this, other stresses and events might further predispose some individuals to increase their use of a drug, as a means of managing distress or anxiety, for example. In general, the more often someone uses a drug, and the more of it they use, the more likely they are to become dependent upon it.

As we have already seen in the case of alcohol, the harms resulting from the use of a particular substance are directly proportional to the extent to which that substance is used, or consumed, within a given population. Amongst these harms we might identify dependence as being a particular concern, as it makes discontinuation of the drug less likely, even where harm is caused, and it tends to further escalate the extent of use by the dependent person.

Of course, the nature of the drug or behaviour which becomes the focus of addiction is also important. Up until this point, alcohol has been used as the main example as it is widely and legally consumed, it is socially accepted, and yet also potentially highly dangerous because of its effects on human behaviour and its potential to cause organ damage (especially to the brain, liver, and pancreas, but also to many other organs). However, alcohol is only one substance about which we need to be concerned.

People do not generally become addicted to a drug unless it has some mood-altering, or other mind-altering, property. Even then, some drugs appear to be more 'addictive' than others. In the case of LSD, for example, the development of tolerance is so rapid as to make true dependence relatively rare. Continued regular use is increasingly ineffective. However, this does not mean that intermittent use of LSD does not cause significant harm – just that the harm is less related to dependence and more related to the particular mind-altering and other effects of the drug.

The legal, and more or less socially acceptable, drugs which can cause dependence include alcohol, nicotine and caffeine. Prescribed drugs which can lead to dependence include various kinds of tranquillisers, and especially the benzodiazepine group (including drugs like Valium, Librium and Ativan). Controlled drugs, possession, sale and use of which are regulated under the Misuse of Drugs Act 1971,[1] include heroin, cocaine, amphetamines, cannabis, ecstasy and LSD. Solvents, although not controlled under the act, are also both harmful and mood-altering. Commonly misused by school-age children, their sale is restricted in the UK on the basis of age.[2] Hallucinogenic mushrooms are also widely used by young people, but possession of these mushrooms, which grow in the wild, is not illegal.[3] It is not possible to go into detail here concerning the effects of all of these drugs and the type and extent of harm that each causes. However, the interested reader may wish to consult one or more of the helpful reports or reference works produced by various organisations, including the Diocese of Southwark, the Royal College of Psychiatrists, and others.[4]

It has been mentioned that behaviours, as well as drugs, can be associated with patterns of dependence. Mostly, these behaviours are not the subject of legislation, although, of course, concerns with gambling, one of the first behavioural patterns not involving drug/substance use to be recognised as a form of addiction,[5] have led to legal regulation of gaming, lotteries and betting. Scientific reports of shopping, exercise and sexual behaviour as forms of dependence do suggest that patterns of behaviour which do not involve ingestion or administration of drugs into the body

1. This Act is subject to various subsequent amendments, including, for example, the Drugs Act (2005).
2. Only persons aged 18 years or above may purchase solvents, including gas lighter refills, certain types of adhesive and aerosol, paints and petroleum-based products, etc. Alcohol sales are similarly regulated. Tobacco products and National Lottery tickets/scratchcards are restricted to those aged 16 years and over.
3. Preparation of extracts from these mushrooms (*Psilocybe semilanceata*) is illegal, however.
4. Brands, B., Sproule, B. and Marshman, J. (1998). *Drugs and Drug Abuse: A reference text* (3rd edition) (Toronto: Addiction Research Foundation); Buxton, P., Drummond, T. and MacNamara, F. (1998). *The Chemical Generation: Understanding young people and drug use* (London: Southwark Diocesan Board for Church in Society); Working Party of the Royal College of Psychiatrists and the Royal College of Physicians (2000). *Drugs: Dilemmas and choices* (London: Gaskell).
5. Moran, E. (1970). 'Gambling as a form of dependence', *British Journal of Addiction*, 64, 419–428.

can display the features of dependence described above.[1] A popular literature is concerned with a much wider range of behaviours including, for example, religious behaviour.[2] Caution should perhaps be urged, lest 'addiction' or 'dependence' simply become labels for people whose behaviour is different from our own. However, limitation of the concept of addiction only to the use of drugs and substances external to the human body would equally appear to miss the point. Addiction is something which, directly or indirectly, concerns us all.

An example: George

> George[3] was a church warden, and a faithful member of the congregation of his local parish church. He was also a local GP, nearing retirement. Several members of the church council had commented that he seemed to smell strongly of alcohol at church council meetings, but one member of the congregation had received a visit from him at home one morning, in his capacity as a medical practitioner, and had thought that he smelled of alcohol then, too. She also commented that he had a marked tremor when attempting to examine her.
>
> Although only George's wife was aware of this, his own doctor had told George to cut down on his drinking. He said it was damaging his liver. George flatly denied that he drank too much, and told his doctor that he would treat himself in future and that he didn't need advice like that. George's wife didn't dare mention the subject, because George always reacted angrily, but she noticed that he no longer spent time with the family, or reading, both of which he had always loved, because he was always going to 'meet some friends'. She was pretty sure

1. de Coverley Veale, D. M. W. (1987). 'Exercise dependence', *British Journal of Addiction*, 82, 735–740; Glatt, M. M. and Cook, C. C. H. (1987). 'Pathological spending as a form of psychological dependence', *British Journal of Addiction*, 82, 1257–1258; Goodman, A. (1998). *Sexual Addiction* (Madison: International Universities Press).
2. Booth, L. (1989). *Breaking the Chains: Understanding religious addiction and religious abuse* (Long Beach: Emmaus).
3. This is a false name, and the case is based on no particular individual, but it illustrates the kinds of things that are very commonly encountered in clinical practice when working with people who are alcohol-dependent.

> that he actually went to the pub, because he always smelled strongly of alcohol when he got home. However, she only ever saw him drinking a couple of glasses of wine with his evening meal.

George illustrates a number of features of alcohol dependence. Salience is especially evident here, as it would appear that George's drinking has assumed priority over his professional, marital and other social obligations, as well as his health. He has also almost certainly been driving when over the legal limit. It would appear that he drinks in the morning, to relieve withdrawal symptoms, but that this is only partially successful at reducing the tremor which he experiences as a part of withdrawal. Although it is not a diagnostic feature of the dependence syndrome, George also illustrates the common problem of denial. Even though everyone else can see that there is a problem, and that his life appears to be self-destructive, he strongly denies it.

Summary of the problem

To summarise briefly, addiction is thus, at the extreme, a pattern of behaviour which is clearly out of the ordinary. It causes significant harm, it is associated with distinctive biological, psychological and social disturbances, and it is characterised by an apparently self-destructive pattern of behaviour which continues either in the face of denial that there is any problem, or else despite the best efforts of the dependent individual to stop. However, addiction is not something which is confined to illicit drugs, or even to socially acceptable but potentially harmful drugs like alcohol. Neither is it confined only to a few people, but rather it touches – even if only indirectly – on the behaviour of us all.

How should it be dealt with?

Can it be treated?

Secular (medical, social and psychological) approaches to the treatment of addiction take a variety of forms. At the simplest level, they might include a brief intervention aimed at recognising harm, or potential harm, and encouraging a corresponding change in behaviour to reduce that harm, or risk of harm. At the most intensive level, they might involve residential treatment over a period of months, aimed at breaking the addictive pattern of thought and behaviour and establishing a stable abstinence from all actual or potential objects of addiction. In between these extremes, there are a variety of out-patient and day-patient programmes, or counselling facilities, which address the addictive behaviour itself and/or the perceived underlying causes of that behaviour.

Brief interventions

Brief interventions have been found to be extremely effective, and especially cost-effective, in the field of alcohol misuse. For someone suffering the early stages of harm as a result of their drinking, an intervention of this kind – usually comprising a short meeting with a nurse, counsellor or doctor – is all that is usually required. However, this should be distinguished from educational measures as a means of prevention of alcohol- and drug-related problems. Generally speaking, educational measures aimed at the whole population (for example, in school) have not been found to prevent alcohol-related harm and, in the case of drugs education, have occasionally increased rather than reduced illicit drug use.

Help for the established addict

For someone with more established or advanced problems, something more than brief advice is likely to be required. A variety of approaches might be employed, but the philosophy of harm reduction is now almost universal. According to this approach, no moral judgement of the rights or wrongs of drug use (or whichever addictive behaviour is the cause of concern) is offered *per se*. The focus of therapy is rather on reducing the harm that the individual and others might experience as a result of that behaviour. This is achieved in a pragmatic and hierarchical fashion. Thus, for example, the advice might be not to use illicit drugs at all but, if the drug user does decide to go on using them, then they are advised not to inject them. Again, the harm reduction philosophy recognises that, when advised not to inject drugs, some drug users will continue to do so, and so such users are advised to use clean needles and a sterile injection technique. In some cases, drug users are maintained for the short- to long-term on prescribed doses of an appropriate drug (for example, methadone) with the aim of eliminating more dangerous illicit drug use.

Interventions to address psychological patterns of behaviour usually involve some kind of counselling or psychotherapy. However, there may be minor or even life-threatening medical complications to address at the outset of treatment, such as abscesses at injection sites or other infections, liver disease or other organ damage. Such problems will require assessment by a doctor or nurse, even if ongoing counselling is to be provided by someone else.

When dealing with dependence, medical input will also be required in order to determine the most appropriate management of the withdrawal syndrome. This can be merely a case of offering reassurance and psychological support, or it can require in-patient admission, but can usually be managed in the out-patient clinic. Amongst the most serious complications of any drug withdrawal syndrome is the condition of 'delirium tremens' in the case of alcohol withdrawal (see above). However, fits (or 'seizures') can complicate various drug withdrawal states (notably those from alcohol and various kinds of tranquillisers). Proper medical advice is therefore essential, and prescription of medication may be required. In the case of alcohol withdrawal, this will usually include a minor tranquilliser and thiamine supplements (to prevent thiamine-related brain damage). In the case of opioid drugs (including many of the stronger painkillers and illicit heroin), a substitute of the same drug group is usually prescribed and then reduced in dose and withdrawn gradually. However, there are also non-opioid medications available which specifically suppress opioid withdrawal symptoms.

Usually, the management of drug withdrawal is a fairly simple medical matter (although, as has been said, not without its complications if neglected or managed badly). The real challenge of treatment lies in the social and psychological measures employed to break the pattern of dependent use. The goal of such treatment may be either to achieve 'controlled' or 'social' use or to achieve complete abstinence, and discussion of this should usually be a matter for negotiation and agreement at an early treatment session. As has already been mentioned, severe dependence will usually indicate that a goal of complete abstinence is most appropriate, and this may be the only treatment goal with any likelihood of success. However, it can be better on occasions to engage someone in treatment with a goal of dose reduction, or moderation, if they are not willing to countenance abstinence, rather than lose them from treatment altogether. A supplementary agreement can usually be reached, to the effect that the goal may have to change from moderation to abstinence if moderation proves impossible to achieve.

Amongst the common psychological approaches employed in treatment are motivational enhancement and relapse prevention. The former recognises that motivation to change addictive patterns of behaviour may vary, and that the addict may be at varying stages of having decided to change or having acted upon a decision to change. The aim is to establish which stage an addict has reached and to work on building motivation for change. Relapse prevention recognises that addictive behaviour tends to relapse and aims at identifying the circumstances in which this is most likely to happen (so-called 'high-risk situations') and developing strategies for coping with such situations. A distinction is also made between a minor failure to adhere to treatment targets, usually referred to as a 'lapse', which may be a learning experience, and a major failure or relapse.

How to intervene if you are concerned

What is the appropriate response to encountering someone in your own family, place of worship or place of work, who you think might be addicted? This is a difficult question to answer briefly. On the one hand, it is obviously not helpful to 'turn a blind eye', or to pretend that nothing is wrong. On the other hand, wading in with confident accusations is unlikely to be constructive. Between these two extremes, there is the place of knowing enough to recognise that expert help might be needed, and that tentative and sensitive steps need to be taken at first if a good final outcome is to be achieved. So, being generally informed is good, and it is that general information that this chapter seeks to impart. But knowing where to get expert help is probably even more important. Where can that be found?

Provision of statutory services for people with drug- and alcohol-related problems and other kinds of addictive disorders is very geographically variable. A good general practitioner (GP) should be well informed about where help can be obtained, and many GP practices will have direct links with specialist agencies. Usually, there is provision of specialist treatment within the health service, often there is provision by charities, and many treatment programmes are provided privately. In addition to all of these professionally led sources of help, Alcoholics Anonymous (AA) and other Twelve Step groups offer mutual help and are widely available. Telephone numbers can be found in local directories, and on the internet.[1] Very often, if contacted in advance, members will be willing to come and make contact with a potential new recruit who is coming to a meeting for the first time.

So, apart from being generally informed and finding out about local services, what are the 'tentative and sensitive' steps that a lay person might take in order to help someone who they think might be addicted? If non-threatening questions can be raised about drinking, drug use, or other behaviour that is a cause of concern, without simply antagonising the person concerned, then a conversation of that sort might be a good place to start. This is unlikely to be helpful if the subject has already become a battleground and defensive positions of denial and mistrust are deeply entrenched. In such circumstances, it might be good to go and speak to a specialist counsellor or drug worker, or other professional person, to get advice on how best to help. In other circumstances, however, the trick is to find a non-threatening, supportive and constructive way of introducing

1. See, for example, www.alcoholics-anonymous.org.uk/ or www.ukna.org/

the conversation. This might be easier if there is already a tangible focus of concern – such as a doctor's recommendation to drink less, or a warning about drinking at work. In any case, it is always important to stick to objective facts and personal concerns, not to speculate, jump to conclusions or blame others.

George revisited

> Gossip was beginning to spread around the parish, with quite a few people saying that it would be wrong to say anything to George, and others that they were sure that there wasn't a problem. Some commented that, in any case, he was soon due to retire. Despite this, Andrew, the other church warden in the parish, decided to challenge him one evening before a church council meeting. Although he took George to one side, several other people were within earshot. George responded angrily, saying that all Andrew could smell was the mouthwash that he (George) used. Shouting that he'd never been so insulted, he marched out of the church council meeting, threatening never to come back again if Andrew was still there.

We don't know exactly what Andrew said to George – but it clearly didn't have a very constructive outcome. Most importantly, George is now not speaking to Andrew, so Andrew has lost the chance to have any further input. If Andrew had spoken first to George's wife, he'd have known that this was not the time and place, and not the right way, to go about trying to get George to see the need for help. However, George's wife is at her wit's end and doesn't know what to do. Sadly, no one in the parish has noticed this and she suffers alone. Despite this, the story could still have a happy ending:

> George's vicar, seeing what had happened, visited George and his wife at their home the following evening. He stressed that he was simply concerned and wanted to help. With a third party present, George's wife was able to express her fears, but she

didn't go beyond what she knew. She simply said that, even though she never saw him drinking more than a couple of glasses of wine, she knew that something was wrong. She had lost the George she knew and loved. They both cried, and George found himself able, for the first time, to admit that perhaps he did need to seek help.

Religious responses

Various responses to the treatment of addiction have been offered from within different religious traditions: Christian,[1] Islamic,[2] Buddhist[3] and Native American.[4] Amongst Christian responses, there have been those from a more evangelical tradition and also those from a more liberal perspective. The former tend to be aimed primarily at a drug-free lifestyle and might be termed 'redemptive' in their theology. Sin and addiction are more or less closely identified in such an understanding. The latter are more likely to be open to a relapse prevention approach and to recognising the need to meet with people 'where they are', perhaps with little expectation of change in the early stages. This might be referred to more as an 'incarnational' theological approach.[5] Methods employed vary widely, and it would be misleading to offer over-generalisations. Some programmes offer an almost entirely secular programme and their Christian ethos provides largely the rationale and motivation for their work. Others focus almost entirely upon Christian discipleship objectives and draw little or nothing from medical and psychological approaches. Most Christian

1. Moos, R. H., Mehren, B. and Moos, B. (1978). 'Evaluation of a Salvation Army alcoholism treatment program', *Journal of Studies on Alcohol*, 39, 1267–1275.
2. Abdel-Mawgoud, M., Fateem, L. and Al-Sharif, A. I. (1995). 'Development of a comprehensive treatment program for chemical dependency at Al Amal Hospital, Damman', *Journal of Substance Abuse Treatment*, 12, 369–376.
3. Barrett, M. E. (1997). 'Wat Thamkrabok: A Buddhist drug rehabilitation program in Thailand', *Substance Use and Misuse*, 32, 435–459.
4. Garrett, M. T. and Carroll, J. J. (2000). 'Mending the Broken Circle: Treatment of substance dependence among Native Americans', *Journal of Counseling and Development*, 78, 379–388.
5. This emphasises the participation of Christ in human form in a fallen world with all its evil and imperfection. According to this model, Christ always precedes us when we seek out those who are in need. This model emphasises the identification of Christ with those who are in need, and sees the drug user more as victim than as sinner. The contrast between these theological positions as expressed in pastoral care is described in more detail by Christopher Moody (1992). *Eccentric Ministry* (London: Darton, Longman and Todd).

programmes probably fall somewhere in between these extremes. However, prayer, Bible study, worship and Christian counselling tend to feature, especially in programmes of the more redemptive theological type.

Spiritual responses

Spirituality is also increasingly recognised as being important even within secular addiction treatment programmes. In particular, this is true within the 'spiritual but not religious' mutual-help approach of Alcoholics Anonymous (AA) and its sister organisations – Narcotics Anonymous (NA); Cocaine Anonymous (CA); Al-Anon, for the families of alcoholics; Families Anonymous (FA), for the families of drug addicts – and the professionally led programmes which adopt their 'Twelve Step' philosophy. This approach has been very influential in North America, and now accounts for a significant part of the provision of non-statutory facilities in the UK; furthermore, AA and NA groups are available all over the UK and around the world. It therefore deserves some further description here.

AA began in Akron, Ohio, USA, in 1935. From the outset it was a mutual help organisation that recognised the help that alcoholics could give to each other in their recovery. It was influenced by medical and religious thinking of the time, including ideas drawn from the Oxford Group, an evangelical Christian movement. However, in its efforts to be accessible to people from all faith traditions and none, it came to emphasise the content of its programme as spiritual but not religious, and might now be considered to offer a form of secular spirituality.[1] The philosophy of its programme is encompassed in its Twelve Steps, which summarise the experiences of the founding members, and so are expressed in the first person:

1. We admitted we were powerless over alcohol – that our lives had become unmanageable.
2. Came to believe that a Power greater than ourselves could restore us to sanity.

1. Kurtz, E. (1996). 'Twelve Step Programs' in Van Ness, P. H. (ed.), *Spirituality and the Secular Quest* (London: SCM), pp. 277–302.

3. Made a decision to turn our will and our lives over to the care of God *as we understood him.*
4. Made a searching and fearless moral inventory of ourselves.
5. Admitted to God, to ourselves and to another human being the exact nature of our wrongs.
6. Were entirely ready to have God remove all these defects of character.
7. Humbly asked him to remove our shortcomings.
8. Made a list of all persons we had harmed, and became willing to make amends to them all.
9. Made direct amends to such people wherever possible, except when to do so would injure them or others.
10. Continued to take personal inventory, and when we were wrong, promptly admitted it.
11. Sought through prayer and meditation to improve our conscious contact with God *as we understood him,* praying only for knowledge of his will for us and the power to carry that out.
12. Having had a spiritual awakening as the result of these steps we tried to carry this message to alcoholics and to practise these principles in all our affairs.[1]

The steps include a number of important theological ideas, notably: that help is needed from a 'Higher Power', subsequently referred to explicitly as God; that recognition of personal moral failings and a desire to be changed are important to recovery; and that an ongoing personal spirituality of prayer, meditation and helping others with similar problems must become a rule of life. The emphasis is upon a personal experience of divine grace, but theological terms such as 'grace' are studiously avoided, as are doctrinal

1. Alcoholics Anonymous (1977). *Twelve Steps and Twelve Traditions* (New York: Alcoholics Anonymous World Services).

statements. The programme must start with recognition of personal powerlessness and an awareness of God, as the individual alcoholic is able to understand God. In fact, for the atheist or agnostic, it is not even necessary to believe in God at all – only to recognise that they must turn to a power greater than themselves, whatever they may understand that to be.

Subsequently, various sister organisations formed which met the needs of those addicted to other drugs and behaviours and the needs of the families of those addicted. Each has adopted its own Twelve Step programme, modelled on the original wording devised by the members of AA. AA itself has grown to become an international network of over 100,000 groups, and over 2 million members, operating in 150 countries worldwide.[1]

There is no doubt that AA has helped many Christians, as well as people from other faith traditions. It has itself drawn heavily from the Christian tradition, and so its principles do not conflict with traditional Christian doctrine. However, for some Christians, the lack of affirmation of Christian doctrine is itself a problem, and so various groups have attempted either to revise the Twelve Steps, or else use them within a specifically Christian environment.[2]

1. www.alcoholics-anonymous.org
2. See, for example: www.overcomersoutreach.org

A Christian response

Various 'models' of (or ways of understanding) addiction have been proposed in scientific writing on the subject. Amongst these, the so-called 'disease model' has been amongst the most controversial and influential. According to this model, addiction is a disease in the same way as many other mental and physical conditions. There is debate and speculation about exactly what the nature of that disease is, but evidence has come to light in support of a genetic basis for alcohol and drug dependence, as well as a variety of biological, psychological and social disturbances that may be identified in the dependent state.

Amongst many benefits of the disease model is that of reduced stigma. The addict has not chosen to be as they are; they are in need of help, not condemnation. They are victims of the disease; it is not their fault. For many, this has been a huge advance from the so-called 'moral model', which is said to have preceded the more medical perspectives that have developed over the course of the last two centuries. According to the moral model, people are addicted simply through their own fault. They are bad – or at least weak – people who are reaping the consequences of their own behaviour.

The moral model is not popular in clinical or research circles interested in addiction today. It is seen as discredited, and is criticised as being little more than blind prejudice. However, it does place responsibility upon the addict for their plight, and the disease model is roundly criticised in some quarters for removing that responsibility. In fact, both criticisms are somewhat unfair. Those who campaigned against 'intemperance' in the nineteenth century were often very sympathetic to the plight of the addict, whom they saw as a victim of society's unwillingness to seriously address intemperance as much as of their own behaviour, and often worked hard to help those who suffered from 'inebriety'. On the other hand, proponents of the disease model have always emphasised the importance of personal responsibility for recovery on the part of the addict. According to this philosophy, no one is responsible for being an addict, but every addict is responsible for engaging with a programme of recovery.

There are, in fact, many other models of addiction. Amongst psychological models, perhaps that of addiction as a learned behaviour is the most widely influential. Addicts learn to use drugs because drug use is strongly psychologically reinforced – both by the mood-altering effects of the drug itself and also by social support. Yet others have criticised the concept of addiction altogether, suggesting that it is either a myth or simply a way of socially labelling deviant behaviour. In different ways all of these approaches tend to normalise the behaviour of the addict.

What are the theological models of addiction? This question could be answered from the perspective of different faith traditions. Thus, for example, we might wish to consider the injunctions of the Qur'an against drinking alcohol and gambling on the basis of their adverse spiritual effects:

> Satan's plan is (but)
> To excite enmity and hatred
> Between you, with intoxicants
> And gambling, and hinder you
> From the remembrance
> Of Allah, and from prayer:
> Will ye not then abstain?[1]

Or else we might wish to consider the importance that Buddhism attributes to the connection between suffering and attachment to things in this world which, in any case, are impermanent.[2] Undoubtedly there is wisdom in such models, and that wisdom might both inform Christian theological reflection and also provide a good starting point for pastoral work with people from other faiths. Indeed, identification of the implicit or explicit theological models that are held by someone who suffers from an addictive disorder might be a very good place from which to start trying to understand how to help them. However, the focus of the present work is on Christian theological reflection and pastoral care, and the present

1. Surah 5:91; Ali, A. Y. (ed.) (2000). *The Holy Qur'an: Translation and commentary* (Birmingham: IPCI: Islamic Vision).
2. Groves, P. and Farmer, R. (1994). 'Buddhism and addictions', *Addiction Research*, 2, 183–194.

author writes from a Christian perspective, so further consideration of theological models here will therefore be undertaken primarily from that perspective.

Within the Christian tradition, various theological models of addiction might be identified. Thus, for example, addiction might be identified as sin, or at least as a direct consequence of sin. According to this model – which looks very much like the moral model in theological clothing – people are responsible for the ways in which they use and misuse drugs – including alcohol – and any suggestion that addiction is a disease is simply unbiblical.[1] We might refer to this as the 'addiction as sin' model.

Another Christian theological model might be to emphasise that addiction is reflective of life lived in the selfish pursuit of life apart from God. This model recognises that people behave sinfully in response to their own pain, that we are vulnerable to addiction, and that in fact addiction is reflective of the human condition – the way that we *all* are.[2] For shorthand, we might call this the 'sin as addiction' model. It has also been pointed out that in Christian Scripture sin is likened to disease, and that this is therefore not as different as it might initially appear, in theological terms, to the disease model.[3] However, it deals with a disease that, in different ways, affects us all. In one sense or another we are all addicted.

Of course, there are various ways in which these models might be modified or combined. Sin and addiction might be understood as overlapping but distinct domains. On this basis, whilst they frequently occur together, each may be found without evidence of the other. Addiction may occur as a result of diverse factors, not all of which are necessarily sinful, but some of which may be.[4] We might also imagine a theological model of health and disease within which addiction is understood as disease but not sin.

If we are looking for a constructive theological model, it should address the theological and scientific realities of the condition. These should

1. Playfair, W. L. (1991). *The Useful Lie* (Wheaton: Crossway).
2. See, for example, Lenters, W. (1985). *The Freedom We Crave* (Grand Rapids: Eerdmans).
3. McCormick, P. (1989). *Sin as Addiction* (New York: Paulist Press).
4. Mercadante, L. A. (1996). *Victims and Sinners* (Louisville: Westminster John Knox Press); Plantinga, C. (1996). *Not the Way It's Supposed To Be: A breviary of sin* (Grand Rapids: Eerdmans).

include the bio-psycho-social, and spiritual, nature of the dependence syndrome on the one hand, and should be consonant with Christian Scripture and tradition on the other. It should also be 'reasonable'. That is, given the theological and scientific realities, it should make sense – it should be intelligible. Elsewhere, I have attempted to construct such a model, drawing particularly upon reflections on two Christian texts – one drawn from Scripture (specifically from Romans chapter 7) and one drawn from Christian tradition (specifically from Augustine's *Confessions*).[1]

Both St Paul and St Augustine talk of an internal struggle or division which affects their ability to choose that which is good. We see this, for example, in these verses from St Paul:

> I do not do the good I want, but the evil I do not want is what I do. Now if I do what I do not want, it is no longer I that do it, but sin that dwells within me. So I find it to be a law that when I want to do what is good, evil lies close at hand. For I delight in the law of God in my inmost self, but I see in my members another law at war with the law of my mind, making me captive to the law of sin that dwells in my members. Wretched man that I am! Who will rescue me from this body of death? Thanks be to God through Jesus Christ our Lord! So then, with my mind I am a slave to the law of God, but with my flesh I am a slave to the law of sin.[2]

Paul speaks here in a vividly self-reflective manner about his ability to recognise within himself a tendency (which he calls sin) to do that which he does not want to do. He sees this as contrary to reason, as enslaving, imprisoning and life-denying. These qualities are themselves evocative of the nature of addiction, but the subjective quality of the inner struggle is especially evocative of the compulsion that is one of the core elements of the dependence syndrome. To what extent are we justified in identifying the two struggles as being the same kind of thing? To what extent can we deny the similarities and insist upon their essential difference?

1. Cook, C. C. H. (2006). *Alcohol, Addiction and Christian Ethics* (Cambridge: Cambridge University Press).
2. Romans 7:19-25 (New Revised Standard Version)

Christian Scripture and tradition, as exemplified in the writings of St Paul and St Augustine, reveal a capacity for self-reflectiveness which is at the heart of what it is to be human. The struggles that this capacity reveals within us must include those which we might want to label 'addictive', although this is not to say that addiction and sin are one and the same thing. However, it does suggest that addiction is a pathology which is particularly human, in that it arises when we find that we wish ourselves to be other than we are, or to behave in ways other than those in which we actually do behave. To deny that there is any similarity between the phenomenon of addiction and the human struggle with sin would appear to be rather implausible. However, this is not to say that we are all addicted (to sin) or that all sin is addiction.

Addiction affects people in all dimensions of human experience – biological, psychological, social and spiritual. Thus, divisions similar or analogous to those of which Paul and Augustine speak can be identified at a physiological level in the process of drug withdrawal, at a psychological level in divided motivation, at a social level in the divisions between those who promote or reinforce drug use and those who are its victims and, finally, in the division that addiction causes between human beings and God. To say that such concerns can be reduced entirely to scientific ones is atheistic, but to imagine that they are purely theological is arguably a denial of the incarnation. A theological reflection upon the nature of addiction thus takes us to the heart of the Christian gospel.

Do's and don'ts

- Do be informed.
- Do seek specialist help.
- Do think about how your church can be involved in helping people who struggle with addiction.
- Do have an alcohol and drugs policy for church employees and church premises.
- Do go to an open meeting[1] of AA or NA to find out more about what goes on and how they work.
- Don't assume that Christian young people have not been offered drugs or that they have never tried them.
- Don't go beyond your expertise.
- Don't collude or enable continuing addictive behaviour (for example, by giving money which might be used to buy alcohol/ drugs, or protecting people from the consequence of addiction in such a way that they don't need to think about stopping or getting help).
- Don't take away a person's responsibility for their own recovery from addiction.
- Don't forget the family and friends of the addicted person – they need help too!

1. AA and NA have open and closed meetings. The latter are for members only. Visitors are usually very welcome at the former. Telephone numbers are available in the local telephone directory and on the internet.

Conclusion

As we have seen, both Christians and members of other faith traditions have developed programmes of addiction treatment or rehabilitation within the framework of their own beliefs, and in response to their differently perceived senses of calling to respond to the needs of those who suffer. However, this is only one level of response. At a wider level, Christians (and others) need to be involved in addressing the economic and social problems that nurture not only addiction but the broader patterns of behaviour of which drinking is a part. For example, Christian attitudes to drinking and drug-taking need to be examined. Outright rejection is likely to be as unhelpful as blind acceptance, but a critical concern needs to be well informed and sensitively conveyed. This sensitivity will also be needed at the narrower level of response: that of dealing with our own behaviour, and the behaviour of those whom we know and encounter. On the one hand, a healthy self-examination may be required, and on the other a compassionate and sensitive willingness to raise questions and seek expert help. However, it is rarely helpful to wade in with an ill-thought-out confrontation. 'You're an alcoholic!' is more likely to elicit denial and hostility than agreement and willingness to accept help.

Recommended reading

- Cook, C. C. H. (2006). *Alcohol, Addiction and Christian Ethics* (Cambridge University Press).
- Edwards, G., Marshall, E. J. and Cook, C. C. H. (2003). *The Treatment of Drinking Problems*, (4th edition) (Cambridge University Press).
- Southwark Diocesan Board for Church in Society (1998). *The Chemical Generation: Understanding young people and drug use* (Southwark Diocesan Board for Church in Society).

Gambling Addiction

—— James Walsh ——

The intention of this chapter is to give essential information to people in positions of management, leadership or pastoral care concerning the nature of compulsive gambling and its impact on gamblers and their families, what treatment options are available, and how Christian faith may guide a response to the proliferation of gambling venues and an appropriate response to the gambler. Most frequently it is the family, friends and employers of compulsive gamblers who seek help first, as the gambler's relationships deteriorate as a result of the erratic and often illegal behaviours necessary to perpetuate the gambling. Mental health professionals and clergy are usually the first line of defence for individuals suffering from the emotional, financial, and spiritual consequences of compulsive gambling. Gamblers and their families are generally deeply distressed when first seeking help for the devastating effects of compulsive gambling; having knowledge about this problem and being able to provide assurance that there is hope is essential to initiating the healing process. I hope to be able to convey this information through case studies and a review of current literature that describes the possible causes and treatment of compulsive gambling, and also provide a Christian perspective on bringing compassionate care to compulsive gamblers and their families.

What is gambling addiction?

According to the Oxford English Dictionary,[1] gambling is defined as an act whereby the participant pursues a monetary gain without using his or her skills. In its more common usage, gambling also includes activities that require skill, such as betting on a sporting game in which one is actually a participant, but in all cases the word 'gambling' is only applicable to the extent that the gambler cannot control the final outcome. That is, in order for an activity to be considered gambling, *there must be risk.* Gambling exists in a variety of forms including placing wagers on card games, sporting events, horse and dog races, a variety of table games typically found in casinos, slot machines, lotteries, and, most recently, each of these games and others that can be easily accessed, legally or otherwise, on the internet. Indeed, with nearly universal access to the internet, individuals of any age or in any location can now gamble in near anonymity with few restrictions at any time of day or night.

With passage of the Gambling Act 2005, the United Kingdom entered a new phase in its legal relationship to gambling. There are three stated intentions to this Act: (a) to prevent gambling from being a source of crime or disorder; (b) to ensure that gambling is conducted in a fair and open way; and (c) to protect children and other vulnerable persons from being harmed or exploited by gambling.[2] In setting legal parameters for gambling, however, the Act appears to allow for expansion of available gambling venues and can be expected to further normalise gambling as an acceptable leisure pastime. The expansion and normalisation of gambling will likely result in a measurable increase in problems related to out-of-control gambling, often referred to as 'compulsive gambling'.[3]

1. As cited in National Research Council (1999). *Pathological Gambling: A critical review* (Washington, D.C.: National Academy Press).
2. Office of Public Sector Information (2007). Gambling Act 2005. Available at http://www.opsi.gov.uk/
3. See literature from Gamblers Anonymous, which can be found at http://www.gamblersanonymous.org.uk/

Case studies

In my experience working with compulsive gamblers and their families I've learned that when you've met one gambler, you've *only met one gambler!* While all gamblers have much in common, compulsive gambling is an illness that affects people in a variety of ways. In order to illustrate the universality *and* individuality of gambling-related problems, I will present two case studies that are typical of the issues associated with compulsive gambling.

Frances G.

At the age of 51, Frances G.[1] could look back at a good life, a life of service to her family, friends, church and community. As the second of four children born to a middle-income family, she first learned responsible behaviour by providing care for her younger siblings while her mother and father were working. Frances married Donald, her closest friend since childhood, when she was barely out of high school, and stayed home to raise their two children in a nurturing environment. Frances was very active as a helper in her parish and surrounding community, respected by family, friends and local leaders. By any standard, Frances's life was a success, one filled with deep love of family supported by deep faith in God. Yet on a rainy afternoon in October of 2000 Frances prepared to commit suicide by driving her car at high speed into a towering oak tree on the side of a winding country road just a few miles from her home.

Frances's suicidal depression illustrates one of the most common effects of compulsive gambling. Frances had gambled for fun with no ill effects for most of her life. Frances's ethnic background is Italian-American and she grew up in an Italian-American neighbourhood where there was a gambling bookmaker on every corner who conducted brisk business every day of the week. Whether he was taking nickels and dimes from the housewives and grandmothers to play the 'daily

1. The vignettes presented in this section are based on composites of actual clients and their families treated for gambling and gambling-related problems. Some facts have been altered to protect their anonymity.

> number', or collecting tens and hundreds and thousands of dollars from the working men and grandfathers of the neighbourhood looking to win big from betting on horse races and all sorts of sporting events, the local bookmaker was a respected figure and an ordinary part of everyday life. For Frances gambling was normal, gambling was fun, gambling was something everyone did and talked about. To have good fortune with one's bets meant generosity and laughter and good cheer, with thanks expressed to the Virgin Mary or the local patron saint by making donations to the neighbourhood parish. Losing only meant that the day was closer when fortune would smile and one's luck would change. Until Frances was 49 years old she never lost more than a few dollars gambling on any day and never won more than a few dozen. When her gambling habits changed drastically and she began to lose so much money that her family was facing bankruptcy, her growing shame and depression drove her to make the decision to take her own life.

Frances's path to compulsive gambling is typical for middle-aged people, particularly women. In 1996 her local government (the State of Delaware in the United States) legalised slot-machine gambling at local racetracks in an effort to stabilise the economic health of the horseracing industry and provide a stream of tax revenue for the state. Coincident with the opening of a 'racino' (race track + casino) within 15 minutes of her home, Frances had fulfilled one of her lifelong dreams by opening a small bridal shop, which happened to be within a quarter of a mile of the entrance to the racino. Frances and Donald's eldest child, their daughter, had married around the same time and Frances had experienced such joy designing and sewing her daughter's wedding gown and the gowns of her bridesmaids that she and Donald decided to take a risk and invest a substantial part of their life savings in a small bridal salon.

At first Frances's business did well and became a welcome supplement to the family's income. But within a year a bridal store that was part of a national chain opened nearby and, with the buying power that a large network of stores enjoys, priced Frances's little shop out of business. As her business failed, Frances fell deeper and deeper into depression. Her husband began to complain when the revenue fell off. He demanded that she work harder and smarter to restore their lost income and pay off the debt they incurred when they opened the store.

Despondent, feeling increasingly helpless and eventually hopeless, Frances began to take her store's revenues to the racino at her doorstep, hoping to win enough money each week to placate her husband and give her the seed money she would need to expand her business and compete with the larger store. As this strategy failed she began to take money from her family's accounts in order to gamble. At first she was still trying to win the money she would need to save her business, but as her losses mounted her gambling behaviour became increasingly erratic, driven by the desperate need to win back the money she had lost by gambling her family's funds. By the year 2000 Frances was over $100,000 in debt, had lost her business to bankruptcy, and had to tell Donald that the family savings were exhausted. She continued to gamble heavily but now it was 'escape gambling', a means to dissociate from her panic, isolation and helplessness. Alone, depressed and ashamed, Frances could see no way out other than to take her life in a terrible accident, an accident that would result in a considerable insurance payment to her family and restore her husband's retirement savings.

Frances's descent into gambling addiction is typical of the middle-aged compulsive gambler with no prior history of gambling problems. Recent research[1] has conclusively shown that when a new gambling venue is opened, there is a 50-mile radius surrounding the local community which typically experiences a doubling of the rates of compulsive gambling within the first year of the opening. It appears that simply making gambling *available* results in the proliferation of gambling problems among vulnerable individuals. The people who appear to be most susceptible to compulsive gambling problems are those at risk for depression and who find themselves with high-stress problems in their lives, such as the failing

1. The Congress of the United States commissioned a report entitled 'The National Gambling Impact Study Commission Report' in 1999. It can be found at http://govinfo.library.unt.edu/ngisc/reports/fullrpt.html.

business venture that Frances experienced. Indeed, as described in the National Gambling Impact Study Commission Report, the psychological literature indicates that nearly 100% of compulsive gamblers also suffer from depression and suicidal thinking or attempts. While it is not true that most depressed people gamble compulsively, it is certain that there is a strong association between compulsive gambling and depression. It is difficult to determine causality, but depressed people are well advised to avoid gambling ventures and compulsive gamblers nearly always require treatment for depression.

Furthermore, it is clear that individuals from ethnic groups where gambling behaviour is considered culturally normative are at greater risk of compulsive gambling.[1] Frances turned to gambling when her business began to fail and as relief from her subsequent depression. Given that gambling behaviour is normative in Italian-American communities and the nearness of the venue, her turn to gambling to resolve her problems comes as no surprise. But the depressed compulsive gambler who starts gambling in middle age and who is seeking escape from life's problems is only a part of the story. Prior to the proliferation of gambling venues through legalisation the most typical compulsive gambler was a male who began gambling in childhood and who preferred games of action. George F.'s story is typical of this more 'traditional' type of gambler, one who can be found in any village, town or city throughout the United Kingdom.

George F.

> George F. is a 55-year-old white male who has been gambling since he was a teenager. Always a gifted athlete, George began placing bets on professional sporting events with a local bookmaker when he was 14 years old. By that time he was renowned throughout his home town as a stellar athlete and leader of every team on which he played. His athletic fame combined with his handsome face and engaging personality made him somewhat of a celebrity in his school, the recipient of

1. See the excellent article by Raylu and Oei titled 'Role of Culture in Gambling and Problem Gambling' in the journal *Clinical Psychology Review*, 23 (8), 1087–1114.

favoured treatment by teachers and coaches. George could do no wrong as a teenager, both on the football pitch and off. His parents, particularly his father, glowed with pride for George and boasted of his great accomplishments. They paid little attention to his gambling, thinking it a passing phase and nothing more.

Like most early-onset compulsive gamblers, George did not consider himself to have a problem with gambling and did not experience any financial hardship as a result of it. He generally broke even with most of his betting or could easily cover his losses throughout his 20s. George's actual losses during the third decade of his life can be more accurately measured in his loss of educational, career and emotional growth, as he devoted most of his energies to working on his betting lines rather than getting an education, a steady job and finding a woman with whom he could fall in love. By the time George was 30 years old his gambling habits were firmly entrenched and dominated his daily routines, and his only friends were fellow compulsive gamblers found in the betting shops and alongside the rail at the track.

George first showed up for treatment in December of 2000 when he was 49 years old. He reported that he had gambled heavily for over 30 years. George stated that he bet heavily, and daily, on all kinds of sporting events and at the blackjack tables in the casinos nearby. He was also alarmed at the increase in his gambling habits after he began playing blackjack over the internet. The online environment, with its easy access to resources through his credit card, proved to be his financial downfall. The somewhat limiting realities of seeing diminishing piles of casino chips or torn betting slips at the racetrack were replaced with the silent persistent online debiting from his credit limit, which seemed to occur unnoticed and uncontrolled. George was now hundreds of thousands of pounds in debt, most of it accumulated in just a few years of nearly constant online betting. Always an upbeat, happy-go-lucky character, George was depressed and suicidal for the first time in his life. Like Frances, he found himself alone, isolated and ashamed. After 30 years of heavy gambling he was finally seeking help.

Understanding the problem

Compulsive gambling is a multidimensional problem in that it affects the gambler, their family and friends, employer and community. In this section I will present a broad overview of the effects of gambling, paying particular attention to the impact of gambling on the families and associates of compulsive gamblers.

Historical perspective on gambling

For as long as humans have gambled, there has been apprehension about excessive gambling.[1] Numerous sources described gambling as a social problem as far back as the early days of the Roman Empire, where gambling was rampant. Indeed, gambling is well documented in both the Hebrew and Christian Scriptures, as seen as early as Joshua's conquest of Canaan, when the Promised Land was divided among seven of the twelve tribes by the casting of lots and at the foot of the cross, where Jesus' garments were distributed by the same means. Gambling was rampant in ancient Rome, and it is thought that the emperors Nero and Claudius would meet modern standards for compulsive gambling. Historical texts note that King Richard the Lionheart limited dice-playing among the Crusaders. The Russian novelist Dostoyevsky described compulsive gambling in remarkable accordance with modern diagnostic ideas in his short story *The Gambler*. During the nineteenth century gambling, alcohol consumption and drug use were the targets of temperance movements on both sides of the Atlantic Ocean, leading to a variety of legislative actions ranging from the limitation of gambling, alcohol and drug availability to outright prohibition. Temperance movements typically adopted a 'moral model', equating gambling, alcohol and drug use with sinfulness. These movements emphasised the need for religious conversion in order to recover from the excesses of gambling, alcohol and drugs.

1. For an excellent review of the cultural history of gambling see National Research Council (1999). *Pathological Gambling: A critical review* (National Academy Press, Washington, DC).

The spiritual and medical models of addiction

In the early part of the twentieth century the American psychologist William James described a model of addiction based on spirituality rather than morality in his book *The Varieties of Religious Experience.* James' understanding of addiction was based on consumption of alcohol, which he believed stimulated a false spiritual awakening in the drinker. He evoked the nature of this spiritual experience when he stated that alcohol 'is in fact the great exciter of the *Yes* function in man . . . making him for the moment one with truth.'

This spiritual way of understanding addiction led to the formation in 1935 of Alcoholics Anonymous (AA). The founders of AA, Bill W. and Dr Bob, were inspired by James' spiritual view of alcoholism and encoded their strategy for recovery from alcoholism in the Twelve Steps.[1] Addressing the spiritual nature of alcoholism, Bill W. composed the movement's basic textbook, *Alcoholics Anonymous,* in 1939. In his book Bill stated that the alcoholic is 'willing to grow along *spiritual* lines. We claim spiritual progress rather than spiritual perfection.'

Nearly simultaneous with the development of this spiritual understanding of addiction, Freud[2] promulgated his view that compulsive gambling was part of an addiction triad. Freud's addiction triad included alcoholism, drug addiction and gambling. Freud rejected both the moral and the spiritual models of addiction, articulating instead a medical model that became the foundation for the psychological treatment of compulsive gamblers. Freud's view of gambling as an addiction and the successful growth of AA across the United States and Europe led to the formation in 1957 of Gamblers Anonymous (GA), the first gambling fellowship. GA adopted the Twelve Steps of AA and modified them to reflect addiction to gambling rather than alcohol.[3] GA is a spiritually based mutual help programme and is the primary intervention for compulsive gambling in most Western countries.

1. The Alcoholics Anonymous website (www.alcoholics-anonymous.org.uk/) is an excellent source of information concerning the history of AA and the nature of alcoholism and its treatment.
2. See Freud's essay *Dostoyevsky and Parricide*, published in 1928.
3. An excellent overview of the history of GA can be found at its American website: www.gamblersanonymous.org/history.html

Psychiatric diagnosis of pathological gambling

The first attempt at psychiatric categorisation of compulsive gambling in the United States was made in 1980 by the American Psychiatric Association in its *Diagnostic and Statistical Manual of Mental Disorders* (3rd edition). This first definition of compulsive gambling (the DSM-III and subsequent editions refer to compulsive gambling as 'pathological gambling') focused on the consequences of gambling, emphasising progressive loss of control, the damage and disruption to the individual's family, personal or vocational pursuits, and issues dealing with money. More recent editions of the DSM have added criteria similar to those for substance dependence, such as the build-up of tolerance and the presence of withdrawal symptoms.

The current criteria for recognising compulsive gambling fall roughly into three broad categories. First, there are those symptoms related to how the gambler thinks about gambling. Second are the physical symptoms. The third set of criteria deals with the behavioural signs of compulsive gambling. There are a total of ten criteria; the presence of five or more indicate that the mental health professional may find a diagnosis of pathological gambling. It is important to note that seven of the criteria are related to observable behaviours.

The first set of criteria relates to how compulsive gamblers think. Typically, compulsive gamblers are preoccupied with gambling, as can be seen by the amount of time they spend handicapping bets, planning gambling ventures, reliving past gambling experiences and thinking about ways to get the money needed to gamble. This preoccupation can become so severe that gamblers will neglect basic needs such as eating, drinking, sleep, bathroom needs and overall hygiene. While it may sound extreme, many counsellors who specialise in treating gambling disorders can tell stories of gamblers who have soiled themselves rather than leave a casino floor, convinced that they were bound to begin winning at any moment. More common but no less destructive are the tales of families neglected and opportunities squandered. One client who presented for treatment several years ago had become so preoccupied with playing dice that he offered the title to his sports franchise (an American football team) in order to cover his wager. When he lost the wager, he lost his team.

There are two physical symptoms to look for, which are directly based on the criteria for substance dependence. First, most compulsive gamblers build up a tolerance, much like substance-dependent individuals, except the tolerance is for risk in terms of the amount of money that is wagered and frequency of gambling ventures rather than a particular amount of a chemical stimulant. For instance, when Frances G., the escape gambler mentioned above, began playing the slot machines with regularity, it was her custom to gamble weekly, bringing $50 to the racino and playing $0.25 at a time. By the time she was planning her suicide she would not gamble with a stake of less than $1,000, was playing $10 per bet, and was going to the racino several times a week. By her own report, to have played with any lesser amount of money or with any less frequency would have been boring and would not have provided the stimulation she needed in order to find relief from depression. Her need to play with more and more money *was not solely* related to her ever-increasing debt, but was driven equally by her worsening depression and the increased stimulation it was taking to feel better. Similarly, George F. was losing nearly $20,000 per day by the time he came in for treatment, stating that he needed bets of at least $200 per hand 'in order to keep it interesting'. Like Frances G., George F. needed a greater experience of excitement and anticipation in order to avoid feeling his deepening depression, and only by betting with extraordinary amounts of money could he generate the levels of excitement he needed.

The second physical symptom is withdrawal, a feeling of restlessness and/or irritability when attempting to cut down or stop gambling. Most compulsive gamblers find that their sleep, appetite, concentration and mood are affected when they stop gambling, and that this disruption may continue for several weeks. It is not unusual for the behaviour of compulsive gamblers to take on a manic quality (little sleep, rapid speech, disorganised streams of thought, excessive risk-taking, impaired judgement) for weeks or even months at a time, as all of their energies can become devoted to gambling activities.

Recent research has shown that there is a relationship between the neurotransmitter serotonin, implicated in a variety of psychiatric disorders (for example, depression and obsessive compulsive disorder) and compulsive gambling. Compulsive gamblers respond well to the same medications used to treat these psychiatric disorders. This research further supports the notion that there are measurable and treatable physical aspects to compulsive gambling. Similar research has found that the brains of compulsive gamblers have a typical hyper-responsiveness pattern when exposed to gambling stimuli, which is not seen in non-gamblers. Whether these differences in brain physiology and responsiveness precede the advent of gambling problems or are the result of long-term compulsive gambling behaviours is not well understood, but there is no dispute in the research community that there are biological dimensions to compulsive gambling that deserve further inquiry.[1]

In addition to these symptoms, there are seven typical behavioural patterns that are classified as symptomatic of pathological gambling. The first, and most obvious, is that the gambler has made repeated, unsuccessful efforts to control, cut back or stop gambling. It is not unusual for compulsive gamblers to make sporadic attempts to return to earlier, non-pathological levels of gambling, usually without success. The second is that gamblers use gambling behaviour as a way to escape from problems (typically financial problems caused by the gambling itself) or for emotional relief, most frequently from depression. A third behavioural symptom is referred to as 'chasing' behaviour; that is, after losing money compulsive gamblers return, usually on another day but not infrequently later in the same day, to try to get even by winning back the money they have lost. Indeed, asking gamblers whether they 'chase' their losses is probably the easiest way to differentiate between a hobby and a very bad, possibly addictive, habit. Simply the gambler's knowledge of what the term 'chasing' means probably indicates that the gambling has become pathological.

A recent treatment episode illustrates these three behavioural symptoms.

> Marion S. was in her late 20s when she went to her pastor for help. She complained that she had occasionally been playing the

1. The BBC presented an excellent overview of research in this area. This report may be viewed at their website, http://news.bbc.co.uk/1/hi/health/1013204.stm

> daily lotto game offered by the National Lottery, but her visits to its website led her to be intrigued by the variety of games offered (for example, 'EuroMillions,' instant win games offering up to £100,000, 'scratch-card' games offering up to £40,000 for life) and their ease of play. After playing more than she intended one day, she resolved to play a bit more in order to win back her money ('chasing'). Because she was able to win back her money on the first occasion in which she chased, she found herself easily tempted to exceed her budget for gambling nearly every day ('loss of control'). As her chasing behaviours regularly failed she began to experience depression and self-loathing, and found that playing at these games online was the only way to relieve her unpleasant state of mind ('escape'). Her descent into compulsive gambling was rapid.

While these first three behavioural symptoms focus on the gamblers' inner experiences and attempts to cope with their gambling behaviour, the final four criteria focus on the social and legal impact of gambling behaviour. The first of these is that the gambler frequently lies to family members, therapists and others to conceal the extent of gambling involvement. As the gambling behaviour becomes less controllable, this secrecy is necessary for the gambler to continue gambling in order to win back the lost revenue, and frequently covers up the final three of the behavioural symptoms. These include illegal acts committed to finance the gambling, loss of job, marriage, educational or career opportunities because of gambling, and obtaining 'bail-outs'; that is, borrowing money from family, friends, commercial lenders and loan sharks in order to relieve a desperate financial situation caused by the gambling.

It is these final four criteria that typically appear when the gambler has lost all control of the behaviour, and they are most closely associated with what most addicted people refer to as 'hitting bottom.' At this point the gambler is finding it more and more difficult to continue gambling, experiencing terrific levels of preoccupation, tolerance and cut-off from financial resources, family, friends and gambling opportunities. For these reasons the gambler who meets all or nearly all criteria for this diagnosis becomes a high risk for self-destructive, and often suicidal, behaviour.

A careful review of these criteria makes clear that there are varying degrees of addiction to gambling. For instance, the gambler may not be suffering any of the physical symptoms but may report gambling out of control (playing more money or more frequently than intended), chasing those losses (sometimes during the same gambling session, but at other times coming back another day with the express intention to recoup recent losses), keeping knowledge of their losses secret from their spouse (or someone significant, such as an employer or counsellor), taking time away from work in order to gamble, and asking friends and relatives for small 'bridge loans' to get through a rough stretch (often with a story, such as 'needed' home repairs or an unexpected financial setback). While this individual may not be depressed or suicidal over their gambling habits, this person has displayed evidence for meeting five of the diagnostic criteria and is now diagnosable with pathological gambling. It is not unusual for a person in this sort of situation to present to a counsellor, employer or local pastor, feeling troubled about gambling but by no means considering themselves to be 'addicted'. How the helper responds to the troubled gambler is essential. The helper's response is generally guided by what they believe about the nature of addiction and how best to treat it, subjects which will be examined later in this chapter.

Gambling-related problems

There are other factors associated with gambling problems that the counsellor or concerned person must take into account when seeking to help a gambling-troubled person. These include the impact that excessive gambling has on the family of the gambler, the overall financial and social impact of gambling on the gambler (an impact which often extends to the gambler's employment) and the frequency of being addicted at the same time to alcohol or other substances.

First, one must pay attention to the impact that gambling has on the family of the gambler. This is often not difficult because it is not unusual for a spouse or family member of the gambler to be the initiator in seeking help. In addition, there is a growing consensus that interventions that include the spouse and/or family of the gambler improves treatment compliance and outcome.[1] Whether it is the gambler or the family of the gambler who presents for help, the caregiver must always assess what help the family needs in order to survive the chaos of addiction, particularly the brand of chaos that gambling tends to bring into people's homes.

The social and economic effects of pathological gambling on the family of the gambler are significant. A survey of the spouses of compulsive gamblers at Gam-Anon, the family component of Gamblers Anonymous,[2] found that most family members had serious emotional problems and had resorted to drinking, smoking, overeating and impulse spending. Similar studies have found that the spouses of compulsive gamblers suffer disproportionately from chronic or severe headaches, stomach problems, dizziness and breathing difficulties, in addition to experiencing emotional problems such as extreme anger, depression and anxiety. In a comparison of children who characterised their parents as compulsive gamblers with those who reported their parents as having no gambling problems, the children of compulsive gamblers were more likely to smoke, drink and use drugs. Furthermore, they were more likely to describe their childhood as an unhappy period of their lives. Each of these problems is clearly related to the experience of chronic stress in the family members, stress created by the erratic and, at times, malevolent behaviour of the gambling family member.

Several studies of gamblers in treatment indicated a great economic cost in addition to the emotional and medical costs inflicted on the family. A 1995 profile of members of Gamblers Anonymous in America found that 28% of pathological gamblers were divorced or separated as a result of gambling. Most had borrowed or stolen from funds designated for family needs, and frequently had stolen from their employers. The average gambler had active debts of nearly $100,000 due to gambling, with the median being $21,000. Average lifetime indebtedness due to gambling

1. For an excellent review of treatment issues in general see Ciarrocchi, J. W. (2002). *Counselling Problem Gamblers and Their Families: A self-regulation manual for individual and family therapy* (Academic Press).

2. Information concerning Gam-Anon can be found at their UK website, www.gamanon.org.uk/.

exceeded $200,000 per gambler. Roughly one third had lost or quit a job due to gambling and nearly half had stolen from work to pay gambling debts.

It is also important to pay attention to the possibility that the compulsive gambler has substance abuse problems in addition to problems with gambling. In a study of 50 male patients admitted to an inpatient programme, 36% of the study sample showed at least one important cross-addiction to alcohol and drugs, and 47% had a problem with drugs or alcohol at some point during their lives. Another study found that among a group of 186 compulsive gamblers receiving inpatient treatment there were very high rates of familial alcoholism (41% of fathers and 18% of mothers), well exceeding the rates found among the general population. The rates of alcohol abuse (34%), drug abuse (6%) and combined drug and alcohol abuse (31%) were also remarkably high.

The same problem for co-occurring addiction to gambling can be found among samples of substance-abusing people (see **Alcohol and Other Addictions**, page 83). A study conducted in an inpatient alcohol and drug treatment programme found that 19% of a sample of 458 patients had gambling problems. Another study of the rates of pathological gambling at an outpatient substance abuse clinic confirmed previous research indicating considerably higher rates of pathological gambling in substance abusers than in the general population. This study also found that the rate of substance abusers that could be classified as problem or compulsive gamblers was 10.7%, significantly greater than general population estimates, which at that time were 1% to 4%. This information should lead one to ask if a person with gambling problems is also drinking (or taking drugs) too much, or if someone with alcohol (or drug) problems has problems with gambling.

How should it be dealt with?

Origins and treatment of compulsive gambling

There are probably as many opinions about addiction, its origins and its treatment as there are people who are either addicted or affected by the addiction of a family member, friend or loved one. Addictions have been given many labels including disease, sickness, moral failure, crime, spiritual vacuum, attitude problem, character defect and the like, but the truth is that addiction is a complex phenomenon that resists any easy categorisation. For those who intend to help the compulsive gambler it is wisest to focus on recognising the signs and symptoms of gambling addiction and the ways it is best treated, and refrain from spending too much time and energy on determining causality. In order to place treatment strategies in the clearest possible context, however, this chapter will provide a brief overview of the theories describing the origins of gambling problems, followed by recommendations for helping compulsive gamblers to find effective treatments.

In coming to an understanding of any theory that describes the origin of a gambling (or any addiction) problem, there are two essential questions one must ask:[1] (a) to what extent is the person considered responsible for the initial development of the problem and (b) to what extent is the person held responsible for changing the behaviour? In responding to these two questions one finds four general models of addiction beliefs:

1. *The moral model,* in which the person is held responsible for both acquiring and solving the problem.
2. *The medical/disease model,* in which the person is held responsible for neither the development nor the solution to the problem.
3. *The enlightenment (spiritual) model,* in which the person is held responsible for the development of the problem but is incapable of changing without the help of a 'higher power'.

1. For a review of the theoretical models of addiction see Brickman, P., Rabinowitz, V. C., Karuza, J., Coates, D., Cohn, E. and Kidder, L. (1982). 'Models of helping and coping', *American Psychologist,* 37, 368–384.

4. *The compensatory model,* in which the person is not held responsible for developing the problem, but is responsible for solving the problem.

Each of these models proposes an approach to treatment of addiction disorders. Perhaps more importantly each model suggests the attitude one should take toward the addiction and the addicted person. Nearly every person who presents as suffering from an addiction will have formed an opinion concerning the causes of addiction and its treatment, which likely guides their own personal response to the problem. It is essential for concerned helpers to be able to recognise not only their own attitudes and beliefs about causes and treatment but also those of the sufferer, as the sufferer's attitudes and beliefs may facilitate recovery as well as impede it. Let's take a closer look at each model.

The moral model

The oldest model of addiction is the moral model. The moral model is based on the belief that the use of intoxicating substances or indulgence in over-stimulating behaviours such as gambling is an immoral choice that the individual makes. In this model the indulgence in these substances and behaviours is understood as a sign of weak character that requires an act of willpower to regain control in order to return to sober and respectable living. Addicted individuals are further understood as being somewhat lazy, lacking in determination to behave according to societal norms. The solution to the problem is the prohibition of use of the substance or indulgence in the behaviour, and this prohibition is achieved through exhortation (frequently of a religious nature), education and law enforcement. The foundation of the moral model is the notion that the world is completely just, so that individuals must stand on their own two feet bearing full responsibility for their fate in life.

The moral model certainly has its appeal in that it makes the treatment of addiction seem simple, but it has little support in any of the research literature. There are two downsides to this model. First, it doesn't seem to help people stop using substances or indulging in addictive behaviours.

Second, it seems to actually make the addictive behaviours worse as the addicted individual feels deeply ashamed and isolated as a result of the judgemental tone of the moral model. In this model addicted individuals are seen as rather weak-willed, pitiful people who should be shunned if they are unable to admit their problems and stop using substances. The shame and isolation heaped upon the addicted individual generally stimulates more of the very behaviours it seeks to diminish, as shame and isolation are factors that are closely associated with the addiction itself. Keeping in mind that it is likely that addicted individuals and their loved ones may adhere to the moral model, application of this model by counsellors, employers or family will likely exacerbate the addictive behaviour. This model is to be avoided.

The medical/disease model

The medical/disease model of treatment marks the beginning of modern treatment approaches, though its point of view certainly stretches back at least as far as the ancient Greek physician Hippocrates, to whom this quotation is attributed:

> Men ought to know that from the brain, and from the brain only, arise our pleasures, joys, laughter and jests, as well as our pains, sorrows, griefs and fears. It is the same thing that makes us mad or delirious, inspires us with dread and fear, whether by night brings sleeplessness, inopportune mistakes, aimless anxieties, absentmindedness and acts that are contrary to habit. These things that we suffer come from the brain when it was not healthy.

Hippocrates' insight that all feelings arise from the action and effects of the brain is consistent with the belief of medical practitioners through the ages that addiction is a medical disease that requires medical treatment. Prior to the early part of the twentieth century the medical treatment of addiction consisted mainly 'of a period of "asylum" from responsibilities and from access to alcohol, to take place in a family-like setting, in a milieu of respect, consideration and social support'.[1] This treatment approach is still widely and successfully used, augmented by the use of psychological and drug therapies, and a growing appreciation for the role of genetic heritage in the origin of an addiction disorder. The medical/disease model, with its emphasis that addicted people are not at fault for developing the addiction but rather suffer from a progressive, chronic disease, frees them from the debilitating shame they typically feel as a result of their addiction-driven behaviour. In essence it teaches that the addiction is more about chemistry than about character. However, in addressing primarily the biological aspects of addiction, the medical/disease model overlooks the role of thinking, behaviours and habits, which is why most if not all treatment programmes integrate the treatment tenets of the compensatory model, which puts its primary focus on the psychological and behavioural aspects of addiction.

The enlightenment (spiritual) model

If the moral model was the dominant model of nineteenth-century addiction understanding and treatment, then the enlightenment or spiritual model has been the dominant popular model throughout most of the twentieth century and into the twenty-first century through the work of Twelve Step organisations such as Alcoholics Anonymous and Gamblers Anonymous. As described earlier in this chapter, Twelve Step organisations ascribe the causes of an addiction to loss of contact with one's 'higher power', most frequently but not exclusively understood as God. In the spiritual model the individual is fully responsible for losing contact with God as a result of the choice of using mind-altering substances and behaviours. Research into the efficacy of AA has consistently found that alcoholics described a judging, condemning, vindictive deity, in contrast with classical religious thought, which understands the deity in terms of forgiveness and love rather than judgement and vengeance. Given this vitriolic image of God, it is no wonder that addicted people frequently feel a spiritual void and sense of alienation from their 'higher power'.

1. Westermeyer, J. (2005). 'Historical and social context of psychoactive substance use disorders'. In Frances, R. J., Miller, S. I. and Mack, A. H. (Eds), *Clinical Textbook of Addictive Disorders* (New York: The Guilford Press) pp. 16-36.

The religion of alcoholics (and addicted people) is not the religion of most other religious people. AA (and Twelve Step programmes in general) restore the classical understanding of the deity, enabling the alcoholic (or addicted person) to restore right relations with God.[1]

While the spiritual model does assign responsibility for the addiction to the addicted person's choice to abuse substances and behaviours, it also teaches that the addicted person is *not* responsible for recovery from the addiction. Rather, the spiritual model teaches that through the intervention of God, facilitated but not caused by the openness of the addicted person to that intervention, the desire to use illicit substances and behaviours will be removed. An examination of the literature of each of the Twelve Step organisations will find numerous examples of this sort of divine intervention leading to sobriety and full recovery. Frances G., whose story was narrated earlier, attests to the power of finding God as the only way she was able to arrest her compulsive gambling. Most mental health professionals are quite familiar with the testimony of Twelve Step members concerning their perception of God's role in restoring them to sanity.

Twelve Step programmes are quite pragmatic in that they recognise that addiction has strong biological and psychological components. As a result one finds that the tenets of the disease and compensatory models, to which I turn next, are promoted in Twelve Step groups.

The compensatory model

The compensatory model of addiction asserts that the individual is not responsible for the development of an addiction because of the complex interaction between biological and learning factors beyond the individual's control. 'Central to the compensatory model is the notion that addiction can best be understood as learned adaptive or functional behaviour in the context of personal and environmental factors – i.e. that drug use or other addictive activity is motivated by the individual's attempt to adapt to stress (including stress associated with the consequences of drug use) rather

1. For a thorough discussion of AA spirituality see Gorsuch, R. L. (1993). 'Assessing spiritual variables in Alcoholics Anonymous research', in McCrady, B. S. and Miller, W. R. (Eds), *Research in Alcoholics Anonymous: Opportunities and alternatives* (New Brunswick, NJ: Rutgers Center of Alcohol Studies), pp. 301–318.

than simple exposure to addictive substances.'[1] The case studies of Frances G. and George F. presented earlier clearly demonstrated how their gambling behaviours helped them to compensate for the consequences of depression and, in time, the addiction itself.

This conceptualisation of addiction as a complex interplay between personal factors (temperament, learned behaviours, biological/genetic vulnerabilities, family of origin problems) and environmental stressors (relationship issues, job and educational problems, poverty, racism, cultural biases, peer pressure) enables helpers to individualise their understanding of the addicted person's problems and to develop specific solutions that take into account the wide variety of treatment options available. This particular approach, when combined with the understanding offered from the world of medicine, alleviates addicted persons from the devastating shame that mires them in their disordered behaviours while giving hope, through its vast array of treatment approaches, that there is a way out of the dreadful suffering of addiction. This approach is also frequently combined with the Twelve Step model with its stress on spirituality, generally for the benefit of those individuals for whom religious and spiritual practices have played a beneficial role in their lives. The spiritual model's emphasis on developing awareness of the need to understand the effects of the addiction is completely consistent with the compensatory model's emphasis on the responsibility of the addicted person to find solutions.

What treatment is available?

A comprehensive review of the treatment outcomes literature is beyond the scope or intention of this chapter. However, readers should be aware of what works and what does not so they can avoid worsening an individual's gambling problems and discern appropriate interventions and referral recommendations.

There has been a great deal of research on the relationship between involvement in Twelve Step programmes and abstinence from addictive

1. Marlatt, G. A., Baer, J. S., Donovan, D. M. and Kivlahan, D. R. (1988). 'Addictive Behaviours: Etiology and treatment', *American Review of Psychology*, 39, 223–252.

behaviour. The literature generally supports that people who actively participate in Twelve Step programmes and incorporate their beliefs and practices do well, except for individuals with severe psychiatric disorder, who do significantly better in structured treatment programmes.[1] Generally speaking, counsellors and those concerned with the gambler's well-being are well advised to be aware of local meetings of Gamblers Anonymous[2] and to facilitate participation in those meetings by people troubled by gambling problems.

Most formal treatment programmes incorporate a blend of treatment approaches, including aspects of the medical/disease model, spiritual model and compensatory model. These eclectic programmes are referred to as 'multimodal model programmes'. Multimodal programmes, which are often referred to as the 'Minnesota model,'[3] include inpatient and outpatient treatment that employs the use of recovering gamblers as peer counsellors, an emphasis on group work including Gamblers Anonymous Twelve Step meetings, and work with the spouse and/or family of the gambler. In addition, these programmes emphasise that avoiding relapse into compulsive gambling requires skillful stress management, acknowledgement of the risks of exposure to gambling friends and venues, and a daily commitment to acceptance that all forms of gambling must be avoided by the compulsive gambler.

Generally multimodal treatment programmes are effective, with most research showing roughly 50-60% of people in treatment meeting their treatment goals in one year follow-up studies. It should be noted that these multimodal treatment programmes utilise specific forms of psychotherapy based on cognitive and behavioural models of treatment, which focus on current thinking and behaviours rather than trying to probe for deeper insight into childhood problems. Also, there is a growing body of literature demonstrating the effectiveness of antidepressants in gambling treatment, particularly the use of the Selective Serotonin Reuptake Inhibitors (SSRI)

1. Project MATCH Research Group (1997). 'Matching alcoholism treatments to client heterogeneity: Project MATCH post-treatment drinking outcomes', *Journal of Studies on Alcohol*, 58, 7–29.
2. List of meetings can always be found on the Gamblers Anonymous website www.gamblersanonymous.org.uk/
3. For an excellent description of the Minnesota model and its treatment approach see the website http://www.hazelden.org/web/public/minnesotamodel.page

class of antidepressants (for example, Prozac, Luvox and similar medications) and medications typically used to manage bipolar disorders (for example, Lithium). Programmes based on the multimodal model typically include a psychiatric component that focuses on discerning the need for medication for the gambler, particularly if the gambler is suffering from a co-occurring mental illness.

How can you help compulsive gamblers and their families?

In my experience as a clinician working with compulsive gamblers and their families, I have often noted how rarely it is the gambler who presents for treatment. When gamblers do present for treatment, frequently their chief complaints concern their money problems and their poor relationships with spouses, family members or employers, or problems with the legal system. The resistance and, at times, outright denial experienced by compulsive gamblers is generally an attempt to redirect attention away from themselves and towards 'fixing' the problems (financial and relational) caused by the gambling. The potential helper must resist becoming enmeshed in the gambler's preoccupation with escaping a temporary crisis. Non-professional helpers especially should find competent gambling counsellors and mental health professionals to begin the process of helping gamblers arrest their gambling behaviours and reconstruct their chaotic living situations. Family members, frequently deeply troubled themselves, should also seek out professional guidance as they begin to address the myriad of problems caused by compulsive gambling.

When the individual with gambling problems presents for professional help it is incumbent on the counsellor to first provide for the gambler's safety given the high rates of suicidal thinking, attempts and completion found in this population. The best way to assess for suicide is simply to ask the individual if suicide is being considered. If so, it is important to determine if the individual has ever attempted suicide in the past, intends on committing suicide in the present, and has access to the means to commit suicide. If the answer to any of these questions is 'yes', then it is best to ensure that the suicidal gambler is evaluated by the nearest inpatient medical facility for admission, whether this facility is a psychiatric or general hospital.

If the gambler is not suicidal, then the helping strategy for the mental health professional should include all of the basic elements of competent counselling: listening, assessing and recommending. First, it is rare for compulsive gamblers to experience compassionate, empathic, non-judgemental listening from anyone in their families or among their non-gambling friends or employers. Generally speaking, compulsive gamblers have 'burned their bridges' through lying about their gambling, irresponsibility in relationships and obligations including family life and work, possible involvement in illegal activities, over-involvement and preoccupation with gambling, and, most especially, by the bail-outs they have obtained from various people, usually through deceptive means. George F., one of the case studies presented earlier in this chapter, had become notorious within his extended family for his variety of borrowing schemes, most of which involved 'emergencies' brought on by purported bad luck or temporary setbacks. Rarely were any family members repaid, and when they came to realise that George was conning them for his gambling money they gradually terminated all relations with him. In time, George's schemes for bail-outs evolved into cheating his employer on his expense account and, eventually, passing bad cheques at his bank, leading to a series of legal problems that continue to plague him.

By the time they are confronted by reality or come in for help voluntarily, compulsive gamblers find they are alone, isolated and out of options. Most typically they see the solution to their problem as getting the money they need to pay off debts and/or provide a stake for the next gambling venture, the one that they feel certain will get them out of the financial hole they have fallen into. Anyone who chooses to help the gambler must exercise caution to refrain from engaging in strategies to fix the financial fiasco, which will be the preoccupation of the gambler. Their preoccupation with their financial problems will sound convincing, and frequently diverts the helper from the real problem: the out-of-control gambling. 'Fixing' the financial fiasco is always a losing strategy for the concerned helper.

The helper must instead focus on the person of the gambler. This can best be done by acknowledgement of the level of distress the gambler is experiencing and communicating this understanding along with the intention to help the gambler find a way to stop gambling. The gambler and, not infrequently, the helper can get caught up in creating inventive ways of 'fixing' the gambler, but the only way to facilitate change is with compassionate, empathic, objective counselling. This may seem unsatisfying to the gambler and, perhaps, to the helper, but establishment of a trusting relationship in which the gambler feels accepted opens other options to the gambler as they seek to make positive change. Once a trusting relationship is established, it is also very helpful for the gambler to experience an assessment of the extent of their gambling problems, something which a competent professional (or the compulsive gambler) can easily accomplish by using the Gamblers Anonymous '20 Questions', which can be found on page 361. Professional treatment should also include assessment for depression and co-occurring addiction disorders. Several instruments useful for assessment of gambling disorders, depression and addictions are included in the appendix on pages 361 and 362.

Upon assessing for the nature and extent of gambling and related problems, the caregiver can and should make recommendations for treatment. If the compulsive gambler is suicidal, then referral to an inpatient facility is an absolute necessity. If the compulsive gambler is not suicidal and is ready for some form of treatment, then the caregiver can make the gambler aware of local meetings of Gamblers Anonymous and local treatment providers familiar with addiction treatment in general and gambling treatment in particular. A full list of Gamblers Anonymous meetings throughout the United Kingdom can be found at the UK website of Gamblers Anonymous.[1] The UK Gambling Commission, which was created subsequent to the Gambling Act 2005, provides a directory of national telephonic helpline services, online help services, financial advisory services, and psychiatric treatment through its website.[2] In

1. www.gamblersanonymous.org.uk
2. www.gamblingcommission.gov.uk

addition the GamAid website[1] provides a directory of gambling treatment providers throughout the UK.

Finally, I would also like to offer a few thoughts on the use of prayer with those suffering from a gambling disorder. Recovery from pathological gambling is a lifetime process frequently complicated by the presence of another psychiatric illness, and nearly always complicated by fractured relationships and catastrophic financial damage. Prayer is not and should never be a first line of defence; attention must be paid to the overall suffering of the individual. But there is research that demonstrates that prayer helps to restore personal well-being to compulsive gamblers, and the restoration of personal well-being is the foundation for establishing gambling abstinence. If the compulsive gambler is to stop the gambling behaviour, it will only be accomplished by the restoration of a sense of satisfaction with life, a restoration that has been shown to be helped by an active and fulfilling prayer life.[2]

1. www.gamaid.com
2. Walsh, J. M., Ciarrocchi, J. W., Piedmont, R. L. and Haskins, D (2007). 'Spiritual transcendence and religious practices in recovery from pathological gambling: Reducing pain or enhancing quality of life?', *Research in the Social Scientific Study of Religion*, 18, pp. 155–175.

A Christian response

In working for many years with compulsive gamblers I have come to realise how difficult it can be at times to maintain the compassionate objectivity that good therapeutic intervention mandates. Though interventional talk therapy is essential to stimulate and facilitate the change process, it cannot occur successfully in the absence of the compassionate yet objective therapeutic relationship described by the founder of person-centred therapy, Carl Rogers, who asserted that the foundation of personal growth rests on the pillars of genuineness, acceptance and empathic understanding. Rogers believed strongly that these three conditions, when present in the therapeutic relationship, constituted the necessary and sufficient conditions for change. There is strong support for Rogers's principles.

The most salient variable in the change process is therapist presence. Toward the end of his life Rogers added the condition of therapist presence to his list of three conditions for therapeutic change. He stated that there were moments in the therapeutic process when he was able to 'relax and be close to the transcendental core of me', when his 'inner spirit . . . reached out and touched the inner spirit of the other'.[1]

Indeed, it is a challenge to establish and maintain therapeutic presence when the suffering person presents with problems that appear on the surface to be the result of greed, hatred and ignorance. Compulsive gamblers, like most addicted people, become quite self-centred as the craving for the gambling game overwhelms any sense of righteous decision-making and application of moral values. Many times I have worked as a clinical supervisor for counsellors of compulsive gamblers, counsellors struggling with remaining non-judgemental and compassionate. Indeed, I can relate to that struggle through my own experiences.

It is fundamental to the helping process that pastoral agents and concerned individuals remain non-judgemental in their world view while working with anyone who is suffering. This is easy to do when the sufferer

1. Rogers, C. R. (1986). 'A client-centered/person-centered approach to therapy', in Kutash, I. and Wolf, A. (Eds), *Psychotherapist's Casebook* (San Francisco: Jossey-Bass), pp. 197–208.

is clearly the victim of another person or circumstance that cannot be controlled. It is a far greater challenge when the suffering seems or is self-inflicted. But there are two key facts that the caregiver can never forget: (1) there is only one thing that Jesus asks us to do concerning our neighbours: to love them unconditionally as we love ourselves; and (2) all of the behaviours of the compulsive gambler, no matter how self-centred and pleasure-driven they may appear to be, are evidence of the gambler's suffering.

Jesus' admonition to love our neighbour as ourselves demands a selfless giving, understood in the early Christian world as *agape*, that is reminiscent of the fellowship of the Twelve Step programmes and of the quality of relational presence described by Rogers. To extend compassion is to be fully present and to offer theological hope in the simple act of listening with an open heart. There is no greater gift for the Christian to give and, it turns out, this gift of listening is therapeutically efficacious. The concerned individual is well advised to listen, assess (with the aim to maintaining safety) and recommend, and to do so from the wellspring of compassion that our Lord gifted to each of us.

Is it enough, however, to offer oneself as a compassionate pastoral caregiver? Though Jesus' preferential option for the poor may be expressed in many fashions, is there not a more public response as an advocate for those who suffer that is demanded of each of us? Compulsive gamblers generally present as people with self-inflicted wounds, making it easy to lose sight of the role that government and society play in the instigation of their addiction. With the increase in legal availability of gambling and the parallel decrease in social and moral barriers, one can see how society has turned a blind eye to the suffering of those addicted to gambling. Yet society enjoys the economic benefits that gambling provides for each of us through the taxes our government is able to collect.

When government and the society that it governs sanction and proliferate a profitable venture that leads directly to addiction, one is led to conclude that its secondary product, pathological gambling, has become a form of institutionalised suffering. While it is necessary to focus on the needs of the individual and that person's family, one is also called to prophetic advocacy on behalf of the victims of gambling at all levels of our society: individually, locally to our communities, nationally to our governments. In his encyclical *Sollicitudo rei socialis* John Paul II wrote that it is the role of Christians 'to animate temporal realities with Christian commitment, by which they show that they are witnesses and agents of peace and justice'.[1] This call to be a witness and an agent of peace and justice is, in essence, a call to prophetic vision. Prophetic language is essentially the language of protest. 'Those who suffer unjustly have a right to complain and protest'.[2] As members of our communities and our Christian Churches, our service to those who suffer demands that we engage actively in a societal-level struggle against the exploitation of the vulnerable. Though this task appears daunting and, perhaps, overwhelming, it is essential that we combine our contemplation with praxis, so that our relationship with God might be informed by our clothing of the naked and feeding of the poor, and our advocacy on behalf of the victims of gambling might be informed by the comfort and wisdom of an all-knowing, merciful God. We must inform our fellow members of society about the suffering of those broken by gambling, as a prophetic warning to them to reflect deeply on the effect of gambling expansion on our values and on our people. To do less would be to express a preferential option for the wealthy.

1. John Paul II (1987). *Sollicitudo rei socialis* (Mahwah, NJ: Paulist Press).
2. Gutierrez, G. (1987). *On Job, God-talk and the Suffering of the Innocent* (Maryknoll, NY: Orbis Books).

Do's and don'ts

- Do recognise any changes in the gambler's usual pattern of gambling behaviours, especially when the gambler's life is stressful.
- Do pay attention to any signs of depression or despair in the person who has been gambling heavily.
- Don't assume that because a person has not had a gambling problem in the past that they do not have a gambling problem now.
- Don't pass off adolescent gambling as a passing phase; the earlier a gambling problem starts, the less likely it is that the gambler will be able to stop.
- Do assess the compulsive gambler carefully for any signs of suicide.
- Do realise that gambling is one of the world's oldest professions, and that there are firmly held beliefs and attitudes throughout all cultures.
- Do recognise that compulsive gamblers suffer morally, spiritually and medically as a result of their behaviours.
- Don't assume that compulsive gamblers are capable of making sound judgements concerning their problem, as the gambling behaviour itself causes impairment to the gambler's biological and psychological self.
- Do recognise that compulsive gamblers descend in stages into their gambling problems, usually beginning with chasing behaviours and loss of control, and progressing to increasing tolerance, withdrawal symptoms and increasingly antisocial behaviours.
- Do pay close attention to the welfare of the family members of compulsive gamblers, as their emotional, medical and financial welfare may worsen precipitously as the gambler progresses into fully fledged addiction.

- Don't get trapped by shaming moralistic responses to the compulsive gambler.
- Do point out the shame the compulsive gambler feels, and offer alternatives to continued gambling.
- Don't get enmeshed in the compulsive gambler's preoccupation with the financial chaos caused by the gambling.
- Do focus on the emotional and medical consequences suffered by the family of the compulsive gambler. Offer them help and support.
- Do facilitate the compulsive gambler's contact with the Gamblers Anonymous community and competent treatment professionals.
- Do learn about the nature of gambling problems and how to recognise compulsive gambling by visiting the various websites provided in this chapter.
- Do recognise the compulsive gambler's behaviour as evidence of their suffering, and not simply self-centredness.
- Do see the compulsive gambling from a larger perspective, as an inevitable consequence of expanded gambling opportunities.
- Do raise awareness in your community that there is a societal price to pay for the economic boon provided by gambling expansion.
- Don't lose hope for even the worst compulsive gambler. Treatment works!

Conclusion

In this chapter I have attempted to present the issues that affect the compulsive gambler and their family. As gambling becomes more available within a community it is inevitable that people will gamble more frequently and that some people will fall into compulsive gambling. While family members of the compulsive gambler will bear the brunt of the emotional and financial devastation associated with this illness, there is a ripple effect throughout the community as well, which is typically experienced by employers, law enforcement and community organisations. Indeed, the National Gambling Impact Study Commission Report in the United States, cited earlier, reported that communities in which gambling venues have been introduced usually experience an increase in a variety of financial crimes, bankruptcies, divorces and suicides. Though gambling expansion provides numerous economic benefits for national, regional and local governments and economies, there is a social price that communities must pay.

The one message I most fervently hope comes through in this chapter is that there is hope for the compulsive gambler and their family. Addiction treatment works. It is difficult work, requiring commitment to long-term treatment and absolute abstinence from gambling, but therapeutic care can help the compulsive gambler to arrest the behaviour and begin recovering from the disorder. Though it is essential to guide the compulsive gambler into treatment, it is equally important to assist the family of the compulsive gambler, as the stress-related illnesses they experience can be as debilitating as the compulsive gambling itself.

I would like to end on one final note. The portrayals presented in the case studies section were based on real individuals. Both are doing quite well at the time of writing. Frances G. has worked hard with her husband to restore their marriage. She hasn't gambled for a number of years and they are living happily and comfortably in retirement. George F. has become a leader in the local Gamblers Anonymous community, where he redirects his drive to gamble into helping newcomers into Gamblers Anonymous. He has not gambled in years, and will break out into a broad smile when asked if he misses betting. 'I miss it every day,' he says, 'but now I place my bets on helping others who are as insane as I once was. It's a safer bet!'

Recommended reading

- Ciarrocchi, J. W. (2002). *Counselling Problem Gamblers and Their Families: A self-regulation manual for individual and family therapy* (Academic Press).
- Heinemann, M. (1999). *Losing Your Shirt: Recovery for compulsive gamblers and their families* (Hazelden Press).

Websites

www.gamblingcommission.gov.uk
www.gamaid.com
www.gamblersanonymous.org.uk

Sexual Addiction and Internet Pornography

Mark Brouwer and Mark Laaser

It might seem strange on the surface to imagine that sex could become an addiction. It's a natural, biological activity; not a chemical that one ingests into one's system. But just as alcohol and drugs can become addictive, so can activities such as sex, when used to excess, or when used as a means of escaping pain or boredom. This chapter will focus on how sex can become destructive, and map out the road to recovery from addiction.

Krista and David's story

> Krista's husband David was a young and successful lawyer. Their new married life was in many ways happy, but also filled with stress and unexpected challenges. Krista felt that David was often withdrawn, and even though he wanted sex very often, he frequently seemed disengaged when they were sexual. She wondered if she was somehow disappointing him, but comforted herself with the thought that he was simply struggling with the pressures of a new career.
>
> She was shocked when, shortly after their third anniversary, he confessed that he had gone to massage parlours several times that year. Over the course of the next several weeks, she learned more: he had received oral sex on his past two visits to the massage parlours. He had been much more sexually active before their marriage than she had previously known. And the pornography use that she thought was just a phase in his single life was still a

common occurrence. He had been viewing pornography on their home computer and masturbating several times a week for virtually all of their married life.

These disclosures swept Krista into waves of confusion, anger and hurt. She and David were committed Christians and very involved in their church. David had never talked to anyone about his sexual struggles, and neither of them knew where to turn. Although Krista knew very little about addiction, she wondered, 'Is David a sex addict?' If so, what could she do to help him? Did she even want to?

What is sexual addiction?

Krista and David are not alone in facing this kind of struggle. As sexual mores change in our society, and as pornography and the sexual activity it portrays become more ubiquitous, millions of people find themselves becoming compulsive in their sexual behaviour. They find themselves engaging in unhealthy and destructive habits, unable to stop. The statistics alone tell the story.

- According to a recent study entitled Internet Filter Review, revenues in the pornography industry for 2006 totalled $97 billion, up from $57 billion in the previous year. In terms of revenue, the pornography industry is larger than the top technology companies combined: Microsoft, Google, Amazon, eBay, Yahoo!, Apple, Netflix and EarthLink. At the end of 2006, 12% of all the sites on the web were pornographic, and 35% of all peer-to-peer downloads, 25% of search engine requests, and 8% of total email traffic were also porn-related. In addition, 47% of self-professed Christians reported in a survey to Focus on the Family that pornography is a 'major problem in our home', and 20% of men admitted to accessing pornography at work.[1]

- Analysis of server data from internet service providers (ISPs) shows that nearly 20% of all internet usage involves pornographic content.[2] CBS news reported recently that in hotels where 'in-room' pornographic movies are available, 55% of hotel guests rent one or more of these pornographic movies.[3]

- These statistics all point to the prevalence and growth of pornography, an important indicator of the growing epidemic of sexual addiction. After ten years of research, Dr Patrick Carnes estimated that about 8% of the total population of men

1. http://internet-filter-review.toptenreviews.com
2. http://publications.mediapost.com
3. www.time.com

> and 3% of women in the United States are sexually addicted.[1] In the UK, the BBC reported a more conservative estimate of 3–5% of the population. However, this estimate is based on the number of people who are seeking treatment, which is much lower than those who are actually addicted.[2]

The sexual behaviours of addicts vary widely. These behaviours vary in social acceptability and harm done to others. Here is a list of the various types of sexual 'acting out', separated into three categories:

Basic or building-block behaviours

- Fantasy
- Masturbation
- Pornography – magazines, videos, internet, TV, books, movies, music
- Affairs – this includes long- or short-term sexual relationships, 'one-night stands' and/or intimate emotional involvement that is non-sexual

Level two behaviours

- Prostitution – on the street, over the phone, and massage parlours, escort services, on the internet
- Anonymous sex – the name of the sexual partner is not known
- Voyeurism – observing unsuspecting people who are undressing, naked and/or having sex
- Exhibitionism – sexual arousal from exposing oneself to an observer

1. Ewald, R. (13 May 2003). 'Sexual Addiction', *AllPsych Journal*.
2. www.bbc.co.uk

- Indecent liberties or frotteurism – touching someone for sexual arousal without their permission or knowledge
- Phone sex/cybersex – talking on the phone or chatting online for the purpose of sexual arousal
- Bestiality – sexual touching or relations with animals
- Sadomasochism – sexual arousal from pain exchange

Offending behaviour

- Incest – sexual relations with relatives
- Molestation – unwanted sexual contact with someone (most often used to refer to sexual activity with minors)
- Rape – unwanted/forced sexual relations
- Authority rape – using the power of role, status, age or authority to gain sexual access

The crack cocaine of sex addiction

By far the most common behaviour associated with sexual addiction is internet pornography, which is often referred to as the 'crack cocaine' of sex addiction. Shortly after it was introduced into the marketplace some years ago, crack cocaine changed the rules of drug addiction and treatment. It was cheap, widely available and extremely addictive. People who did not fit the typical profile of a drug addict became addicted to crack. The cycle time between someone's first sample of the drug and their addiction to it shortened with the onslaught of crack.

The same is true with internet pornography. Several years ago, sex researcher Dr Al Cooper predicted that because the internet is so affordable, accessible and anonymous, it would radically expand the use of pornography and facilitate new kinds of sexual acting out, ushering in a sexual revolution greater than that experienced in the 1960s. He was right. People who might not otherwise find themselves sexually addicted are drawn in by the power of internet pornography. And people are lured into pornography and other sexual activity through the internet very quickly.

For example, one pastor's wife we worked with was given a computer for Christmas one year. She was new to computers, but since her children had grown and recently left home, she had time on her hands and caught on quickly. She discovered chat rooms in January and quickly became a heavy user. Soon she was engaging in sexual chats (cybersex). By February she had developed several online sexual relationships, and by March had met several men for in-person sexual encounters. Such rapid escalation of addictive sexual behaviour is extreme, but by no means isolated. And it is fuelled by the affordability, accessibility and anonymity of the internet.

Sex addiction centred around pornography and masturbation can be challenging because people tend to minimise its destructiveness and may not identify it as problematic. As the statistics about pornography cited earlier suggest, many people are growing dependent on this sexual behaviour, even though they may not realise its power over them. Since they haven't tried to stop the behaviours, they don't realise how much of a grip they have. It's similar to the situation where college students become binge drinkers and don't realise they are becoming addicted to alcohol. They don't sense their growing dependence on alcohol because heavy drinking is common and accepted among their peers. It doesn't feel problematic. But when challenged to cut down their consumption, they discover alcohol's power over them. What about pornography? What happens when people who think it's OK to view pornography are challenged to stop using it?

The writer of a humour website called 'A Pointless Waste of Time' conducted an informal study of 100 online pornography users – basically people he knew who looked at porn – and challenged them to go without pornography for two weeks. These were people who didn't view their pornography use as problematic, but they decided to take him up on the challenge. Of the 100 pornography users, 6 dropped out of the study, 52 were unable to go even a week without pornography, and 24 couldn't last for three days. In the end, only 28 of the subjects were able to go through the two-week period without pornography.

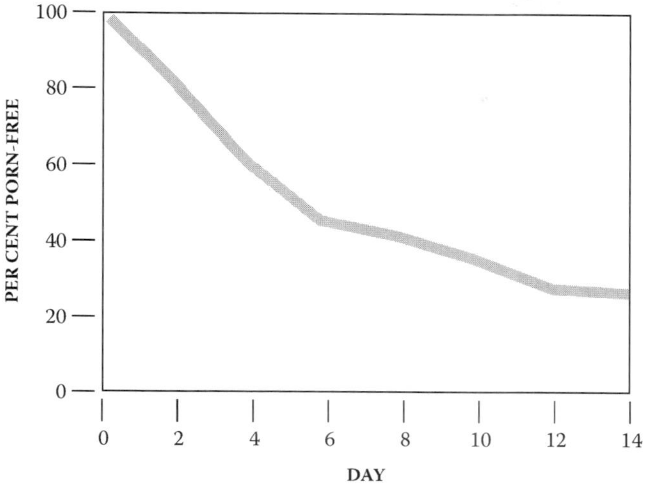

The author of the study noted that even though the subjects did not view themselves as addicts, they tended to describe their experience with the study in 'addict's terms'. He writes:

> The participants were not strangers to me and were largely people I know in an online sense. And while I had heard lots of jokes over time about them being alcoholics or hopelessly fat or hopelessly poor, I had never, ever heard any of them talk about being porn addicts.
>
> Until we did the study.
>
> From the first hours on, lots of these guys were suddenly talking about 'withdrawal' and talking about how tomorrow was going to be a 'tough day' with time alone and high-speed access. They were using the language recovering addicts use, which I admit both surprised me and creeped me out a little.[1]

When does sex become an addiction?

When does someone become a sex addict? Where is the line that separates a normal, healthy sex drive from sexual addiction? It might be helpful to think of sexuality in terms of a spectrum of behaviour, and to think in three categories. The first category is normal, healthy sexual behaviour. The

1. http://www.cracked.com/article_15725_great-internet-porn-off.html

second category is sexual behaviour that is unhealthy, inappropriate and destructive. The third category is behaviour that is compulsive or addictive. It is possible for someone to engage in unhealthy, destructive sexual behaviour, but not be addicted. A person might occasionally succumb to the temptation of pornography, for example, but still not be an addict. The line is drawn when that person is unable to stop, or when they repeatedly go back to the same behaviour, despite negative consequences.

The medical and counselling community has established several universal criteria for determining if a substance or behaviour is an addiction:

Use of the substance or behaviour has become unmanageable

This means that the addict has tried to stop, over and over again, but can't. There is a history of failed attempts. The word 'powerlessness' has also been used to describe this pattern. Sometimes addicts refer to themselves as 'out of control'. Even when an addict creates destructive consequences for themselves with sexual behaviour, it's not enough to get them to stop. Sexual addicts may be able to stop their behaviours for periods of time, but until they find healing they will always return to them. Over time, a pattern of repeated failure will be evident.

The addiction gets worse over time

This means that more and more of the substance or behaviour will be needed over time to achieve the same effect. The chemistry of the brain adjusts to whatever an addict puts into it. Over time the brain demands more to achieve the same effect. For alcoholics, the brain adjusts to alcohol and requires more. Thinking about sex and engaging in sexual behaviour requires the brain to produce the brain chemistry to achieve sexual response. New research is finding that the sexual chemistry of the brain can also become tolerant, which means more and more stimulation is necessary to have the same brain chemistry effects – the feelings of arousal, excitement and pleasure. This escalation can take two forms.

The most basic is that the addict does more and more of the same kind of behaviour. An addict might start out masturbating once a month and progress to once a day – or more – in the course of their addiction.

For other addicts, progression means that they will need new kinds of acting-out experiences to achieve the same high. So they will look for new, novel or more risky forms of sexually acting out. Almost every addict can point to certain behaviours that at one time they said they would never do and later find themselves doing. Maybe they would look at pornography in print or online but not watch a video. Then they start watching videos.

It's important to note that, while this pattern of escalation helps explain how some addicts degenerate into offending behaviours (such as molestation or rape), it is rare for this to happen. Only a very small percentage of sex addicts become sex offenders. But for addicts, the pattern of escalation over time is universal and inevitable.

Because of the brain chemistry involved, addicts use the thoughts and behaviours that produce the neurochemical highs to either raise or lower their moods

This is what is meant by saying that addicts 'medicate' their feelings. If an addict is depressed, lonely or bored, they can think of exciting sexual encounters – either remembered or imagined – and the arousal part of the sexual response produces chemicals that raise their mood. If an addict is stressed, anxious or fearful, they will tend to think of the relationship or romance quality of a sexual encounter. These associated brain chemicals create a feeling of well-being and contentment that lowers their mood. Most addicts are capable of both kinds of thoughts and, therefore, can both raise and lower their moods depending on their feelings at the moment.

Finally, addicts act out despite negative consequences

Addicts don't pay attention to negative consequences and are in what is commonly called 'denial'. They usually minimise or rationalise their acting out, despite the consequences. Until an addict decides to surrender control of the fears that prevent them from getting help, they will continue to act out. As the addict experiences more and more negative consequences for their behaviour, feelings of depression and self-hatred will grow. Unless they are somehow helped to find hope and guidance for change, these negative feelings could create the fuel for further sexual acting out.

How should it be dealt with?

Can it be treated?

Sex addiction can indeed be successfully treated, but it is a multifaceted problem that requires multifaceted solutions. One helpful way of thinking about the variety of issues related to successful recovery from sex addiction is to think in terms of dealing with past, present and future issues.

Coming to terms with the past

Addicts are often mystified about why they fail to keep their resolve to abandon destructive behaviours. Addictions are more powerful than mere habits, which can be formed and changed at will. Sex addicts have become dependent on sexual behaviour as a way of dealing with the stress, grief and pain they faced in their past. Most sex addicts found sexual behaviours early in life to be a solution to medicate pain that was overwhelming to them. Very often these addicts find themselves being triggered into these same feelings of shame, loss and stress as adults, and find themselves reaching for the same solutions. As the saying goes, 'old wounds, old solutions'. Until they learn to deal with these past feelings and hurts in ways that are healthy, they will continue to struggle with addiction.

Coming to terms with the ways we've been hurt

Wounds from abuse suffered as children will affect addicts for the remainder of their lives, unless they understand and come to terms with them. Full recovery from sexual addiction won't take place until a person comes to a conscious awareness of what happened to them in childhood.

In this connection, people may wonder if sex addicts aren't just trying to blame their families or their abusers for their behaviours. The fact is that unrecovered sex addicts do indeed blame many other people, including family members. But focusing on past abuse as a way of shifting responsibility for present behaviour is unhealthy and detrimental to recovery. Recovering sex addicts seek to understand their abuse in order to heal from it.

Understanding abuse allows people to recognise what happened to them and see how they cope with it through their addictions. It helps them to understand how painful the abuse was, how frightened they were, how alone they felt, and how angry they are. Acknowledging these feelings and finding healthy ways to express and cope with them can heal them.

There are two kinds of abuse: invasion and abandonment. Invasive abuse is what occurs when interactions that shouldn't take place happen in families or in other significant relationships. These destructive interactions may damage people in several ways:

- emotionally – yelling, screaming, put-downs, name-calling
- physically – hitting, slapping, pushing, shoving, spanking in rage
- sexually – touching or penetrating genital area, teasing about body, sexual humour
- spiritually – judgemental and angry messages about God, self-righteousness, overly negative messages about sex

When these kinds of boundaries are crossed, victims of the abuse feel afraid, alone and ashamed. Invasive abuse is extremely stressful and traumatic for children to endure and sets them up to look for relief and consolation in unhealthy ways.

The other kind of abuse is abandonment, which is often harder for people to identify from their own past. It is one thing to remember certain traumatic experiences and identify them as unhealthy. It's quite another to identify normal, healthy, positive things that *should* have happened, but never did. Abandonment occurs when children do not get the love, attention and nurturing they need to thrive. When children are not listened to, when they receive few (if any) displays of affection, when they are left alone for extended periods of time, when they receive inadequate food, shelter or clothing, when they are not taught appropriate physical self-care or given information about intimacy or sexuality . . . they grow up confused and damaged.

When children are abused emotionally, sexually, physically or spiritually, they are too small and helpless to defend themselves against these injuries. What are children to think about themselves when they are being invaded or abandoned? They come to a very logical conclusion: 'If this is happening to me, I must be bad, because bad people are punished.' Or, 'If no one loves me, it must be because I am bad. Good people are loved.'

Sex addicts believe that sexual activity is the only way to meet their needs for love and nurturing. For many of them, sex was the only way they received attention and physical touch. They learned to make the connection between love, nurture, touch and sex. Sex became their most important need because it was the only association they had between having needs and having them met.

Healing versus mourning

To recover, the sex addict must *come to terms* with his or her own past. To suggest that 'healing' of the past is necessary may create an unrealistic standard or expectation. What does it mean to be 'healed' of past wounds? For many, it means that the feeling of sadness or hurt will go away, or that relationships will be restored.

Many addicts come to us looking for the magic bullet – some way of magically finding healing from the pain of their past. Often the assumption is that they will remain stuck in their addiction until they have some kind of powerful breakthrough, where they confront parents or other people who mistreated them in the past. Usually those confrontational conversations are unsatisfying, and sometimes can even set a person's recovery back.

Instead we counsel people to simply *grieve* the losses and hurts they experienced. Addicts must learn to acknowledge the painful feelings of anger and loss, and deal with them appropriately, rather than try to cover them up or run away from them. In the Beatitudes, Jesus promises 'comfort for those who mourn.' Addicts must learn to mourn, so that they can be comforted. What they have learned to do is to cover up feelings of sadness by distracting themselves with sexual behaviours instead of letting themselves mourn.

Creating an environment in the present that provides accountability and support for recovery

Our 'personal environment' includes the relationships we have with friends and family, the habits we develop, the hobbies we take up, the homes and neighbourhoods we live in, the work we do, the music we listen to, the books and magazines we read, the television and movies that we watch . . . in short, all the things that surround us and make up our daily lives. Some aspects of our environment are beyond our control, but many are not. We can change them, if we really want to. The goal in recovery is to create an environment that supports a life of emotional health and sexual well-being.

Many people underestimate the power of their personal environment to shape behaviour. They try to change their lives by exerting willpower, rather than by changing their environment. As a result, they try to live in ways that run counter to the environment they live in and expend Herculean efforts to no avail. Instead, they need to create an environment around them that supports and reinforces their values, and encourages actions that lead to their goals. Creation of a supportive environment includes the following:

Find a safe community of recovering addicts

This is the most frequently prescribed strategy for recovery, and for good reason. It is vitally important for recovering sex addicts to be in community with other people who understand their struggle and support them in it. In all our work with addicts in recovery, we have yet to find a person who established long-term recovery who was not part of some kind of support group. Even an individual 'accountability partner' is not enough. A person in recovery will need a multiplicity of people who will help them in this journey. By being a part of a group, recovering addicts are exposed to a variety of challenges and solutions, successes and failures, ideas and insights.

There are a variety of support groups available for people struggling with sex addiction. There are several Twelve Step groups specifically focused around sex addiction, and many church groups as well. We encourage addicts to focus on groups who understand and deal with sex addiction in particular. Sex addiction is unique. It carries its own brand of shame, and is frequently misunderstood not only by the population in general but also by other addicts. Recovering sex addicts need a place where they can be honest and where other addicts can be honest with them.

Another reason support groups are so important is that most sex addicts are starved of friendship. Sex addiction is an isolating syndrome. Addicts live 'in their heads', distracted by thoughts of sexual fantasy, plans for acting out, or shame for having acted out. They objectify and fantasise about the people around them, rather than relating authentically with them. Furthermore, sex addicts are isolated because they have created walls of deception to hide their behaviour. They live in fear and shame, convinced that 'if people really knew the truth about me, they wouldn't love me'.

The only way to overcome this isolation is to develop safe relationships where addicts can be honest about their stories and find acceptance and love. And this can be found in support groups with like-minded sex addicts in recovery.

Get rid of stash and triggers

For the same reason that an alcoholic should not spend time in a bar, the sex addict needs to monitor the people and images around them, and limit the things that will trigger sexual thoughts and fantasies. Certain TV channels may need to be blocked, and internet filter or accountability software put in place. The recovering sex addict may decide not to go to certain movies, or visit certain sections of town, beaches, etc. The temptations found in these places are just too powerful.

One area of particular importance is to go through the home and office to make sure that any stash of sexual material is taken away. This obviously includes pornography, but also may include secret e-mail accounts, post office boxes or mobile phones.

One pastor we worked with was addicted to pornography, and his addiction came to light in a very public and painful way. He worked hard to rebuild his life, his marriage and his ministry. He went to therapy and attended support groups. But in the midst of all the good work he was doing, he kept a DVD of pornographic images hidden in his basement. After two years of sobriety and a public restoration to ministry, he went through a difficult struggle in his marriage. During this vulnerable time, he went to the basement one afternoon, retrieved the long-hidden DVD and renewed his involvement with pornography. Not long after, he was discovered viewing pornography by his church staff, and lost his marriage and ministry position.

Be hyper-vigilant about emotional health

People in recovery from sex addiction need to learn ways of dealing with the emotional ups and downs of life without acting out sexually. In the past, they have turned to fantasy and sexual activity as a way to manage painful feelings. So when painful feelings arise, addicts must realise that their sobriety is at risk. They have learned to deny or minimise the negative feelings they have, and instead use fantasy and sexual activity as a way to manage these emotions. The process of recovery involves gaining a new sensitivity to the feelings that come up and developing strategies to deal with them.

In all our groups with addicts we begin by having each member identify and tell the group what he or she is feeling. It's surprising how hard this exercise is for many people. They don't know what they are feeling because they have grown accustomed to pushing their feelings aside. The journey of recovery involves developing a new attentiveness to one's emotional state and implementing healthy coping strategies for painful emotions such as sadness, anger and fear.

Work towards reconciliation and health in marriage

Most addicts who are married have significant issues to work through with their partners and there is much healing to be done. Sex addiction is especially destructive for marriages. Its very expression violates the commitment to sexual fidelity made in marriage and creates tremendous hurt and alienation. Acting-out behaviours are almost always accompanied by some form of dishonesty – and often an extensive web of lies – so trust has also been broken and needs to be rebuilt.

Sex addicts need help developing intimate relationships. Their addiction and the lies and guilt it fosters have created a distance and superficiality in their marriage. Most addicts don't know how to process their anger towards their spouse in a healthy way. Because they are used to feeling guilt and shame about their actions, they can't find ways of accepting and expressing their own needs and hurts. When they felt anger in the past, they often acted out sexually instead of dealing with the disappointment or hurt that caused the feeling. Now they need to learn to do this.

Sex addicts need to learn how to be honest about their feelings and needs with the spouse that they have hurt deeply. Their spouse – because of the pain caused by the acting-out behaviours – will likely be struggling to demonstrate acceptance and compassion to them. Many addicts struggle to deal with the mixture of feelings they have towards their spouse – often love, compassion and remorse combined with disappointment and anger. If nothing else, addicts need the support of their recovery group and other trusted friends to help them go through the transition from disclosure of their addiction to openness and healing with their spouse. This will take time.

One more thing needs to be said about marriage. While it is true that working towards restoration of the marriage is an important part of recovery, it must remain a secondary priority. The top priority for the addict is their own recovery. Many addicts come to treatment because of fears of losing their relationship, and much of their 'recovery' is dominated by concerns about how to get back in their spouse's good graces. This is evidence of a lack of commitment by the addict to well-being for its own sake. They must want healing for themselves, regardless of what this healing will mean for their marriage. If addicts aren't committed to their own recovery, and simply want to please their spouse, two things are likely to happen. (1) If they start the journey of recovery, and things go well with their marriage, they may stop the process too early. Once the pressure from their spouse eases, they will quit doing the internal work, and stop attending support groups. (2) If they start the journey of recovery, and things *don't* go well in their marriage, they may get discouraged and drop out. Addicts need to commit to work on their own recovery, regardless of what their spouse does.

Establishing a vision for a healthy future

One of the important issues in recovery from addiction is to know what to fill one's life with when confronted by the void created by ending the behaviour. As the saying goes, 'It's hard to say no until you know what yes is.' It's hard for an addict to give up sexual behaviours that have brought comfort and excitement to life without having hope that other healthy things can meet those needs.

A vision is a picture of the future that draws us forward. For sex addicts, one of the many losses associated with their addiction is a loss of vision. Many addicts are so filled with shame that they have lost hope for a positive future. It is likely that their addiction has created chaos in their lives. They may have lost jobs because of their addiction, or at least struggled with diminished productivity. As addiction escalates, it eats up more and more of an addict's time. Consequently, many addicts lose touch with the hobbies and pastimes that brought a healthy balance to life in the past. Life feels increasingly grim and a positive future increasingly remote.

A vision for a healthy future is essential for recovery, but it takes time to develop. In this sense, vision is like a Polaroid picture. When a Polaroid picture is taken, it immediately slides out of the camera, but the 'picture' is just a black box. After a few seconds shapes begin to emerge but they are still vague. As time passes, the dark shapes become brighter and clearer, and more detail comes into focus. Eventually the picture sharpens into a colourful landscape or portrait. This is how vision usually works – it rarely flashes into our minds with sharp clarity. It emerges, coming into focus over time.

This is especially true for people in recovery. In early recovery, addicts' lives are often still filled with the chaos created by their addiction, and their minds are clouded by denial, rationalisation and hopelessness. The future orientation of early recovery must centre around a vision of a life free from the power of addictive sexual behaviour. Many addicts have lived so long with their addiction and struggled with attempts to stop their behaviours for so long that they have lost hope. They wonder if living sexually sober lives is even possible for them. Spending time with other people who have experienced the struggle and come through on the other side is helpful at this stage. Seeing other addicts who have established long-term sobriety establishes the beginnings of a vision for an addict, as they start to think, 'If they can do this, maybe I can too.'

It's also important for addicts to spend time thinking of healthy ways to experience renewal. Often addicts have lost touch with healthy ways of getting their needs met. Jeff was a sex addict we worked with who had lost touch over the years with anything that brought him joy. Married with four children, his life revolved around family responsibilities and a demanding career. At one point in a group session he noted wryly, 'There is nothing in my life that I do for fun any more. It's all about work: work at the office and work projects at home. The only thing I do for myself is look at pornography.' For Jeff, part of the recovery journey involved re-establishing a long-neglected hobby of woodworking. Finding ways of directing his creative energy towards positive pursuits, combined with space for solitude in his life, was an important part of the balanced life needed for recovery.

As time goes on, and the addict finds the emotional and spiritual clarity that comes from extended sobriety, their vision becomes more clear. Time that used to be spent in fantasy and acting out can now be invested in ways that tap into the addict's innate gifts and passions. Our sex drive is, at its most basic level, a creative and passionate urge. Recovery from sex addiction does not involve suppressing this drive, but rather channelling its energy towards other pursuits which can become outlets for one's creativity and passion. In their addiction, many addicts lost touch with the things they were passionate about and invested more and more of their passion and creativity in acting-out behaviours. The process of recovery involves putting that same amount of energy, passion and creativity into healthy pursuits.

What to look for

With these thoughts in mind about how treatment takes place, how can you tell if someone you know is having trouble with sex addiction? While sexual addicts will work to conceal their behaviour, they usually exhibit some observable symptoms. People who live, work or are friends with a sex addict might notice some of these.

Preoccupation with sexual behaviours

Sex addicts will first of all be preoccupied with their own sexual fantasies. This preoccupation leads them to search for sexual expression of their fantasies. They will devote more and more time to the preoccupation until they reach the point where sexual thoughts and activities are the central organising principle of their lives.

There are many ways to observe this symptom. Is pornography of any type present? Does the person watch sexually explicit videos? Does the person notice or point out sexually oriented places like bookstores, massage parlours or strip clubs? Do they do double-takes of attractive people? Does their conversation seem to centre on sexual activity?

Sex addicts may use sexual humour a great deal in their conversations. They may engage in frequent sexual teasing or telling sexual jokes, which in most contexts is considered a form of sexual harassment. Sex addicts sexualise most situations and see some sexual humour in almost anything. Sexual jokes can be used to recruit new sexual partners. Sex addicts can gauge the reaction of the person hearing their sexual joke, and if that reaction is favourable, the level of sexual engagement might be taken one step further.

Acting distant or withdrawn

As the pattern of sexual activity escalates, sex addicts seem more distant and withdrawn because they are preoccupied with their sexual activity, guilt, shame and/or fear of getting caught. They are unavailable mentally and often physically to the people around them. They may seem distant or distracted. They may seem cold, and they may become angry if badgered about what they are thinking. Ask them what the trouble is, and they deny any problem. More and more, their work, activities, interests and relationships suffer from lack of attention.

Depression and mood swings

Sex addicts may be alternately depressed and then excited, even giddy. In the sex addiction cycle the withdrawn character of preoccupation is followed by the excitement of the ritual or the chase – the high of acting out, and then the despair of shame afterwards. Asking them about these mood changes may elicit elaborate denials and perhaps anger.

Sex addicts try to avoid their feelings and avoid being found out. They create enormous defences. If anyone asks questions that come too close to the truth or simply challenges their story, addicts can become greatly agitated. Their behaviour makes them angry with themselves and angry with others. Past abuse issues that have not been dealt with also create hidden resentments and anger. Triggers that remind them of these past events may set off anger that seems unrelated to the importance of the event. Simple questions, insignificant events or basic statements may incite an angry reaction that will surprise you because the reaction is out of proportion to the event.

Resistance to supervision or criticism

Since they hide a large part of their daily behaviours, sex addicts are not very open to criticism, whether or not it is constructively given. They may live with people who would very much like to correct their behaviours and who continue to turn up the volume of their criticisms in order to be heard. This simply drives addicts deeper into withdrawal, because they do not want their sexual behaviours to be challenged. Because sex addiction often consumes a great deal of time and preoccupies addicts' minds, their work may suffer. They may be gone longer than is necessary for errands or tasks, because they are engaging in fantasy or acting out while they should be doing their work.

Inappropriate sexual behaviour and sexual advances

If you know what to look for, you can likely spot a sex addict at a party, a grocery store or even at church. They tell sexual jokes, they touch people in ways that don't feel right, they give too many hugs, and they are looking, *always looking*. Their eyes dart around the room continually, taking everything in. They follow certain attractive people.

As sex addiction progresses, inappropriate sexual behaviours get worse. Spouses should be aware that sex addicts will become increasingly frustrated with sexual activity in marriage. They may avoid sex altogether because of frustration or as a result of sexual activity outside of marriage. Sex addicts may make increasing demands for sex and certain types of sexual activity, or they may not seem to be interested in sex at all.

An unaware spouse may feel guilty at not being able to fulfil the sexual desires of their partner. He or she may feel angry or repulsed by the demands put on them by their addicted partner. It is difficult for some Christian spouses to confront inappropriate sexual demands in marriage because they may assume it is their duty to be submissive. However, they need to assert their right to have sexual standards and preferences.

Once a partner becomes aware of what is happening, he or she will realise that no amount of sexual activity or attractiveness will be enough to satisfy an active sex addict. Even if the sex in a marriage may seem quite good, he or she might not be aware of the partner's frustrations because the sex addict doesn't have the ability to articulate them.

Occupational, social, professional and legal difficulties

As the sex addiction progresses, increasing amounts of time are spent thinking about or obtaining sex. This means less time for work, social life, family, professional responsibilities or other obligations. Ignoring these activities is evidence that energy is being used somewhere else.

A concerned person should demand to know what is going on. Family members have a right to know because they are being hurt by the addiction. Employers also have responsibilities and other legitimate concerns. If work is ignored, jobs and income will be lost. Friendships or other social relationships will be lost. Unethical conduct can result in the loss of professional licences or the ability to practice a profession.

If illegal behaviour is involved, a sex addict may be arrested and could go to jail. Many sex addicts try to explain away arrests – such as soliciting prostitues – as isolated events that won't happen again. These arrests are rarely, if ever, isolated. More than likely they are part of a long-standing pattern.

In situations before the addict experiences serious losses and consequences, look for signs that the addict is ignoring obligations, duties, jobs, and relationships. Even if you discern sexual addiction, you might not be able to help a sex addict. Sadly, it appears that some sex addicts need to experience consequences before they are willing to get help.

Intuition

The last symptom is observable not in the sex addicts but in those who are in relationship with the sex addict. Be an observer of your own intuition. This means taking your own feelings and perceptions seriously, and not being too hard on yourself for ignoring them in the past. Often spouses, managers, colleagues, pastors or friends of sex addicts have a sixth sense that something is wrong. This may take various forms and could simply be a combination of impressions from certain events. Friends and family may feel they are not getting the full or the real story. The explanations of sex addicts of where they were or what they were doing on a certain occasion simply don't make sense.

Trust your instincts and act on them. Looking the other way and hoping things will get better is not a caring reaction because the sex addict's behaviour will become increasingly destructive, and things will only get worse.

A Christian response

For recovery from addiction, three important spiritual questions must be resolved.

Do you want to get well?

In John 5, Jesus heals a man who has been paralysed for 38 years. For all that time he had been lying by the pool of Bethesda, which was said to have healing properties. Jesus knew about this man, and his question to him might seem surprising. We might expect Jesus to ask how he came to be this way, or how he felt, or what Jesus could do to help. Jesus' question doesn't seem to be very compassionate: 'Do you want to get well?' Why ask such a question?

Jesus understands human nature deeply, and the paralysed man's answer gives us a clue about why Jesus had asked. The man says, 'Sir, I have no one to help me, and when I go down, someone gets in my way.' Rather than answering in the affirmative, the man explains why others have found healing, but he hasn't. In some way, it seems that the man had adopted the identity of being paralysed. Jesus knew that for the man to be healed, he had to want to change.

In addiction, part of the addict wants to be free and part doesn't. To use the language of the apostle James, addicts are 'double-minded' (James 1:8). Many addicts question how they could give up their sexual behaviours – for years these behaviours have been the way that they coped, survived and had their needs met. Even though addicts may have a deep religious faith, part of them resists trusting God and surrendering their sexual lives to God.

The strategies for healing are not complicated. The key, however, is whether or not addicts really want to change. If they don't, no strategy, however simple, will work. Anyone who wants healing must get past the hurts and anger of the past in order to say yes to God. Addicts must learn that there are alternative ways to find the love and nurture they need. This requires a lifetime of discovery, but it all starts with willingness.

Alcoholics Anonymous (AA) learned over 50 years ago that it is easier to help alcoholics when they 'hit bottom' – when their lives are so shattered and broken that denial, delusion and excuses are wiped away. One of our favourite AA expressions is 'My own best thinking is what got me here.' When addicts have nowhere else to turn, and when they have totally lost it, then they are willing to turn to God.

What are you thirsty for?

Several years ago one of us (Mark Laaser) counselled a famous actor in southern California. He claimed to have been sexual with over 3000 women, including a number of famous actresses and models. His sexual exploits had also included extensive involvement with prostitutes, whose services had cost him over $3 million. He was a depressed, drug-addicted and hopeless man. As he reflected on his experiences, he said, 'All that sex was never enough. I always wanted more.' He was obviously a sex addict. Mark suggested that he was really thirsty for God and that sex does not quench spiritual thirst.

John 4:6-26 tells of a Samaritan woman who had been married five times and was currently living with another man. She had come to a well to draw water at noon to avoid the 'respectable' women of her town, who came early in the morning. There she found Jesus. She was lonely, frightened and ashamed. She was looking for love and nurture and had failed to find it in a series of relationships with men. Jesus knew all of this. The woman offered to help Jesus draw water from the well, but he said to her, 'Anyone who drinks of the water from this well will thirst again.' Jesus offered the woman at the well 'living water', the water of salvation. This water, Jesus promised, would truly satisfy.

Only in a relationship with God can we quench our deep spiritual and emotional thirst. The desires for intimacy, acceptance and ecstasy that we associate with our yearning for sex are closely tied to – and often confused with – our spiritual yearning for communion with God. As G. K. Chesterton pointed out years ago, 'Anyone who knocks at the door of a brothel is looking for God.' In order to heal, addicts must see how their strivings to satisfy their thirst for intimacy with sexual activities have been a failure. They must discover and embrace that for which they truly thirst.

Are you willing to die to yourself?

The apostle Paul tells us that we should lead lives of love, just as Jesus loved the Church and gave himself up for her as a living sacrifice (Ephesians 5:1, 2). Paul says we should be 'imitators of Christ', for we can never be truly like him. Christ died for us – he was willing to pay the ultimate price for our sins. As imitators of Christ, we are also challenged to be willing to pay such a price; to die to ourselves.

This is especially important in our context, because the energy and focus of sex addiction is self-absorption. Because of the suffering addicts endured in their formative years, they came to believe that they could not trust anyone else to meet their needs. If needs were going to be met, they had to meet them by themselves. This coping strategy – while understandable – establishes a destructive pattern of isolation and self-centredness. Spouses, children and friends are often hurt by the self-absorption of the addict.

Few people are ever called on to physically die for someone else. But if they want to heal, addicts must be willing to die to their selfish desires. They must be willing to endure the suffering that will take place as a result of doing the internal work of recovery. They must face the vulnerability of honest relationships. They must be willing to experience the sense of deprivation that is an inevitable part of recovery, as certain acting-out behaviours now are laid to rest. It is important for addicts to make the connection between these recovery behaviours and 'laying down one's life' for others.

Do's and don'ts

- **Do prepare before confronting a sex addict.**
  Ask yourself some important questions about your motives and goals for confrontation: (a) Are you in a codependent relationship with the addict? If you need an addict's approval, you may not have the strength or objectivity to confront him or her on your own. (b) Is your own conscience clear in relation to sexual behaviour? If not, be very careful about confronting someone else. (c) Will you be able to follow through with any intervention or ultimatums you give as part of this confrontation? Don't attempt a confrontation if you are not strong enough to do what you say you will do. To that end, find out ahead of time where help is available and how to get it. Collect a list of phone numbers for counsellors, treatment centres, and Twelve Step fellowships.

- **Don't insist on the label of sex addiction.**
  There is much confusion and baggage associated with this term that is not important to resolve in the early stages of recovery. In our work with clients, we don't impose this label. What matters is whether people acknowledge they are struggling to establish and/or maintain healthy boundaries in their sexual life. The label one chooses for the experience of powerlessness over sexual behaviour is less important than one's willingness to ask for help and make the changes necessary to recover.

- **Do expect denial and minimisation when initially confronting sex addicts.**
  Since sex addiction is surrounded by so much shame, and since addicts live in fear of being found out, expect the truth to come out haltingly and in pieces. It is very common for addicts to tell only 'part of the story' when they are initially confronted. Then, as they gather more courage, they become willing to tell more. While this is frustrating, and further damages trust, understand

that it is common. Work patiently to get at the truth, asking clarifying questions whenever vague language is used.

- **Don't blame the spouse for sexual addiction, especially if you're the spouse.**
  Many spouses of sex addicts struggle with feeling responsible for their partner's addiction. Often influenced by the blame-shifting rationalisations of the addict, spouses come to believe that if only they were more attractive or more sexually available, their spouse wouldn't have this problem. Not true! We remind spouses of what we call 'The Three C's' – 'You didn't **cause** this addiction, you can't **control** it, and you can't **cure** it. It's not about you.' As we've pointed out in this chapter, the sexual desires of addicts run deeper than the biological sex drive – they are looking for intimacy and validation that will heal their woundedness. No amount or variety of sexual experiences will accomplish this. The addiction was present before the spouse came on to the scene, and its presence says nothing about the spouse's lack of desire or desirability.

- **Do find a place of support for the spouse as well as for the addict.**
  The spouses of addicts need to find safe friendships – and ideally a safe group – where they can share their struggles and be heard. They need outlets for conversation and support where they can share their anger, so that their addicted spouse does not have to be on the receiving end of all of it. Without these additional places of support for the spouse, either the addict will be overwhelmed by the sadness and anger of the spouse, or the spouse will hold back their genuine feelings and progress will be slowed. Spouses also need support for decisions they have to make about how to support the recovery of the addict, and how to deal with their marriage and family if the addict is not staying sober. Spouses need support as much as addicts.

- **Don't attempt to rush the process of forgiveness.**
  Forgiveness is not a simple, one-time event. It is a process that takes time. Many spouses of sex addicts struggle because they feel they should forgive their spouse, but don't feel ready to do so. Or if they do extend forgiveness, they may continue to have feelings of hurt and anger, and not know how to express them. Both addicts and spouses need to understand that the *decision* to forgive is different from the *process* of forgiving. The process of forgiving is much like the process of grieving: feelings of sadness, hurt and anger will come and go like waves. Instead of being squelched ('I shouldn't be feeling this way'), they need to be accepted and heard. Then, over time, the waves will diminish.

Conclusion

Sexual addiction, while painful and destructive, does not need to be a life sentence. Recovery is possible, as our lives – and the lives of countless others on this journey – attest. Recovery happens when addicts come to terms with their past, adjust their present environment to align with their goal of sexual purity and health, and establish a clear and compelling vision of a recovered life for their future.

Recommended reading

- Laaser, M. (2004). *Healing the Wounds of Sexual Addiction* (Zondervan). This book provides a great overview of sexual addiction and insights into the process of recovery from a Christian perspective.
- Laaser, D. (2008). *Shattered Vows: Hope and healing for women who have been sexually betrayed* (Zondervan). This book provides wisdom and guidance for spouses of people caught in the grip of sexual sin.
- Carnes, P., Delmonico, D., Griffin, E. and Moriarty, J. (2004). *In the Shadows of the Net* (Hazelden). This is a workbook that provides teaching and guidance about the specific issue of online sexual compulsive addiction, including exercises to work through for your own recovery.

Websites

www.faithfulandtrueministries.com – the home page for Dr Mark Laaser, which offers resources for understanding sexual addiction and information about workshops, training events and intensive counselling experiences to help people find recovery.

www.markbrouwer.com – this weblog contains a host of important information about sex addiction, with many links to articles and research material about addiction, recovery and healthy leadership.

Dealing with Difficult People

Jocelyn Bryan

Difficult people are those whose communication style and behaviour patterns serve to manipulate the behaviour and attitudes of others, causing them to feel inferior, threatened, intimidated or frustrated. They have a negative impact on organisations, lowering morale, creating confusion, reducing satisfaction, and impeding the efficiency and effectiveness of a team. People often leave a team or organisation because of the impact of such a person.

When I first worked in management it became apparent very quickly that the major challenges were not necessarily meeting targets and delivering client satisfaction, but managing the difficult people within the two teams for which I had overall responsibility. The most difficult of these was a team leader who was arrogant and aggressive. He always believed he was right and would not listen to others. He lacked sensitivity and self-awareness. When confronted with the effect of his behaviour on the effectiveness of the team, he became very aggressive and threatening. Another difficult person within the team was a friendly, sociable man who was always willing to take on any job you asked of him. Nothing was too much trouble and he was never resistant to anything. However, it became obvious that he was often unable to fulfil all the commitments he made. This was especially difficult when he was promising clients a service which he could not deliver. He had good intentions, but was unable to say 'no' to anyone. This was a source of frustration amongst both his colleagues and the clients for whom he had responsibility.

We have all encountered difficult people in various contexts and we are all, at times, 'difficult'. Being difficult is not a clinical condition but it can be on the borderline of personality disorder. Difficult people chronically use problematic behaviour and communication styles which have a negative effect on others and the effectiveness of any team or organisation they are part of.

I will explore some of these habitual behaviour patterns and suggest ways in which they might be modified and how others may cope with them. It also offers the opportunity for us to hold a mirror up to ourselves so that we might be more self-aware and attentive to the times when we become a difficult person. The psychology of anger is presented as a major explanatory tool in the understanding of these behavioural responses. This theme is developed further in the final section which seeks to explore how we can engage with anger theologically.

Introducing Jim, Sue and Mary

Jim

> Jim has been passed over for a number of new opportunities in the organisation he works for. He carries the label of being a 'difficult person'. He works in a team but his colleagues do not experience him as a team player. Jim is often negative and critical in meetings, but this is expressed in an indirect way, for example in sarcastic humour. He makes asides, niggles and has a tendency to list reasons why change would be impractical or difficult. His attitude is negative but this is expressed indirectly. He is unwilling to volunteer to help other members of the team in new projects, but will do if asked. In such cases he accepts the responsibility willingly, but he is inwardly resistant and often misses the deadlines agreed and lets down others in the team. He is afraid of conflict and avoids any confrontations.

Sue

> Sue is very involved with her church. She is a church steward and pastoral visitor, organises church bookings and is secretary of

the pastoral committee. She works full time and has two children. Sue is friendly, responsive and always willing to do whatever anyone asks of her. She rarely disagrees with anyone and never confronts anyone, whatever their point of view or behaviour. She is very uncomfortable with conflict and often when there is a disagreement in church over who holds responsibility for a particular task, Sue will step in and take on the responsibility rather than let the situation lead to conflict. She is sociable and outgoing; most people would say they liked her. She therefore seems unlikely to be a difficult person to deal with. But she frequently makes unrealistic commitments and then lets people down. She makes promises in good faith but then is unable to keep them. The minutes of meetings are never circulated before the meeting and have to be tabled so members do not have time to give them sufficient attention. There is frequent confusion over who has booked the church premises for what, because Sue has promised it to two different groups at the same time, hoping she can please both parties and then not resolving the difficult situation she has created. Bookings are not recorded promptly or are sometimes inaccurate, so people feel frustrated and let down by her. She often can't attend the meetings she is required to be at, but doesn't let the church minister know until the last minute. She avoids sharing negative or difficult information, which leads to misunderstandings and a misrepresentation of the way things really are.

Mary

Mary also carries the label of being a 'difficult person.' She is described as forceful and often aggressive. Mary is impatient and when her plans are met with resistance or encounter obstacles, her impatience spills over and she becomes indignant and angry. She has a strong sense of what others ought to do and expresses this forcibly and with confidence. It is rare for Mary to acknowledge anyone else's skills or abilities verbally or

> in the manner in which she behaves. Mary is seen as hostile, condescending and sarcastic by her colleagues. She is prone to shouting at them and they find her behaviour and communication style intimidating. Mary is particularly difficult to manage as she is unable to receive feedback and shows little awareness of the impact of her attitude and behaviour on colleagues.

It is difficult to maintain positive relationships with these characters. Together, they represent the most challenging types of difficult people. There are obvious contrasts between them and hence they present very different challenges to those who are their colleagues or those who manage them. Jim and Sue show many of the characteristics of what has come to be labelled passive aggression. Jim disguises hostility by seeming to be nice. He might say he agrees with something but in reality he doesn't and this manifests itself in a lack of commitment and not following things through. He says what he thinks people want to hear and then expresses his actual thoughts and feelings in indirect comments. His words and behaviour are not consistent. He is difficult to deal with because he appears agreeable and compliant, yet his behaviour is problematic.

Sue is super-agreeable, which is often associated with passive-aggressive behaviour. She desperately needs to be liked and accepted. She is super-agreeable as a means of seeking and achieving approval, hence she does not express her actual thoughts, especially if they are contradictory. This means that she is not always honest. Like Jim, her words and actions are sometimes inconsistent. She over-commits herself because she fears saying 'no' will result in disapproval or negative feelings towards her and she always has a plausible excuse for her shortcomings. Many of her actions are rooted in her fear of conflict and disapproval. She frustrates those who work with her and is easily threatened when confronted with any criticism. Sue suffers from frequent headaches and has other symptoms related to stress. She believes it is 'unchristian' to express anger and that her role in the church community is to be 'nice' to everyone. Sue also fears expressing anger because this may result in others not liking her.

Mary, by comparison, behaves in ways which have been characterised as hostile-aggressive. Mary expresses her aggression and frustration openly and is hostile to those who disagree with her, challenge her or obstruct her in achieving her goals. This can express itself physically and verbally. She has to win. She is intimidating and powerful.

The common psychological feature of all three characters' behaviour is that they manage or mismanage their feelings of anger and aggression in such a way that their relationships with others are damaged or dysfunctional.

Bramson[1] describes difficult people as an ubiquitous phenomenon which has gone unnoticed and unexamined. It is evident that dealing with difficult people, whether they be colleagues, parishioners, clients or managers, is a frequent source of stress. Difficult people also present a problem to a team or organisation and can have a fundamental effect on the team or organisation's well-being and effectiveness. Bramson, as a management consultant, provides descriptions of the characteristics of 'difficult people' and how to cope with them. He describes a number of patterns of difficult behaviour which are categorised as the complainers, know-it-all experts, silent responsives, super-agreeables, indecisives and hostile-aggressives. He proposes that all these various behaviour patterns are motivated by a desire to gain control over other people.

In response to this analysis, the coping strategies he outlines focus on ways which enable the 'power balance' in the relationships with these people to be redressed and also minimise the impact of their behaviour on the immediate situation. A key factor in these strategies is acting with purpose and preparing possible responses to the difficult behaviour patterns. Evidently, it is necessary to ensure that the difficult person does not maintain control in the relationship, by using behaviour patterns which enable them to exploit others and exercise a destructive use of power. The effectiveness of coping strategies and also changing behaviour patterns depends largely on understanding the motivation for the difficult behaviour and factors which influence it.

Outline of approach

It is important to recognise what characterises difficult behaviour patterns and how they impact on other people and an organisation. These

1. Bramson, R. M. (1981). *Coping with Difficult People* (New York: Dell).

characteristics will be described in detail before the behaviour patterns are analysed. I will base my analysis on current psychological theories and use these to inform our understanding of the motives and factors which affect difficult people.

I have chosen Jim, Sue and Mary to serve as key examples. The main reason for this choice is the common psychological ground between them; namely anger and aggression. They also all have self-esteem issues and represent the three types of difficult people which people often report as being the most difficult to deal with.[1]

Difficult people are only experienced as difficult in the context of a relationship. It is the way they communicate with others and react to the situation they find themselves in that elicits the behaviour pattern that people find difficult to cope with. Their behaviour is interpreted and experienced as aggressive, negative, condescending, irrational, critical, abusive and frustrating. In other words, it is the way difficult people communicate and present themselves to others which is problematic. This is often accompanied by a lack of awareness regarding the impact of their behaviour on others and poor sensitivity and empathy. For this reason, any coping strategy must focus on how to manage the relationship and communicate with the difficult person in a way which allows thoughts and feelings to be dealt with sensitively and with respect. It requires good communication and listening skills.

There are many writers in managerial literature who make no attempt at this type of analysis. What they offer is a description of the behaviour and suggestions for coping strategies. In contrast, I want to suggest that by seeking to understand the difficult person's motives and the factors which influence these behaviour patterns, we can handle difficult relationships with greater insight and sensitivity, and increase the likelihood of achieving sustainable positive outcomes.

1. Anecdotal evidence: B. Geary.

Characteristics of difficult people

The identification of 'difficult people types' is well documented.[1] Here Jim, Sue and Mary's behaviour patterns are summarised.

Jim: Passive-aggressive

Key characteristics

- Desire for approval and general agreeableness
- Negative attitude and comments
- Subtle defiance
- Ambivalence towards most things
- Frequently uses misunderstandings, excessive demands, as excuses for their inefficiency
- Criticises others outside their presence
- Avoids conflict
- Sulks and refuses to discuss contentious issues
- Resistance to suggestions of others
- Lateness and forgetfulness
- Complaining
- Does not express anger or hostility
- Manipulative
- Procrastinates over decisions

Passive aggression describes a pattern of behaviour which carries a pervasive negative attitude. It is described as passive because there is normally little direct expression of resistance in interpersonal situations.

1. Bramson, R. M. (1981). *Coping with Difficult People* (New York: Dell); Brinkman, R. and Kirschner, R. (1994). *Dealing with People You Can't Stand* (New York, NY: McGraw-Hill); Keating, C. (1984). *Dealing with Difficult People: How you can come out on top of personality conflicts* (New York, NY: Paulist Press).

So the person complies with others in their demands or needs but is passively resistant to them and becomes increasingly hostile and aggressive as a consequence of this. The pattern of behaviour is understood as a defensive response leading to the avoidance of something the person fears. Often, this is fear of authority, competition, dependency, intimacy or conflict. A common expression of passive aggression is complying with the wishes of another and even committing to work to achieve these with enthusiasm, then failing to carry out the necessary task or action on time, or in a way which is unhelpful and puts the desired outcome in jeopardy.

In the past decade passive aggression has been recognised as a common syndrome. Examples of behaviours which fall into this category are agreeing to meet a friend for dinner at 7.15pm and arriving at 8.00pm, consistently failing to meet deadlines at work, being angry with someone and refusing to talk to them about it, always having a list of excuses for any shortcomings, agreeing to changes in procedures then gradually reinstating old ways of doing things. In daily life, in ministry and in occupational settings, passive aggression presents itself frequently, but by its very nature can be difficult to identify and deal with. It is a behaviour pattern which disguises underlying emotions.

Sperry[1] notes that passive-aggressive employees are relatively common in organisations but far less common in leaders. Interestingly, he goes on to comment that this is not the case in non-profit organisations such as religious communities, diocesan offices and non-profit making public-sector institutions where passive-aggression is a characteristic of leaders and employees and is associated with low morale and productivity.

Sue: Super-agreeable

Key characteristics

- Agrees with other's point of view
- Cheerful and socially outgoing
- Eager to volunteer
- Does not like to say 'no'

1. Sperry, L. (1990). 'Passive aggression in organisations', *Human Development,* 11 (2), 41–42.

- Over-commits
- Does not see things through
- Dislikes conflict and the expression of anger or discussion of anything unpleasant
- Makes promises in good faith
- Avoids confrontation whenever possible
- Fails to meet deadlines or is late
- Affirms others and makes them feel liked
- Never expresses anger
- Is negative about others when they are not present
- Minimises problems

Super-agreeable people are difficult to deal with because of their agreeableness. It has been suggested that the super-agreeable manipulates the presentation of reality to gain approval.[1] The fear of conflict and disapproval are significant factors in their behaviour patterns and this is undoubtedly linked to issues of self-esteem and the need for affirmation and acceptance by others. The expression of anger is often interpreted as a sign of weakness and lack of self-control and hence it becomes associated with fear of rejection and the lowering of self-esteem. This is especially apparent in church settings where cultures are created in which anger is often denied (and disapproved of) and conflict avoided. It is also the case that many churches are experiencing a decline in membership and there are more and more demands made on the existing members of the church community. Hence there is considerable pressure on individuals to be agreeable and take on additional responsibilities. This, coupled with the desire for approval as a Christian who lives out their discipleship in acts of service and puts others before themselves, makes super-agreeableness a problem in many churches. There are some obvious examples of how within

1. Bramson, R. M. (1981). *Coping with Difficult People* (New York: Dell), p. 90.

church communities passive aggression and super-agreeableness combine to result in a stagnant community where the psychological and spiritual well-being of both the people and the community is at risk.

The 'nice' church which is so fearful of conflict that it resists making any changes becomes stagnant and members drift away.

The parish priest who 'loves' everyone, agrees with everyone and is afraid to say 'no'. He is overworked, increasingly stressed and fails to meet his deadlines.

The church treasurer who grumbles to anyone who is willing to listen about the amount of money being wasted throughout the church, but never raises it as an issue in the finance committee meeting or makes suggestions to improve funding.

Mary: Hostile-aggressive

Key characteristics

- Impatience
- Abrupt and intimidating in interaction with others
- Needs to prove to themselves and others that they are right
- Presents as self-confident
- Aggressive and abrasive manner
- Lack of care for and trust in others
- Lacks capacity to receive and accept feedback
- Poor listening skills
- Lack of empathy
- Arrogant, with a strong sense of how others should think and act
- Lack of control of anger and frustration expressed verbally and sometimes physically

Hostile aggression is associated with a variety of characteristics as the list above illustrates. However, it is important to recognise that hostility and aggression are different, but that both are negative responses and inflict hurt, either physical or emotional, on another person. A person can be hostile but not aggressive, for example, by ignoring someone or being unresponsive to another. Emotional hurt can be inflicted intentionally without aggression being present. It is also the case that aggression can be an expression of caring for someone, or one might respond with aggression through indignation on behalf of a friend or relative. In the context of relationships, aggression and hostility are frequently expressed in response to conflict or a perceived threat and as such have a high emotional intensity. It is evident from the characteristics listed above that aggression in hostile-aggressive behaviour is a means of asserting power and establishing increased self-esteem. It seeks to intimidate the other person into submission or undermine or ridicule them or provoke them into a state of irrational anger. If an aggressive person holds a position of power within an organisation then they can be extremely difficult to deal with.

Jim, Sue and Mary's behaviour patterns reveal difficulties in their management of conflict, anger and aggression. When anger is not recognised or worked with constructively, it results in personal and social difficulties. Aggressive behaviour is often an expression of anger and frustration and manifests itself verbally and non-verbally in relationships. It is a response mediated through the sympathetic nervous system and the 'fight or flight' reaction stimulated by adrenalin. Hence, in the case of the behavioural characteristics such as those listed above, we are dealing with a universal innate human response which is being managed or mismanaged in the particular social setting and which is usually influenced by the personal goals of the individual.

Understanding aggression

These insights enable us to understand the nature of aggression and make it possible to understand not only our own aggressive tendencies but those of others. They also help us to develop strategies which enable us to manage relationships which are characterised by anger and aggression.

What factors influence aggressive behaviour and how does our expression of anger and aggression develop?

In Jim's case, his aggression and frustration is suppressed and then expressed in his negativity, sullenness, resentment and lack of commitment. Sue believes that if she shows her anger she will be rejected and it will damage the affirming relationships she desires, and so she disguises her anger and seeks alternative channels to express this. On the other hand, Mary's hostile-aggressive behaviour is an expression of her mismanagement of her aggressive feelings in her social context, and this leads to abrasive, angry, threatening and, in extreme instances, violent, physical behaviour. In each case, the mismanagement of aggression leads to relationships which are difficult and damage the social unit which they operate in.

Motivation for aggressive behaviour

Anderson and Bushman[1] see all aggression as including the intent to harm. However, they distinguish between hostile and instrumental aggression. Hostile aggression is defined as impulsive, driven by anger and motivated by the goal of harming the other.

It is conceived as being in response to a perceived provocation and is sometimes called *reactive* aggression. In contrast, *instrumental* aggression is seen as a premeditated means of obtaining a goal other than harming the other person. It is defined as *proactive*. A person may be verbally aggressive towards someone in order to bully them into supporting one of their proposals, but not to harm them as such.

Current theories of aggression

There are a number of different theories of aggression which help us to understand how aggressive behaviour develops and what influences it. These are outlined briefly below.

Social learning

Undoubtedly some people are more aggressive than others, but what determines this depends on how they have learned to express aggression and anger through their upbringing, observing others, and the beliefs and

1. Anderson, C. A. and Bushman, B. J. (2002). 'Human aggression', *Annual Review of Psychology* 53: 27–15.

expectations regarding social behaviour which they have been taught and exposed to. This draws on social learning theory which explains how we develop our understanding of the expectations of the social world we inhabit and behave accordingly. We observe and experience aggression in our early lives, and through these experiences and observations we learn when and how to express aggression in our social world. The key influences in this learning process are the observed aggressive behaviour patterns in families and other significant social settings such as school.[1]

Script theory

Heusmann[2] suggests that we store our experience and awareness of patterns of aggressive behaviour in what he calls 'aggressive scripts'. A script is defined as a well-established concept held in our memory which is essentially a set of connected actions linked to goals and likely outcomes. It contains causal links so that the relationship of 'If . . . then . . .' is programmed into the script. We hold scripts for numerous behaviour patterns ranging from catching a bus or eating in a restaurant to dealing with a distressed child. When behaviour patterns are well rehearsed or frequently repeated they are activated or accessed more easily. They also have a large number of links and associations connected to them in memory. This increases the chances of these behaviour patterns being activated across a number of situations. In this way the behaviour becomes generalised across a number of situations through the association network which it accumulates in the memory system.

This theory is particularly helpful in accounting for how a child who has frequently witnessed aggression in their parent's marriage as a means of establishing power and influence, acquires a script incorporating this pattern of behaviour which is then readily activated across many situations in their subsequent interpersonal and social relationships. So when the child can't get its own way in the playground, the script is activated and it behaves aggressively towards its peer group. The cue for activating the

1. Anderson, C. A. and Bushman, B. J. (2002). 'Human aggression', *Annual Review of Psychology* 53:27–15
2. Heusmann, L. R. (1998). 'The role of social information processing and cognitive schema in the acquisition and maintenance of habitual aggression', in Green, R. G. and Donnerstein, E. (Eds.), *Aggression: Theories, research and implications for policy* (New York: Academic).

script for aggressive behaviour is the child being obstructed in achieving its goal. Likewise, the child is more likely to throw a tantrum which includes physical violence towards its parents and teachers if it has frequently seen and experienced such outbursts as resulting in obtaining power and influence. Hence, a behaviour pattern of aggressive behaviour is evoked when they feel threatened or want to exert power and influence over someone or a particular situation.

Social interaction theory

Another theory which has significant explanatory power in this field is social interaction theory. This explains aggressive behaviour as a form of social influence behaviour. It suggests that aggression is used to produce changes in the behaviour of another person. This is particularly helpful in understanding our example of Mary as it begins to draw light on the motivation behind her aggressive behaviour. Aggression is seen as a coercive behaviour which is used to obtain something of value – for example, support for a proposal, money, help, goods – or to exact retribution and right a perceived wrong, or to build up a self-image or social identity of, for example, power, influence, competence. In this theory, aggressive behaviour is a set of premeditated actions directed towards achieving a desired outcome. Hence there is a reasoned goal motivating the aggression which could be anything from inflicting punishment on someone as negative reinforcement for a perceived provocation, to bolstering one's social image of being a tough person who is determined to achieve a particular end result.

Recent findings[1] suggest that aggression is often elicited by threats to high self-esteem, in particular in cases of unwarranted inflated self-esteem. The theory explains many aggressive behaviour patterns in teams and communities where aggressive behaviour is used as a means to enhance one's self-image and self-esteem.

An extension of this theory is related to parenting style. This has been used to explain the development of passive-aggressive behaviour patterns

1. Bushman, B. J. and Baumeister, R. F. (1998). 'Threatened egotism, narcissism, self-esteem and direct and displaced aggression: Does self-love or self-hate lead to violence?', *Journal of Personality and Social Psychology* 58:156–63.

which the individual uses to cope with either threatening, restrictive parenting or inconsistent parenting. In the case of inconsistent parenting, many of the characteristics of passive-aggressive behaviour – for example, indecisiveness and contradictory behaviour – were modelled by parents. The child then does not develop either the cognitive understanding or emotional maturity to assess what is expected of them socially or emotionally. This contradictory parenting style results in a lack of assertiveness and poor self-esteem in the child which continues into adulthood. The child becomes fearful of commitments, unable to predict confidently the responses of others, uncertain of their abilities and afraid of expressing emotions overtly. In parenting styles where the child's needs and desires are frustrated, the child may not risk losing attention or may fear possible rejection from expressing anger directly. Hence, the frustration and anger are expressed indirectly in negativity and resistance but at the same time maintaining compliance for fear of rejection.

Other factors to consider

Personality traits

Some people are predisposed to higher levels of aggression.

Sex

Males have a higher tendency to aggressive behaviour linked to their levels of testosterone. Males are more likely to express aggression directly, but females prefer indirect aggression. This may well be linked to gender differences in social learning, with parents and schools modelling and reinforcing different behaviour patterns of aggressive behaviour according to gender.

Beliefs

If a person believes that aggressive behaviour can lead to the outcome they desire, they are more likely to be aggressive in a given situation. However, if a person's faith tradition views aggression as negative and a sign of weakness or moral failure, then a person is less likely to express their aggression directly.

Provocation

This is probably the most significant single cause. This may include insults, criticism, thwarted plans. Baron,[1] studying workplace aggression, found perceived injustice as positively related to aggression in this context.

Frustration

When someone can't attain or obtain what they want they become frustrated. Sometimes this leads to aggressive behaviour towards the person who has been identified as responsible for the lack of goal attainment, but it is also the case that the target of the aggression may not be this person and the aggression is displaced and directed towards another person or organisation. In both Jim and Mary frustration is a key situational factor in the behaviour patterns shown.

Jim's aggression

In the case of Jim, a passive-aggressive, we can see how these factors combine to lead to some of the characteristics of his behaviour. Jim is frustrated in his work and feels undervalued and overlooked. He has an overwhelming need to be liked and avoids and resists any conflict. He is frustrated and angry about his position. His self-esteem is being lowered by his current situation. However, he believes that if he shows others in his organisation that he is angry about the number of opportunities for which he has been overlooked, he will risk damaging his chances for the future and face rejection or condemnation. Jim believes that showing aggression has a negative effect on relationships and seeks to exert social influence in other ways. Hence he expresses this anger and frustration indirectly by being inefficient, being negative and critical of others behind their backs and resistant to any new ideas. As is often the case with passive aggression, he may be unaware that these are expressions of his anger or of the damaging effect he is having on the organisation and his relationships within it.

1. Baron, R. A. (2002). 'Social and personal determinants of workplace aggression: Evidence for the impact of perceived injustice and the Type A behaviour pattern', *Aggressive Behaviour* 25:281–96, quoted in Anderson, C. A. and Bushman, B. J. (2002). 'Human aggression', *Annual Review of Psychology* 53:27-15.

Sue's aggression

The identification of how Sue manages her anger and aggression is more difficult, because they are avoided. Like Jim, she avoids conflict and she sees anger as a negative emotion. From social interaction theory Sue's behaviour can be understood as the repression of aggression helping her to achieve her desired outcome of maintaining affirming relationships and being accepted. Her motivation for repressing any feelings of anger is that she believes this would put her relationships at risk and in her understanding of social norms she believes that displays of anger are unacceptable and show lack of self-control and weakness. Hence, she is fearful of the consequences of expressing anger and the effect it will have on her relationships. From social learning theory the influence of Sue's parents' attitude towards the expression of feelings and the influence of her church background will also be affecting her behaviour. However, it is likely that Sue will be expressing aggression in ways she is unaware of. Some of her inefficiency may well be unintentional, but she excuses herself by listing the demands she is facing rather than learning to say 'no'. The same can be seen in her increasing tendency to be forgetful. Alongside this she might well become increasingly resentful about her workload for the church for which she receives little reward and no thanks! In addition her symptoms of stress may well be related to the repression of her anger.

Mary's aggression

Mary is a hostile-aggressive. We see some of the factors described above working out in her in a different behaviour pattern. Mary is motivated by proving herself and having power and influence in the team. It is important that she achieves her objectives and this is an important factor in her self-esteem. When others resist her ideas or plans, she becomes irritated and frustrated. Her self-esteem is threatened. To bolster her self-esteem she uses aggression to threaten others and achieve power over them in order to achieve her goals. She is forceful and self-confident. She does not listen to others and firmly believes she is right. Some of her anger she understands to be 'righteous anger'. In Mary's case this is a learned behaviour pattern which has a reasoned goal.

When Mary is thwarted or frustrated, her aggressive script is activated and she adopts the behaviour pattern which she has acquired through observation and experience.

Self-esteem

Another important psychological factor in each of our characters is their self-esteem.

Self-esteem is defined as an overall affective evaluation of one's own worth.[1] It is evident in each of our characters that their difficult behaviour patterns are related to their self-esteem. Branden,[2] in his book on how to raise your self-esteem, suggests that low self-esteem causes people to be less ambitious, less creative in their work and less likely to treat others respectfully. Furthermore, they are less likely to assume responsibility and will look for others to blame.[3]

Research using adolescents and college students found that low self-esteem was associated with a tendency to reject or be overly sensitive to criticism, an avoidance of making decisions and a resentment of being told what to do.[4] Hostile-aggressive behaviour is frequently elicited when criticism is voiced. The confrontational response and bullying behaviour of hostile-aggressives acts as a facade to hide the wound that criticism causes to an already low self-esteem. Their behaviour pattern may also include sarcasm, boasting, arrogance and over-estimating their abilities to appear superior. All of these are strategies to establish a sense of power or inflate their self-esteem.[5]

In the case of passive-aggressives, low self-esteem is expressed as a fear of being rejected or behaving inappropriately, so they procrastinate when

1. Balscovich, J. and Tamaka, J. (2001). 'Measures of self-esteem', in Robinson, J. P., Shaver, P. R., Wrightsman, L. S. (Eds), *Measures of Personality and Social Attitudes* (San Diego, C A: Academic Press), quoted in Rayens, B. L. (2001). 'Predicting difficult employees: The relationship between vocational interests, self-esteem and problem communication styles', *Applied H. R. M. Research,* 6 (1) 33-66.
2. Branden, N. (1988). *How to Raise Your Self-Esteem* (New York: Bantam Books).
3. Hamachek, D. E. (1987). *Encounters with Self* (New York: Holt, Rinehart and Winston).
4. Rosenberg, M. (1965). *Society and Adolescent Self-Image* (Princeton, NJ: Princeton University Press).
5. Rayens, B. L. (2001). 'Predicting difficult employees: The relationship between vocational interests, self-esteem and problem communication styles', *Applied H. R. M. Research,* 6 (1) 33-66 .

making decisions, they offer very little input in meetings, they may be negative and will not volunteer for any new responsibilities since they risk being disliked or rejected.

Super-agreeables classically fear rejection and have an overwhelming need to be accepted and affirmed. Their self-esteem is fragile and anything they perceive as potentially threatening to their relationships and their acceptance is resisted. They fear the consequences of saying 'no', disagreeing with others and expressing their anger.

Whilst low self-esteem can manifest itself in difficult behaviour patterns, it is also the case that inflated self-esteem is associated with problematic behaviour, especially in communication and relationships. When someone with high self-esteem feels that their authority or competence is being threatened, they respond with an aggressive communication style. Individuals with high self-esteem make unrealistically positive claims about themselves.[1] Consequently, they set themselves unrealistic goals which can lead to failure. When failure threatens their egos, they compensate for their deflated self-esteem by using sarcasm and negative communication styles to intimidate others and make them appear inferior, thus restoring their feelings of superiority.

1. Baumeister, R. F., Heatherton, T. F. and Tice, D. M. (1994). *Losing Control: How and why people fail at self-regulation* (San Diego, CA: Academic Press).

How should it be dealt with?

Many of the people who we have so far considered do not have diagnosable personality disorders or suffer from mental illnesses (although this may sometimes be the case). While many people can benefit from therapy, it is not always necessary, nor will everyone be open to benefiting from this. There are, however, interventions that can be helpful.

Super-agreeables often need to learn how to be more assertive. They have difficulty saying 'no', and can create difficulties for themselves that can lead to frustration, resentment and feelings of not being appreciated. They can also benefit from group therapy where their avoidance of conflict and negative emotions will be challenged in a supportive setting. This can provide the corrective emotional experience that will give them greater resilience in interpersonal situations. Adjusting to new behaviours may lead to a period of clumsy interactions; however, after a period of time the super-agreeable, by learning their own limitations and respecting the boundaries of others, can become an asset to the church or organisation. Many church groups now provide training in conflict management and assertiveness to help clergy, volunteers or workers to deal with uncomfortable emotions, especially anger. There are also training agencies that provide similar training for therapists, psychologists, social workers and people in other work settings.

Passive-aggressives can be more difficult to help as so much of their energy is invested in avoidance and denial. They can also be helped by workshops on communications and assertiveness, although this may need to be supplemented by therapy that focuses on emotional expressiveness, as they have difficulty owning and articulating their own feelings. Group therapy can also be helpful for them. Irvin Yalom, who has worked extensively with psychotherapy groups, writes:

> Members of dynamic therapy groups, which have ground rules encouraging open feedback, may obtain considerable information about maladaptive social behaviour. A patient may, for example, learn about a disconcerting tendency to avoid looking at the

> person with whom he or she is conversing; about others' impressions of his or her haughty, regal attitude; or about a variety of other social habits that, unbeknownst to the patient, have been undermining social relationships. For individuals lacking intimate relationships, the group often represents the first opportunity for accurate interpersonal feedback.[1]

Passive-aggressives often require feedback in a safe setting in order to identify, understand and begin to change their behaviour. Individual therapy can also be helpful, but group therapy is probably more valuable and effective for people who behave in this way.

Aggressive individuals often resist any kind of help. However, they too can benefit from workshops on assertiveness and aggressiveness where they can see how their behaviour is affecting other people and experiment with new behaviours that enable them to get their needs met without trampling on the needs or feelings of others. They can also benefit from cognitive-behavioural therapy that helps them to reflect on their life goals and their values, and whether or not their behaviour is helping them to achieve what is important for themselves or the organisations they belong to. The comments made about group psychotherapy for passive-aggressive individuals also relate to aggressive people. They can benefit from receiving feedback in a safe setting. Other group members can be helped to give direct feedback which is often difficult – and difficult for the aggressive individual to hear – in social or work settings.

1. Yalom, I. D. (1995). *The Theory and Practice of Group Psychotherapy* (New York: Basic Books), p. 16.

A Christian response

I have suggested that the management of anger and aggression is a significant factor in the three types of difficult patterns of behaviour described. Anger is a powerful emotion which is often expressed in aggressive behaviour patterns. Within the Christian tradition, anger and aggression are responded to negatively. However, it was only in the nineteenth century that the psychological category of emotions was established. Prior to this time these psychological states were understood as passions and affections of the soul.

Passions were seen as signs of and punishment for the original sin of Adam and Eve. They were interpreted as manifestations of the disobedience to the will and were in tension with the affections of the soul which were viewed as the more refined, spiritual and aesthetic desires which drew the person towards beauty, truth and goodness.[1] Hence anger was understood as an emotion to be tamed, avoided, repressed or controlled. It was associated with sin, disobedience and failure. The challenge for the Christian Church over the past century has been to develop a response to emotions which is consistent with our understanding of the nature of God, of relationships and of our human nature created in the image of God in the light of our ever-increasing knowledge of human psychology.

Throughout psychology's history as an academic discipline, the complexity of our emotional landscape has challenged understanding and theory. Many conflicting and complex theories of emotions have been proposed, and these too have contributed to the confusion in the Church and the continued dominance of the historical negative interpretation of emotions such as anger, depression and anxiety.

The biblical narrative also presents a picture of contrasting and contradictory responses to the expression of anger. The New Testament gospel of Good News reveals the God of love, mercy and grace, whose sacrificial love for us led Jesus to the cross in loving obedience to his heavenly Father. But alongside this we have to place the anger of God portrayed in a dreadful destructiveness in the Old Testament.

1. Watts, F. (2002). *Psychology for Christian Ministry* (London: Routledge), p. 67.

There are over 400 references to God's anger in the Old Testament. Responses to this aspect of God's nature probe at the heart of our understanding of the very nature of God and how God interacts with his creation. One approach sees his anger as a reflection of his holiness and part of his relationship with humankind. Another emphasises the passionate nature of God where 'love is experienced not only as peaceful creativeness but as violent breakthrough.'[1] Jurgen Moltmann[2], a German theologian, develops this in his understanding of the suffering God, suggesting that 'love is the source and the basis of the possibility of the wrath of God . . . As injured love, the wrath of God is not something which is inflicted, but a divine suffering of evil'.Although this is appealing in the sense that it maintains the love of God as the central core of his being and at the same time does not deny God's anger, it falls short of explaining the divine destructiveness and terror which we find in some of the Old Testament texts.[3]

There remains a degree of mystery and unease in God's anger. Part of the challenge of our spiritual journey is not only to engage with and respond to God's grace in our lives but also to explore within our dynamic relationship with God how to live with the mystery of his being and active presence in creation.

The condemnation of expressed anger is echoed throughout the New Testament. Jesus in the Sermon on the Mount says, 'if you are angry with a brother or sister, you will be liable to judgement.'[4] Likewise Paul in the Letter to the Ephesians writes, 'Lead a life worthy of the calling to which you have been called, with all humility and gentleness, with patience, bearing with one another in love, making every effort to maintain the unity of the Spirit in a bond of peace.'[5] And later in this chapter he writes, 'Be angry and do not sin; do not let the sun go down on your anger.'[6] In this letter, the link between how we behave and our spirituality is clearly

1. Haughton, R. (1981). *The Passionate God* (London: Darton, Longman and Todd), quoted in Campbell, A. V. (1986). *The Gospel of Anger* (London: SPCK), p. 8.
2. Moltmann, J. (1974). *The Crucified God* (London: SCM), p. 272.
3. Campbell, A. V. (1986). *The Gospel of Anger* (London: SPCK).
4. Matthew 5:22
5. Ephesians 4:1-3
6. Ephesians 4:26

recognised. The Christians in Ephesus are instructed in this chapter to deal with anger appropriately. Paul quotes Psalm 4:4, saying that anger should not lead them to sinful behaviour. In other words, they need to manage their anger and deal with it before they sleep at night because if not, they are vulnerable to the devil. What you do when you are angry reflects your spirituality and the holiness of your living. We are called to Christian living which demands expressing our anger in ways which reflect the life and love of God. But the tendency to deplore human anger as sinful continues in Christian communities and this has a negative effect on both Church communities and the spiritual growth of individual Christians.

Yet, there are obvious examples of Jesus expressing anger. The memorable scene in the temple after his triumphal entry into Jerusalem, when Jesus overturned the tables of the money changers is arguably when his anger was most dramatically expressed.[1] Here we have a significant example of Jesus exhibiting a necessary expression of anger in response to the misuse of God's house, but its significance goes beyond this as it illustrates that anger can be justified in the face of abuse and injustice.

The acknowledgement of anger leading to a positive outcome goes back to early Christianity. Lactantius[2] in *The Wrath of God* makes the helpful distinction between righteous and sinful anger, but as Watts[3] notes, the acceptability of displays of anger was most likely dependent on the person's status in society. However, the distinction between different types of anger, and whether it can be either constructive or destructive depending on the circumstances, is found in much of the psychological literature.[4] There are many situations when anger can lead to positive developments in human relationships as well as the reversal of acts of injustice and exploitation. This demands a more positive and functional approach to anger. Righteous anger – anger expressed on behalf of others in response to situations of injustice, exploitation and victimisation, or in

1. Matthew 21:12, 13
2. Lactantius. 'The Wrath of God', in *The Fathers of the Church*, vol. 54, ed. Defarri, R. J. (Washington, DC: Catholic University of America), quoted in Watts, F. (1997). *Zygon*, 32 (2), p. 255.
3. Watts, F. (1997). *Zygon*, 32 (2), p. 255.
4. Bowlby, J. (1980). *Attachment and Loss, vol. 3. Loss, Sadness and Depression* (London: Hogarth Press); Fromm, E. (1973). *The Anatomy of Human Destructiveness* (New York: Holt, Rinehart and Winston).

personal situations when something significant is threatened – can be a catalyst for positive development in relationships and eventual outcomes.

The more people care about something or someone, the more likely they are to feel angry when situations lead to disappointment or frustration. Campbell[1] develops this and suggests that the closeness between anger and love can be approached creatively by considering how a loving anger might overcome both apathy and enmity. Anger is also ignited when a person's sense of vulnerability or inadequacy is touched. By reflecting on the circumstances in which anger is elicited, self-knowledge is increased and the emotion managed more appropriately. Any Christian response should therefore incorporate the adaptive nature of anger and its positive outcomes, as well as the negative effects of its expression, in its framework.

One of the most fruitful ways to proceed through this maze of contradictory understandings is by building on the distinction between the emotion or feeling of anger and its expression. Condemnation of the aggressive or passive-aggressive expression of anger which leads to physical or emotional hurt is a very different matter from condemnation of the emotion itself. This point was recognised earlier in the discussion of Ephesians chapter 4.

Anger is part of our daily lives and it has an effect on our health and well-being. Luther warns that without anger we might reach a state of oblivion where nothing changes and where in the end love itself loses all power. The way we deal with anger is connected with spirituality.[2] Spirituality is not something to be kept in our hearts but touches all of life including the words we speak and the way we relate to and interact with others. Many difficult pastoral situations arise through the use or abuse of anger. The confusion and uncertainty it gives rise to, both theologically and personally, causes many Christians to feel lost and lacking in confidence when dealing with it. Frequently the expression of anger is ignored or avoided. This view is supported by Fox[3] who observes that the avoidance of anger in Christian communities may remove justified anger

1. Campbell, A. V. (1986). *The Gospel of Anger* (London: SPCK), p. 95.
2. Ferder, F. (2000). *Words Made Flesh* (Ave Maria Press), p. 68.
3. Fox, M. (1979). *On Becoming a Musical Mystical Bear* (Philadelphia: Paulist Press).

from the centre of Christian prayer life. This leads to love of neighbour being confused with 'being nice'. Such 'niceness' can result in a number of negative effects in the ministry of pastoral care,[1] including negative feelings being repressed, the accumulation of resentment and a pattern of denial in relationships which engenders a culture of conflict suppression. Likewise, Campbell argues that while anger can be denied it cannot be eliminated from human life.[2] He suggests that the more we refuse to face it, the more it will undermine the possibilities of true Christian love through a cloying 'niceness' or ill-concealed resentment.

How can we respond to anger and the difficult behaviour patterns that arise from it in a way which is hopeful, positive and incorporates our understanding of the gospel and Christian living? An approach of personal re-education and management can lead to changes within the Christian community's approach to anger and passive aggression. This involves discovering the cause of personal anger, working with this constructively, avoiding both angry outbursts and any indirect expressions of the emotion. It also seeks to reduce the anxiety concerning the effect of expressing disagreement in relationships and looks to develop an approach which includes respect for self and others. This requires trust, honesty, and, to some extent, taking the risk of vulnerability with others. Recognising our anger, owning it, trying to understand it and communicating it constructively are envisaged as key stages in this process. Wicks claims that once Christians and religious communities stop seeing anger as being either good or bad and recognise it as a sign of personal vitality, they will be able to distinguish between experiencing the emotion and expressing it.[3] This is essential to managing anger constructively and eliminating the avoidance, passivity, denial and suppression which has led to difficult behaviour patterns in many individuals.

In leadership the inability to express personal anger or cope with the experience of anger in others can be a major factor in the avoidance of dealing with difficult people. In Christian leadership it is often the case

1. Augsburger, D. (1979). *Anger and Assertiveness in Pastoral Care* (Philadelphia: Fortress Press).
2. Campbell, A. V. (1986). *The Gospel of Anger* (London: SPCK), p. 94.
3. Wicks, R. J. (2004). 'A threat to Christian communities: Angry people acting passive aggressively', *Human Development* 25 (3) 8-16.

that shame is associated with personal feelings of anger and also with the discovery that the leader may elicit anger in others. As I have already illustrated, such responses can be the source of difficult behaviour patterns in leadership and organisations.

Dealing with difficult people is a necessary task in enabling the body of Christ to flourish and to fulfil its mission. For some Christians, to define another human being as difficult is to be judgemental and to show a lack of compassion and respect which is out of keeping with the commandment to love our neighbours as ourselves. However, it is undoubtedly the case that there are patterns of behaviour which are difficult to deal with and have a detrimental effect on relationships and the effective functioning of organisations. The mismanagement of anger is arguably one of the underlying causes of some of these common difficult behaviour patterns. By managing our own anger and the anger of others in constructive ways, the vitality encapsulated in this emotion can be directed positively towards building up the body of Christ for its service in the Church and the world. This depends on good methods of communication, empathetic listening and a more positive approach to our emotional life.

Do's and Don'ts

Dealing with difficult people

How do we manage these difficult people in ways which enable them to modify their behaviour patterns and improve the quality and effectiveness of their relationships?

Do's

- Do identify the behaviours which are presenting the problem and analyse these in more detail. What, when and how often? Is there a pattern?
- Do ask questions. Keep them simple: 'What makes you feel angry about what is happening in the project at present? I am aware that you have taken on this new project, but you already appear to be fully stretched with your other commitments. Would it be better to ask someone else to take on this project?' Asking questions of others in the team or organisation is also helpful.
- Do name the problem and listen to the response of the person concerned with empathy, asking gentle probing questions to uncover what the person is thinking and feeling.
- Do identify possible solutions. Identify a number of options to address the issue positively.
- Do follow through the chosen plan and monitor regularly.

The passive-aggressive

Do's

- Passive aggression arises out of the mismanagement of anger and aggression. It is repressed and hidden. To recognise it, it is helpful to be attentive to unexpected feelings of anger in ourselves and others. Passive aggression is covert and the person behaving in this way may not be sufficiently self-aware to realise the effect of their behaviour on others. They are trying to avoid being seen as aggressive even though they feel negative and angry about something.

- Empathise and probe gently. What makes the passive-aggressive angry? Within the relationship encourage the discussion of feelings in a non-judgemental way. Build up trust in the relationship.
- Attend to inconsistencies between their actions and words. Give them feedback and probe what this might suggest about their feelings.
- Affirm assertive behaviour. They are frustrated and annoyed and they cannot express this in an appropriate manner. Affirming their assertiveness encourages them to express their emotions and thoughts and reduces their fear of being judged negatively for doing so.
- Manage your own expectations of their efficiency and inability to complete tasks. Work with them to set realistic achievable goals which can be reviewed regularly. This will increase their self-esteem through the achievement of goals and reduce your feelings of frustration with the passive-aggressive.

Don'ts

- Don't agree with their complaints and negative comments but do listen to them.
- Don't be afraid at times to interrupt, especially if you are having difficulty controlling the structure of the conversation.

The super-agreeable

Do's

- Reassurance of personal acceptance and respect for their honest opinions will encourage trust and openness within the relationship. The super-agreeable has low self-esteem and is fearful of conflict and disapproval. The more accepted and affirmed the super-agreeable feels, the more likely they are to be honest about their feelings and limitations.

- Affirm assertive behaviour. Conflict avoidance is a controlling factor in their behaviour pattern, so the affirmation of assertiveness and saying 'no' to requests will enable them to manage their commitments more realistically.
- Be clear with them on priorities and help them plan their commitments.

Don'ts

- Don't allow them to make unrealistic commitments.
- Don't allow tension and disagreement to escalate. When tension increases they are more likely to agree to things they can not achieve.

The hostile-aggressive

Do's

- Give them some time to 'calm' down.
- Listen and try to ascertain what the cause of conflict/frustration is, and how they are feeling about it. It is also necessary to be able to express your feelings. Good listening skills and the ability to express yourself well are important in resolving a problem involving hostile-aggressive behaviour.
- Draw attention to the way you are being treated without becoming hostile.
- Share how you feel but do not attack the person.
- Watch the non-verbal expression of anger and control. If they have not sat down, encourage them to do so.
- Maintain eye contact.
- Be empathetic and try to establish the facts.
- Stand up to the hostile-aggressive without fighting![1]

1. Bramson, R. M. (1981). *Coping with Difficult People* (New York: Dell), p. 25.

Don'ts

- Don't attack the person.
- Don't worry about always being polite – you may need to interrupt.
- Don't argue with what they say or try to demean them.

Conclusion

Difficult people are encountered throughout all organisations. I have already examined three types which are commonly cited as the most testing to manage: passive-aggressive, hostile-aggressive and super-agreeable. These all share difficulties with handling anger, conflict and aggression. I have suggested that the psychological understanding of anger and aggression provides useful insight into analysing these difficult behaviour patterns and developing coping strategies to work constructively with the emotional response which is elicited.

There is confusion and avoidance surrounding anger and its expression in the Christian tradition. This has led to Christian communities failing to deal with difficult people and sometimes to a cloying niceness and lack of growth. This has been explored in the discussion of a Christian response. Many theological questions arise from this, but I have sought to focus on our response. The question of God's anger, to name but one, has received grossly inadequate attention. What is abundantly clear is that when anger is elicited, it will be expressed. How it is expressed can determine whether the outcome results in a difficult behaviour pattern or not. The consequences of the management of this potent emotion can damage relationships and the effectiveness of an organisation. The way in which anger is expressed by an individual has been shown to be influenced by a number of interacting factors including parenting style and self-esteem. Dealing with anger requires recognising our own anger, the positive function of anger and how it can be used constructively in relationships and organisations.

Recommended reading

- Bramson, R. M. (1981). *Coping with Difficult People* (New York: Dell).
- Campbell, A. V. (1986). *The Gospel of Anger* (London: SPCK).
- Keating, C. (1984). *Dealing with Difficult People: How you can come out on top of personality conflicts* (New York: Paulist Press).

Adult Bullying

— Brendan Geary and Edmund Montgomery —

The word 'bullying' almost immediately brings to mind the playground and the way that some children are badly treated by others. There has been considerable research in recent years on the phenomenon of bullying in childhood, with books, articles, television and radio programmes, helplines and resources for teachers dedicated to eradicating this destructive behaviour. The purpose of this chapter is to look at the disturbing and distressing world of bullying in adulthood.

A search of the professional literature on adult bullying will show little written before the 1970s. Since then there has been an almost exponential growth in research, particularly in the Scandinavian countries, and more research, books, reports, websites, TV and radio programmes devoted to this topic. It is clear now that bullying is pervasive and, as many authors have pointed out, exists wherever human beings have opportunities to use power and can exploit, manipulate, threaten or inflict pain and unreasonable demands on others.

The issue of bullying in the workplace was given considerable publicity with the award in August 2006, of £817,317 to Helen Green, an administrator at Deutsche Bank in the City of London, as a result of suffering treatment from one male and four female colleagues which led to a nervous breakdown.[1] She described their behaviour as 'offensive, abusive, denigrating, bullying, humiliating, patronising, infantile and insulting'.[2] The high award, which was controversial, was partly to compensate for

1. Clarkson, P. (2008). *Beating the Bullies* (London: John Blake), p. 28.
2. http://www.guardian.co.uk/print/0,,329544249-103680,00.html, retrieved 8 November 2007.

loss of future earnings. This, however, is only one in a series of cases that have changed the legal landscape regarding the issue of workplace bullying.

Further evidence of the change in society's sensitivity to this issue appeared in an edition of *The Daily Telegraph* which carried an article on bullying in the workplace[1] and one that related to bullying in the Church.[2] These two reports demonstrate that in both business and church contexts it is sadly not unusual to find examples of behaviour that could be characterised as bullying. The fact that both were reported coincidentally in the same edition of a national newspaper indicates the prominence that this topic has now achieved in terms of media and national awareness.

This chapter will provide a definition of bullying and a description of bullying behaviour and its consequences. There will then be a discussion of the characteristics of perpetrators and victims, as well as a section on bystanders who witness this behaviour. In trying to understand bullying, there will be a discussion of characteristics of workplace cultures that appear to facilitate bullying behaviours, before going on to look at the law on bullying and harassment in Great Britain. The chapter will conclude with suggestions for intervention and treatment, and a discussion of a Christian response to this phenomenon.

1. *The Daily Telegraph*, 5 September 2007, p. 11.
2. *The Daily Telegraph*, 5 September 2007, p. 3.

What is adult bullying?

'It is axiomatic that wherever there is power it is likely to be abused, and wherever there is vulnerability there is likely to be exploitation.'[1]

Stephanie's story

> Stephanie was an administrative officer in a community health centre. Just after joining the centre she was invited to a party by Michael, one of the doctors, which led to a period of dating. Michael was also the office manager, as a result of his gift for organisation and capacity to work with the local health board. Stephanie, however, found Michael possessive and controlling. She suggested that they stop seeing each other as a couple. Michael was not pleased, but appeared to accept her suggestion. After that he was cool towards her and began to find fault with her work. He criticised her at meetings of the practice, but did not find support as the other doctors were pleased with her work. As office manager he decided to reorganise the administrative assistants' responsibilities and areas of work. He significantly lightened Stephanie's workload and increased the workload of the others. It was obvious to Stephanie that he was using his position to manipulate the situation to make it look as if she was not necessary and could be made redundant.

Before going further, it is important to provide a description of the phenomenon that is the focus of this chapter. Bullying has been defined as 'the aggressive behaviour arising from the deliberate attempt to cause physical or psychological distress to others.'[2] There are three important components to this definition. First, it involves aggressive *behaviour*. Bullying involves behaviours that can be identified, observed and, in an empirical sense, measured. It is not sufficient for someone to claim that another person does not like them or is 'out to get them' in some unspecified sense.

1. Randall, P. (1997). *Adult Bullying: Perpetrators and Victims* (Routledge), p. 49.
2. Randall, P. (1997). *Adult Bullying: Perpetrators and Victims* (Routledge), p. 12.

Bullying involves actions that can be located on a scale of frequency and intensity. For example, a manager might inform an employee about poor work performance as part of job appraisal. This ought to be done in private, in a respectful manner, with appropriate professional vocabulary which describes work behaviours in relation to expected outcomes or agreed procedures. On the other hand, the manager might speak to the employee in public, using sarcasm, and in a loud, hectoring voice. This could result in public humiliation, belittlement and intimidation.

Secondly, bullying is deliberate. This takes us into the murky waters of evaluating the intention of another person. We will return to this when considering the legal issues around harassment and bullying. To some extent an accusation of bullying relies on the subjective experience of the victim. At the same time, if an action is done repeatedly, whether or not it is witnessed by others, it is reasonable to assume some measure of deliberate choice on the part of the perpetrator. It appears that bullying can be both premeditated[1] and opportunistic. A great deal of bullying appears to happen when an opportunity presents itself – for example, a sarcastic comment, or belittling someone because of alleged poor work. It is, however, an intentional act, over which the perpetrator has control.

The use and abuse of power is a central focus of the study of human relationships. Political science concerns itself with ways in which human societies distribute, monitor and control the use of power. In any group of people there will be a pecking order and variations in the amount of influence that different people possess. Power can be used positively to help groups achieve their aims and to enable others to use their abilities in pursuit of a group task and personal goals. It can also be used negatively, to manipulate, dominate or coerce others, in order to achieve the goals of one individual or group, with no care for the well-being of others who might be involved.[2] This can be seen, for example, in countries where one ethnic or linguistic group is favoured at the expense of the others. Bullying involves the deliberate misuse of power in a way that has a specific, negative impact on another person (or group).

1. Clarkson, P. (2008). *Beating the Bullies* (London: John Blake), chapter 19.
2. See Arbuckle, G. A. (2003). *Confronting the Demon: A Gospel response to adult bullying* (Collegeville, Minnesota: Liturgical Press), p. 20.

The third important component of the definition is the physical or psychological distress which is caused to another person. It can be reasonably argued that leadership and management require injecting a certain amount of stress into a group, parish, organisation or diocese to generate some energy in order to motivate people to achieve important goals. Research on stress suggests that there is a kind of pressure which generates some adrenalin, increases motivation and raises levels of performance. This is called *eu*stress and is distinguished from *dis*tress, which is the kind of pressure that leads to anxiety, decreased motivation, performance deficits and a range of mental health and psychosomatic illnesses. Bullying leads to distress. No matter how charismatic the leader, if their actions lead to physical or psychological distress, then this may be bullying behaviour, even if it is dressed up as aggressive management.

Bullying is mainly a psychological phenomenon and it may be hard to distinguish between 'work place banter' and bullying. It tends to begin subtly then develop into systematic 'criticism' or 'negative remarks'. It is often done in private and can be harder to prove as there may be no witnesses. Harassment can be psychological but can also be physical – for example, sexual harassment. It can be easily recognised as harassment due to the overt nature of the behaviour and the specific nature of the language used in legal definitions. It has a clear focus – for example, ethnicity, gender or sexual orientation. There is more awareness generally regarding harassment and it is a more serious allegation and can result in criminal action.

It may be helpful to consider some of the following data regarding adult bullying:

- Amicus suggests that the cost of bullying in the workplace to the economy may be as much as £1.8 billion a year.

- On average, 16 school students commit suicide each year as a result of bullying.

- It is suggested that up to 100 people in Ireland commit suicide each year as a consequence of bullying.

- The Andrea Adams Trust, set up to prevent workplace bullying, takes around 80 calls a day from people seeking help or advice.[1]
- Research by Professor Cary Cooper concluded that 53% of their sample had experienced being bullied at work and 77% of respondents had witnessed bullying at work.[2]
- Up to 18.9 million working days each year are lost as a result of bullying.[3]
- The National Workplace Bullying Advice Line received 5,156 enquiries and 4,598 cases of bullying between January 1996 and May 2001.[4]

It is clear from these statistics that we are dealing with a subject of major importance to the economy and public health. A significant number of people have been or are victims of bullying, have witnessed others being bullied, or are perpetrators of behaviours which should have no place in churches or the workplace. This has now been recognised and people have the protection of law, as has been shown above.

Examples of bullying behaviour

Jonathon

Jonathon was a member of a legal co-operative in a South London borough. The co-operative was committed to equal opportunities practice, and actively worked with low income families, people from ethnic minorities, immigrants and young people who had become caught up in the criminal justice system. Jonathon, however, was intolerant of anyone who did not show the same commitment to the ideals of the organisation as he (and a select group of friends) did. He frequently berated people at meetings who appeared to be backsliding on the co-operative's values and

1. Andy Ellis, http://www.workplacebullying.co.uk/aethesis.html
2. http://www.workplacebullying.co.uk/employerind.html
3. http://www.andreaadamstrust.org
4. Peyton, P. R. (2003). *Dignity at work* (Routledge).

philosophy. He had alienated the trustees (many of whom worked for prominent City firms) who raised funds for the co-operative's *pro bono* work. He was also impatient, sarcastic and belittling of new colleagues who were struggling to adjust to the new work culture and ethic. He was particularly critical of male colleagues whom he would accuse of sexism, racism, patriarchal bias or abuse of power. Individuals gradually left, with a number breaking away to form their own legal practice.

Joan

Joan was a parish assistant in an inner-city parish. She was employed after completing a degree in theology by Fr Frank, a priest whom she had met at some workshops and conferences. Many demands were made on Frank's time by the parish and diocese, and with the decrease in vocations to the priesthood, he saw employing Joan as a way to share the workload and promote lay partnership in ministry. Things went well for three years and then Fr Frank was transferred to another parish. He was replaced by Fr Joseph who, though younger, was not enthusiastic about having a lay assistant. He reminded Joan continually of the cost of her salary to the parish and quickly began to be critical of her work. Nothing she did seemed to be acceptable. He would humiliate her at meetings and, on one occasion, when she was playing the organ at mass, shouted at her from the altar because music was prohibited at that part of the mass in this liturgical season. Joan struggled on as she felt a sense of loyalty to the parishioners. However, her self-esteem plummeted, she began to forget commitments, was awkward when speaking from the pulpit or making presentations to parishioners, and found herself apologising continually for mistakes and shortcomings. She took time off work due to stress, and after two months received a letter saying that she was no longer employed at the parish. She had no contract and felt she would have no redress if she took the case to a tribunal.

> In any event, she was too afraid and psychologically battered to face going over all that had happened. She eventually returned to live with her parents, entered counselling, and took almost a year before beginning to think about putting her life back together and beginning a new career.

These stories highlight a number of features about adult bullying. In the first place it involves behaviour by a person who has either *position* power, like Fr Joseph, which is conferred as a result of a role or elected position, or *referent* power, which is given to someone by other people. This would be the situation with Jonathon who was technically an equal in the co-operative, but who was given power by the other members of the group. This also happens in prisons and in neighbourhoods where some families can terrorise other people. In one survey 71% of respondents said that they were alarmed by the behaviour of some people in their community and the threat they represented.[1] Power imbalances are the breeding ground for bullying behaviour, particularly where there are individuals who are vulnerable because of personality, economic or social factors.

Bullying is systematic – that is, it is repeated over time, is deliberate and designed to cause hurt or embarrassment, or increase the power and control of the bully in ways that are oppressive or demeaning. It leads to decreased self-esteem, loss of confidence, poor morale in the workplace and unpleasant or hostile atmospheres. The intention of the perpetrator is to bring about pain, distress or belittlement to the victim. Bullying behaviour can involve physical violence, and there is plenty of evidence of violence against employees.[2] However, in most cases the following range of behaviours are involved:

- Aggressive shouting
- Public humiliation
- Work overload
- Unjustifiable or inconsistent discipline

1. See Randall, P (1997). *Adult Bullying: Perpetrators and Victims* (Routledge), pp. 35–46.
2. See Randall, P. (1997). *Adult Bullying: Perpetrators and Victims* (Routledge,) pp. 48–49.

- Constant use of insults
- Unpredictable changes in work routine or holidays
- Exclusion from social events
- Gossip/rumour-mongering
- Intimidation through home contact, text or email messages.
- Sexual/racial harassment[1]
- Marginalisation (being sent to Coventry)
- Intimidation
- Discrediting someone's professionalism, directly or through insinuation
- Ridiculing people's arguments at meetings (using scorn)
- Poking fun at people's accent, ethnic features, pronunciation, weight, body shape, disfigurement or mannerisms

The development of the internet and text messaging has provided more opportunities for bullying to take place. There has been considerable publicity given to cyber-bullying among school children, but it can also happen in the adult world. Helen Green, who was mentioned at the beginning of this chapter, reported that her name was removed from the firm's global intranet directory and from circulation lists.[2] A group of students at Kent University created a Facebook site which posted offensive and cruel comments about a librarian who was unpopular because he implemented the policy on the need for quiet in the library. Emails can also be used to harass and threaten someone. As has been seen with children,[3] text messages can also invade a person's home and privacy, leading to a feeling of never being able to escape the cruelty of the oppressor(s).

Negative emotions used aggressively, especially anger, are often a component part of bullying, although people can also be victimised without

1. Ellis, A. (2007). 'Bullying in the workplace – An acceptable cost', p. 18. http://www.workplacebullying.co.uk/aethesis.html, retrieved 8 November 2007
2. Clarkson, P. (2008). *Beating the Bullies* (London: John Blake), p. 15.
3. Clarkson, P. (2008). *Beating the Bullies* (London: John Blake). (Various chapters demonstrate this.)

loud aggressive shouting. Fr Joseph, for example, undermined Joan over a period of time by reminding her of how much she was a drain on the finances and by pointing out her faults. When Joan was shouted at during mass, it came at the end of a systematic process of belittlement and hostile acts. By that point Joan was afraid to do anything in case she got it wrong and would later pay for it at a public or private meeting.

It appears that most workplace bullying is covert rather than overt. It tends to be cumulative, corrosive of well-being and self-esteem, and is carried out over the long term. People can become the butt of jokes or the focus of the ire of a manager, colleague or group of employees. Scandinavian authors[1] write about the phenomenon of 'mobbing', which involves a group of people who systematically bully another individual. Mobbing can easily happen where a group takes pleasure in ridiculing another person. One author gives an example of a gay man who became the victim of a work crew. What may appear as harmless fun can quickly become part of a work culture where certain behaviours or kinds of humour are tolerated, even though they cause considerable distress to the victim. It is extremely difficult for someone to stand up to this without being ridiculed for being soft or overly sensitive. The consequences, though, can be very destructive. In some cases this kind of behaviour has led to mental breakdowns or suicide.

While most research in Britain has focused on bullying by individuals, Charlotte Rayner suggests from research she conducted with over a thousand part-time students at Staffordshire University that, in fact, most people (81%) are bullied by groups. This can also be seen in offices and workplaces where individuals side with the bullies or patterns of bullying behaviour to curry favour or protect themselves from being victims. It may appear as harmless fun, but it is unlikely that the participants would relish finding themselves on the receiving end of their own behaviour. Rayner also suggests that bullying by groups lasts longer, and is more difficult to resolve.[2] An accountant who had worked in a number of firms as trainee,

1. Leymann, H. (1996). 'Mobbing and psychological terror at workplaces', *European Journal of Work and Organisational Psychology*, 5, 119–126; Salmivalli, C., Lagerspetz, K., Björkqvist, K., Österman, K. and Kaukiainen, A. (1996). 'Bullying as a group process: Participant roles and their relations to social status within the group', *Aggressive Behaviour*, 22, 1–15.

2. Rayner, C. (1997). 'The incidence of workplace bullying', *Journal of Community and Applied Psychology*, 7, 199-208.

accountant and manager made the observation that it is fairly easy to deal with a 'shouter', someone who tries to get what they want by being loud and aggressive; however, subtle group bullying is more insidious and more difficult to challenge and change.

Two special cases: racism and sexual harassment

While bullying has only recently achieved prominence in people's consciousness, the subjects of sexual and racial harassment have long been given attention in law, if not always in employment and social practice.

Racism

What we are describing here is discrimination, or harassment and bullying based on a person's ethnicity. The use of the word 'racism' is seen by some people as unhelpful as it suggests that people differ on the basis of race. We all belong to the human race; what is different is our ethnic origin. Bullying and discrimination often happen on the basis of perceived difference, and skin colour or ethnic features are very obvious ways of noting difference. This also happens on the grounds of religion, as happened, for example, with Jewish people over the centuries, or in Northern Ireland or the West of Scotland, where Catholics were often disadvantaged because of their faith.

Discrimination is a way of keeping power – economic, political or social – in the hands of one group. This can be particularly strong at times of economic difficulty. (It has been shown, for example, that lynching of black people in the United States tended to increase when white workers felt under threat in terms of employment or economic hardship.) In a study of workplace bullying among junior doctors, it was shown that 37% of junior doctors identified themselves as having been bullied in the previous year, but that black and Asian doctors were much more likely to be bullied than white doctors. Of significance for the next section is that female junior doctors were more likely to be bullied than the male junior doctors.[1] Racial bullying achieved national prominence as a result of the

1. Quine, L. (2002). *Workplace Bullying in Junior Doctors: Questionnaire Survey* http://www.bmj.com/cgi/content/full/324/7342/878, retrieved 18 October 2007

treatment of the Bollywood actress Shilpa Shetty by 'bully-in-chief'[1] Jade Goody on *Celebrity Big Brother*.[2]

The current rise in Muslim fundamentalism, with the involvement of a minority in terrorist incidents, can lead to bullying and discrimination against Muslim people. A report commissioned by the former Mayor of London, Ken Livingstone, showed that 91% of articles related to Muslims had a negative slant.[3] A recent Channel 4 *Dispatches* programme,[4] however, also highlighted the issue of bullying and violence within the Muslim community against those who convert to Christianity. In the programme Sheikh Ibrahim Mogra, a senior member of the Muslim Council of Great Britain, condemned attacks on individuals. This, however, does not appear to prevent such behaviour from occurring. Here we are dealing with the difficult issue of a clash of cultural values. The Qur'an forbids apostasy, but the Western political tradition values people's freedom to make their own choices in the areas of religious adherence.

Discrimination, harassment and bullying thrive where prejudice and ignorance go unchallenged. Groups which are disadvantaged can find themselves victims of abusive, unfair and violent behaviour, which is often a result of misplaced aggression, or jealousy at the achievements and good fortune of others.

Sexual harassment

One of the significant historic achievements of the twentieth century in developed countries was the granting of political power to women through the right to vote, and the admission of women to politics, the professions, universities, the armed forces, etc. While there has been rapid advance, it is recognised that women still fall behind men in terms of proportion of promoted positions, high-status jobs, equal pay and political influence. Alongside this 'glass ceiling', there is also the reality of sexual harassment.

1. Jeremy Paxman (24 August 2007). Quoted in Chris Tryhorn, 'After the trust has gone – Executives reflect on a turbulent year for TV', *The Guardian*, p. 9.
2. http://newsvote.bbc.co.uk/mpapps/pagetools/print/news.bbc.co.uk/1/hi/magazine/627397, retrieved 8 November 2007
3. *The Guardian* (14 November 2007). p. 17. Press Association, study shows 'demonisation' of Muslims.
4. *Dispatches*: 'Unholy War', Channel 4 (17 September 2007).

Sadly this is still a feature in places of war, where women (and men or boys) are raped or humiliated sexually in various ways. There is also a growing awareness of the numbers of women (and girls) forced into prostitution. However there is also sexual harassment in the workplace, which can involve flirting, sexual humour and the use of calendars that present women as sexual objects. It can also involve unwelcome attention, coercion for sexual favours, or withdrawal of promotion prospects if sexual favours are not granted. This is not exclusively a female phenomenon as men have also suffered as a result of the unwelcome attention of female managers. Michael Douglas used this as the basis for the film *Disclosure*.[1]

One of the difficulties in this area is that men and women tend to perceive the issue of sexual harassment differently. It has to be borne in mind that men are often in a dominant position in organisations, and humour may be experienced as a way of maintaining power imbalances. The important point, however, is that if a woman finds a behaviour offensive and demeaning, then an employer who believes in creating a healthy and respectful work environment should make it clear that such behaviour is not acceptable.

Another significant area where bullying is all too often present is in the treatment of homosexuals (this also affects other sexual minorities such as transgender individuals). Homophobia, which can be defined as 'an unreasonable fear of or antipathy towards homosexuals and homosexuality,'[2] is best understood as a prejudice against homosexual people. Research suggests that homophobia is more common among people who have strong feelings about traditional gender roles, who are strongly religious, consider sexual orientation as a matter of personal choice (rather than genetic influence) and are less well-educated. It is also more common in men than women. While homosexuals constitute around 4–5% of the population, around 30% of young people who commit suicide are homosexual. Research from the United States suggests that 80% of gay, lesbian and bisexual young people have experienced verbal insults, around

1. Levinson, B. (Director) (1994). *Disclosure* (Motion Picture). Warner Bros International.
2. Miracle, T. S., Miracle, A. W. and Baumeister, R. F. (2003). *Human Sexuality: Meeting your basic needs* (New Jersey: Prentice Hall).

35% have been chased or followed, 25% have been sexually assaulted and around 8% have been assaulted with a weapon.[1] 'Gay bashing' has led to murder both in the United States and in Britain. (The murders of Matthew Sheppard in the United States and Jody Dobrowski[2] in England both achieved national prominence and, partly as a result of the levels of violence used in the attacks, generated revulsion in the media.)

Women and sexual minorities enjoy the protection of the law, and the Christian Churches, which may disapprove of different sexual behaviours, condemn violence and discrimination. There are, however, some areas, such as the ordination of homosexual clergy in the Church of England or adoption by homosexual partners (particularly for the Catholic Church) which can cause conflict both within the churches and between the Churches and some aspects of public policy. However, it remains the case that women and sexual minorities are often victims of harassment and bullying.

The effects of bullying

In her book, *Dignity at Work*, Pauline Rennie Peyton refers to a Health and Safety Executive claim that 30–50% of all stress-related illnesses in the workplace are a consequence of workplace bullying.[3] Victims of bullying have reported a range of symptoms, including loss of confidence, stress, a generalised sense of not being able to cope with life, and lowered self-esteem. Some have reported thoughts of suicide and, as noted at the beginning of this chapter, some victims resort to suicide as a result of bullying behaviour. Ellis, a researcher at Ruskin College, Oxford, conducted research in the retail industry and compiled the following list of medical consequences of being bullied from the 30 questionnaires which were returned:[4]

1. Miracle, T. S., Miracle, A. W. and Baumeister, R. F. (2003). *Human Sexuality: Meeting your basic needs* (New Jersey: Prentice Hall).
2. http://newsvote.bbc.co.uk/mpapps/pagetools/print/news.bbc.co.uk/1/hi/england/london/5, retrieved 6 June 2007.
3. Peyton, P. R. (2003). *Dignity at Work: Eliminate bullying and create a positive working environment* (Routledge).
4. http://workplacebullying.co.uk/aethesis.html

Consequence	*Cases recorded*	*%*
Losing sense of humour	8	47.1
Depression	6	35.3
Migraine headaches	6	35.3
Skin disorders (dryness, rashes)	3	17.6
Chest pains	3	17.6
Constant fatigue	4	23.5
Hypertension	4	23.5
Muscular tension pain	3	17.6
Vomiting at thought of going to work	2	11.8
Diarrhoea	2	11.8
Coughs and Asthma	1	5.9
Abdominal pains	1	5.9

While the size of the sample is relatively small, the conditions referred to are consistent with the information offered by others.[1] This list is also helpful as it offers a perspective on the most common effects of bullying. Others have noted the impact on self-esteem and self-confidence of the victims. Being bullied is a profoundly shaming experience. People are

1. Randall, P. (1997). *Adult Bullying: Perpetrators and victims* (Routledge); Peyton, P. R. (2003). *Dignity at Work* (Routledge); Arbuckle, G. A. (2003). *Confronting the Demon: A Gospel response to adult bullying* (Collegeville, Minnesota: Liturgical Press).

suddenly put in a position of exposure and become vulnerable. There is a cultural expectation that once people leave school they should be able to 'stand on their own two feet' and look after themselves. 'Life isn't fair and you just have to get used to it,' is often the unstated position taken by bullies or some bystanders. People often fail to realise that the systematic, unrelenting nature of bullying significantly undermines the capacity of victims to be more assertive or to defend themselves. A favourite tactic of bullies (and, indeed, torturers) is unpredictability.

Martin Seligman, an American psychologist, noticed that when shocks were administered to dogs in an unpredictable way, – where they had no control, not even being able to prepare for the effects of the shock – they ceased trying to escape even when it became possible. As Seligman noted, 'Nothing they did mattered.' He labelled this phenomenon 'learned helplessness.'[1] This parallels what we know about approaches to torture which seek to break down the resistance and defences of victims. A similar phenomenon can be seen in bullies, who use their power to demoralise and weaken their victims, often on the basis of whim, rather than as a direct consequence of particular actions.

Some victims of bullying develop the symptoms of post traumatic stress disorder (PTSD). This is a diagnostic category which is used for people who meet the following criteria:[2]

The person has been exposed to a traumatic event in which both the following are present:

1. The person experienced, witnessed or was confronted with an event or events that involve actual or threatened death or serious injury; or a threat to the physical integrity of self or others.
2. The person's response involved intense fear, helplessness or horror.

People who are diagnosed with PTSD re-experience the trauma in various ways, including distressing recollections, nightmares or flashbacks. They

1. Seligman, M. E. P. (1990). *Learned Optimism* (New York: Pocket Books), p. 20.
2. American Psychiatric Association (1994). *Diagnostic and Statistical Manual of Mental Disorders (4th edition).*

also go out of their way to avoid anything that will remind them of or result in having contact with the source of the trauma. Other symptoms include psychosomatic illnesses similar to those noted by Ellis above, cognitive dysfunction (memory and attention deficits), avoidance of others, either flatness of affect (appearing neither depressed nor interested in life) or extreme mood swings. These will impact all aspects of the person's life. PTSD victims also tend to be hyper-vigilant, anticipating danger and attack at all times.

Victims of bullying, instead of using their energy to achieve important goals, tend to be more focused on avoiding situations where they will encounter the bully. Avoidant striving, as this is called, is a less effective way to manage one's life than achievement striving. Emmons[1] shows that people with a large number of avoidant strivings experience more distress than people who are motivated by positive life goals. Avoidant goals set up the person for failure, as they are never rewarded by achievement. They constantly use up their energy by being vigilant to escape opportunities for contact with the bully. Examples of avoidant strivings for victims of bullying could be:

- Avoid offending the bully by maintaining a safe distance
- Avoid eye contact with the bully
- Avoid disagreements or opportunities for discussion
- Avoid social situations where the bully will be present
- Avoid tasks where they might fail or be criticised
- Avoid conversations that relate to work or performance

Stress-related illnesses have a significant negative effect on the lives of individuals and on the economy. As we have seen, there are links with a number of illnesses, and this includes some cancers. People who are under severe stress are also more accident prone, which, of course, tends to offer the bullies more opportunities for criticism. The mental health charity,

1. Emmons, R. A. (1999). *The Psychology of Ultimate Concerns* (New York: Guilford).

MIND, suggests that 30–40% of all absence from work for sickness is a result of mental and emotional disturbance.[1] While not all alcohol, suicide, heart disease or mental health problems are due to stress or bullying, it is clear that there is a direct effect of bullying on mental health and that this has an impact on productivity and well-being.

Employers are also beginning to become aware of the costs of bullying on productivity. The price is paid in resentment, lowered morale and its impact on motivation, and a reduced sense of loyalty. This is particularly important in charitable organisations[2] or voluntary organisations like churches. A considerable amount of money is lost due to absenteeism, and replacing workers who leave. If an employee contacts a union representative or uses legal means, then time and money will be spent in hearings and trials. It is often the economic cost that is leading to a change in work culture rather than concern for the well-being of employees.[3] While bullying may bring short-term benefits to bullies, and sometimes managers, the long-term costs are increasingly considered unacceptable.

How does bullying develop?

A key question regarding bullying is how people become bullies, given that the word has such a pejorative connotation. There are two main approaches to this question. The first approach looks at the personalities of bullies and victims, and the second looks at the cultures or systems which enable, facilitate or encourage bullying.

The bullies

It is important to bear in mind that all of us are capable of bullying behaviour; we may have memories of participating in the bullying, mocking, or humiliation of someone else while at school. However, most of us learn how to curb our tongue and adjust our behaviour when tempted to act in this way. Research on children has shown that children are most vulnerable in the early teenage years, but by late teens most young people find bullying

1. http://workplacebullying.co.uk/aethesis.html
2. '40% of charity workers are bullied, reveals study' (26 December 2007). *The Herald*, p. 7.
3. Randall, P. (1997). *Adult Bullying: Perpetrators and Victims* (Routledge).

behaviour distasteful and do not want to be involved.[1] There is also research which suggests that childhood bullies develop into adult bullies, and that they are at risk for a range of negative outcomes, including antisocial behaviours and involvement in crime. A study of 500 children suggested that children who were aggressive at 8 years of age were more likely to be involved in criminality and violence when they were 30.[2]

The study of childhood development has shown the importance of early attachments in healthy development. In the first years of life infants have a range of needs, and are not able to communicate verbally. It is crucial that children experience care and soothing when they experience distress for whatever reason. It is also important that care-givers enable children to learn how to regulate their own strong feelings. The early experiences of soothing and warmth can be built on once children are able to speak. They learn that internal emotional stress or experiences of frustration, emotional arousal or conflict can be resolved using language and negotiation, rather than resorting to coercive strategies to release tension.

Children also learn from what they see and experience. If parents model aggression, inconsistency and rejection, then that is what the child will learn. Parents, and later teachers, have the important task of socialisation; explaining and maintaining rules and boundaries, encouraging the development of empathy, disapproving and punishing appropriately any solutions which infringe the rights and well-being of others. Children who come from aggressive backgrounds learn aggressive tactics. Likewise, children who see their parents treating others in a disrespectful or exploitative way will learn that this is an acceptable (and effective) approach to achieving their own goals.

Bullies also often have a core sense of self that says, 'I am bad', which can lead to poor self-esteem. Parental styles that are authoritative (rather than authoritarian or *laissez-faire*),[3] where children can express anger and

1. Pepler, D. J., Craig, W. M., Connolly, J. A., Yhuile, A., McMaster, L. and Jiang, D. (2006). 'A developmental perspective on bullying', *Aggressive Behaviour*, 32, 376–384.
2. Eron, L. D., Husemann, L. R., Dubow, E., Romanoff, R. and Yarmel, P. W. (1987). 'Aggression and its correlates over 20 years', in Crowell, D. H., Evans, I. M. and O'Donnell, C. R. (Eds). *Childhood Aggression and Violence: Sources of influence, prevention and control* (New York: Plenum), pp. 249–262.
3. Santrock, J. W. (1999). *Life Span Development* (McGraw-Hill).

other feelings, but learn how to verbalise their feelings rather than act them out or repress them, tend to lead to children who are socially mature and morally responsible.[1] On the other hand, harsh discipline and parental neglect or rejection can help to sow the seeds of aggression and poor self-image which ripen into bullying and poor self-control in adulthood.

There are a number of other factors that can contribute towards the development of an aggressive, bullying personality. These include issues related to poor mental health in the parents, especially the child's mother. The presence of parental conflict, economic difficulties, addictions and other stressors all have their part to play. The presence of one of these stressors may not cause insurmountable problems; however, it is difficult for a child to overcome the effects of multiple deprivations. It is important to make clear that this is not a class issue; bullies can be found at all levels of society.

Bullying personality

Bullies often carry a great deal of 'baggage' from their childhoods. This can result in being envious of others, feelings of loneliness and inadequacy, a fragile self-image, limitations in expressing emotions, and a need to be in control as the world is perceived as dangerous and hostile. They are often loud, taking up more 'emotional space' than their colleagues, and can have an overpowering manner. Unlike mature adults who find the distress of others embarrassing (which is a component of empathy), bullies can continue to inflict pain when a person is clearly at the point of humiliation. They tend to be selfish, self-promoting and indifferent to the needs of others. They are noted liars; they may forget agreements, hide important papers, withhold or provide false information. They also lead the victim to believe that he or she is in the wrong.[2] They tend to have favourites, but, as Arbuckle points out, they can create unhealthy relationships where someone becomes dependent on them. The recipients can feel obliged to behave in

1. Randall, P. (2001). *Bullying in Adulthood: Assessing the bullies and their victims* (Brunner-Routledge).
2. Peyton, P. R. (2003). *Dignity at Work: Eliminate bullying and create a positive working environment* (Routledge).

submissive ways. The choice of favourite can also change rapidly, with a previous favourite becoming the next victim.[1]

Some bullies fit the description of antisocial or narcissistic personality disorders, or have identifiable features of these two disorders. People (mostly men) with antisocial personality disorder lack empathy, tend to be impulsive, can have superficial charm, but are callous and irritable. They are easily aroused to anger and can be unpredictable in their behaviour and relationships. Adolescent units and prisons contain a high percentage of these individuals as they tend to be contemptuous of social norms, and their need for excitement leads them into criminal behaviour and substance abuse. Churches are not immune to these people. There have been cases of embezzlement and, of course, the behaviour of some clerical child molesters. There are also some church personnel whose behaviour seems far from the values of the Gospel and leaves many hurt individuals – fellow clergy and parishioners – in its wake. These people surround themselves with sycophants and use religion for their own purposes. They are, of course, spiritually shallow, often going through the motions rather than being open to personal conversion.[2]

Narcissistic people have an inflated sense of their own importance and use people to gratify their own needs. They tend to be superficial but can be outwardly charming and personable. Like people with antisocial personality disorder, they can be exploitative, but tend not to be aggressive or recklessly impulsive. They tend to over-promote themselves and then blame others for their failures. They are intolerant of criticism and cannot accept responsibility for failures or mistakes. Such individuals may bully others to reduce their frustration when they are not promoted or appreciated in the way that they feel they deserve.[3]

1. Arbuckle, G. A. (2003). *Confronting the Demon: A Gospel response to adult bullying* (Collegeville, Minnesota: Liturgical Press).
2. Sperry, L. (1998). 'The psychopathic minister', *Human Development*, 19, 2, 34–37.
3. Randall, P. (2001). *Bullying in Adulthood: Assessing the bullies and their victims* (Brunner-Routledge).

Differences between men and women

One of the clearest differences between men and women is in the area of aggression. Simply put, men appear to be more violent and prone to use force to solve problems and get their own way than women.[1] Whether this is an innate drive or a learned behaviour is not important here. There are significantly more men than women in prison, and almost 90% of sex offenders as well as higher percentages of violent criminals are men. The play of boys and girls is also different, with more rough-and-tumble play among boys, and more relational and conversation-based play among girls. This difference also appears to manifest itself in bullying behaviour. Adolescent girls tend to use indirect methods of aggression such as backbiting, gossip, social exclusion and belittling, and boys appear to use more direct methods, such as physical hitting, pushing, shoving and taking revenge in games.[2]

In adulthood both men and women make use of covert aggression, but men tend to focus on performance, and use aggression that has a 'pseudo-rational' basis in the context of work – that is, the focus of the bullying will appear to relate to an aspect of poor work performance. Women, on the other hand, are more likely to use social manipulation or find ways to criticise personal features or belittle the person. This can be seen, for example, in the *Celebrity Big Brother* incident, where Jade Goody criticised Shilpa Shetty's accent, appearance and cooking.[3] The tendency of women to use social manipulation and covert forms of bullying may make it more difficult for a manager to confront the problem, as tensions may be explained away or may masquerade as personality differences. While bullying of women by women may not be given as much prominence as bullying or sexual harassment by men, it can be no less destructive or harmful to the well-being of the victim or to the morale in an office, parish or workforce.

1. Baron-Cohen, S. (2005). *The Essential Difference: Men, women and the extreme male brain* (Penguin).
2. Björkqvist, K., Lagerspetz, K. M. J. and Kaukiainen, A. (1992). 'Do girls manipulate and boys fight?', *Aggressive Behaviour*, 18, 117–127.
3. http://newsvote.bbc.co.uk/mpapps/pagetools/print/news.bbc.co.uk/1/hi/magazine/627397, retrieved 8 November 2007

Victims

Bullies often choose people who are vulnerable as their victims. People who are different – for example, homosexual men and women or people from religious or ethnic minorities – are often chosen as the victims of bullying. Victims are often highly conscientious, law-abiding, and afraid to take risks or assert themselves. They tend to have low self-esteem, be submissive and sensitive, and are more prone to experience anxiety and depressed moods.

Those who have studied the personalities and developmental histories of victims have noted that children who were bullied often become victims in adulthood. The film *Mystic River*,[1] for example, shows a group of three boys, one of whom is a victim of sexual abuse. In adulthood, one of the boys becomes a detective and one a criminal, but the victim of abuse, played by Tim Robbins, has achieved very little in life and communicates failure and submissiveness. It has been shown that children with parents who are under- or over-controlling in their parenting style can grow up feeling anxious and insecure, lacking in social awareness, with poor ability to be assertive in the face of aggression. One author[2] used the phrase 'submission reaction pattern' to describe their default coping strategy. They often have problems in interpersonal relationships, are lonely and in need of friends. Sadly, they often elicit little sympathy from their peers, and teachers (and later supervisors and managers) may do little to intervene to help them when they are bullied. It is not unusual to hear people say, 'He asked for it'.

The bystanders

Many people have seen their colleagues being bullied. A Finnish study on aggression among university employees, for example, reported that 32% of the respondents had witnessed bullying,[3] and research in an NHS Community Trust suggested that 42% of employees had witnessed one or

1. *Mystic River* (2004). (Warner Bros Entertainment).
2. Olweus, D. (1993). *Bullying at School: What we know and what we can do* (Oxford: Blackwell).
3. Björkqvist, K., Österman, K. and Hjelt-Back, M. (1994). 'Aggression among university employees?', *Aggressive Behaviour*, 20, 173–184.

more types of bullying.[1] Witnesses to bullying are often afraid to act in case they become the next victim, or they simply may not want to become involved. Witnesses can also be affected by stress and insecurity, and it appears that one in five may leave their place of employment.[2] One Catholic Sister, who was a teacher in the languages department of a secondary school, said to a colleague who had been bullied by the head of department, 'When you see one person's head on the chopping block you don't volunteer to put your own there.' This was said after the head of department had been disciplined for unprofessional conduct towards colleagues. Lucy Witheredge, the chief executive of the Andrea Adams Trust,[3] which is committed to preventing workplace bullying, encourages observers not to remain as bystanders but to intervene by saying that the behaviour is unacceptable.

Organisational factors

Bullying has been looked at as the outcome of a relationship between bullies, victims and the organisation they are part of. Each organisation has its own culture which embodies a set of values, with behaviours that are acceptable and those that are unacceptable. Bullying is tolerated or even flourishes in certain cultures. A culture can be defined as:

A pattern of shared meanings and values, embodied in a network of symbols, myths and rituals, created by a particular group as it struggles to adjust to life's challenges, educating its members about what is considered to be the orderly and correct way to feel, think and behave.[4]

Some cultures – such as politics, management and football – appear to encourage or value people who can dominate and abuse others. Tom Bower's biography of Gordon Brown[5] provides plenty of examples of bullying behaviour. Some football managers have been admired for their bullying attitudes to the players. In the world of entertainment, the TV

1. Randall, P. (2001). *Bullying in Adulthood: Assessing the bullies and their victims* (Brunner-Routledge).
2. Higginbottom, K. (3 November 2007). 'Innocent bystanders?', *The Guardian*, Work section, 1–2.
3. www.andreaadamstrust.org
4. Arbuckle, G. A. (2003). *Confronting the Demon: A Gospel response to adult bullying* (Collegeville, Minnesota: Liturgical Press), p. 67.
5. Bower, T. (2004). *Gordon Brown* (Harper Perennial).

show *The Apprentice* appears to enshrine bullying as a management tactic in testing prospective entrepreneurs.[1] Patriarchal systems encourage oppressive behaviour towards women, and some cultures are permissive of racism and sexual harassment. Church cultures also have features that can facilitate bullying behaviour.

The quality of the work environment is an important factor in understanding bullying. Lack of effective leadership, poor opportunities to exercise personal control over work, and role conflict all contribute to a culture where bullying can emerge.[2] Bullying is also more likely to occur where there is an extremely competitive environment, especially if people fear for their job security. This can also be compounded by authoritarian management styles and the uncertainty caused by organisational change or excessive workloads. Work cultures that place a lot of emphasis on targets may also contribute to cultures of bullying.[3] Melanie Reid writes:

> The right targets force the system to respond . . . but in so many areas we have reached the point when the pressure becomes pressure for its own sake; when it amounts to institutional bullying and causes mental ill health and leaves the workforce sour and miserable. Unremitting targets ultimately result in exhaustion and jiggery-pokery, not greater efficiency.[4]

While bullying can be done by peers, and sometimes by people in lower positions than the victim (see Dirk Bogarde in the film *The Servant*,[5] where a servant bullies and controls the rich young man he is paid to look after), it is most often the case that a manager, boss or supervisor is the bully. A teacher, for example, is quoted as saying, 'The bullying governor is the parish priest and, as such, he is unassailable.'[6] One author writes that 90.9% of the respondents in a survey of employees in the retail industry indicated that the person who bullied them was in a position of authority.[7]

1. Jones, F. (2006). 'More questions than answers', *The Psychologist*, 19, 10, p. 640.
2. Rayner, C. and Hoel, H. (1997). 'A summary review of literature relating to workplace bullying', *Journal of Community and Applied Psychology*, 7, 181–191.
3. www.workplacebullying.co.uk/aethesis.html
4. Reid, M. (4 February 2007). *The Times*, p. 19.
5. Losey, J. (Director). *The Servant* (Motion Picture) (Springbok Films).
6. www.workplacebullying.co.uk/aethesis.html
7. www.workplacebullying.co.uk/aethesis.html

The Church as a culture where bullying can develop

There have been a number of reports in the press recently of Church leaders being accused or found guilty of bullying, including the Archbishop of Granada, in Spain, who was fined 3,750 euros after being convicted of bullying a former canon of the city's cathedral.[1] There have also been instances in the Church of England, with a vicar being found guilty of bullying by a church tribunal,[2] and of an Oxford College being accused of bullying by a former member of the lecturing staff.[3] The Churches, which exist to promote the values of the kingdom of God, are just as liable to be places where bullies can be found as anywhere else.

The website www.balmnet.co.uk exists as 'A resource for damaged ministers'. It makes available stories of ministers who have felt bullied by their congregations (or significant groups in congregations), by superiors or colleagues. Members of religious communities, curates, deacons, parish assistants and lay workers can all become victims of bullying in church contexts. In some ways the Christian theology of offering forgiveness, turning the other cheek and loving your enemies can be distorted or misapplied in situations of exploitation or abuse. One person described a church worker as 'pastoral aggressive' in her ability to use Christian principles, guilt and moral manipulation to bully others into doing what she wanted.

Ministers are often encouraged to pray for those who cause them harm, to see this as a test of their faith or commitment or to extend understanding to the perpetrator. Church cultures are often uncomfortable with anger and the expression of strong feelings, so bullies can thrive as many church-going people would rather rationalise, deny or repress conflict than confront it honestly. Often in circumstances of conflict between an incumbent and a curate or worker, the worker or curate is moved and the incumbent is allowed to continue as before. The characteristics of bullies, victims and organisational cultures described above all apply to church contexts. The

1. 'Bullying archbishop convicted' (15 December 2007). *The Tablet*, p. 31
2. Gledhill, R. (24 January 2008). 'Vicar branded a liar and a bully and should be sacked, tribunal rules', *The Times*, p. 37.
3. Yeoman, F. (8 January 2008). 'Christian broadcaster sues Church college', *The Times*, p. 19.

lack of clear roles, poor leadership and unclear lines of accountability can contribute to stress at times when a priest, minister or other superior is changed. Recent unpublished research on Catholic deacons shows that the arrival of a new priest can result in considerable distress and anxiety on the part of deacons who are almost completely dependent on the goodwill and attitude of the priest. Deacons also indicated a desire for role clarity. This makes sense as they would then be less susceptible to the whims and priorities of changing parish priests.[1]

Bullying, harassment and the law

Before going on to explore what can be done, it is important to look at the law regarding bullying and harassment. All people have the right to go to work and be free from discrimination, harassment and any other form of interference with their legal right to seek employment and be safe and secure in the workplace. Yet it is clear, given the weight of case law in this area, that discrimination, harassment and bullying do occur and, sadly, often. The law protects both the employee and the employer from this kind of action and has enacted several statutes to provide legal mechanisms for the resolving of such situations.

The law is at pains to distinguish between bullying and harassment in the workplace, not least because harassment implies a greater degree of trauma than bullying. At present there is no legal definition of bullying either supplied by statute or common law (Act of Parliament or precedent). This creates a problem because bringing an action against the alleged bullies has to be done on a subjective and case-by-case basis, with the court or, more likely, the employment tribunal having to be convinced that behaviour amounting to bullying has taken place.

There do not seem to be any plans at present to introduce a statutory definition to add to the already numerous statutory provisions detailing prohibitions against lesser forms of harassment.

1. Geary, B. (2007). Unpublished research data on 247 Catholic deacons in England and Wales, and Scotland. Ushaw College, Durham, http://www.ushaw.ac.uk/PDF/BGPresentation2007.doc

Current law

Health and Safety at Work Act 1974	Obliges employer to provide for welfare of their staff by ensuring workplace is safe.
Sex Discrimination Act 1975	Prohibits intimidation and having to work in hostile environment, and defines sexual harassment.
Public Order Act 1986 s.4(a)	Criminal offence if one causes another 'distress or alarm' either by actions, signs, writing, or other visible signs or actions.
Protection from Harassment Act 1997 ss.1-3, s.7	Along with the SDA 1975, this is the most common statute for taking action against cases of bullying and / or harassment.

The Acts detailed above are available in full from www.hmso.gov.uk.

Legal issues

The two Acts of Parliament that have become central in action against bullying in the workplace are the Sexual Discrimination Act (SDA) 1975, and the Protection from Harassment Act 1997. The statutory definition of sexual harassment in the SDA 1975 is extremely useful to persons wishing to seek redress of unwanted hostility in the workplace. By having such inappropriate behaviour codified, albeit broadly, the complainant is able to quickly identify that such conduct is not permissible.

Likewise with the Protection from Harassment Act 1997. This law not only codifies the offence, but also provides a remedy to the ill. The Court is empowered by Parliament to take such action as necessary to prevent the abuse occurring, including punitive measures such as restraining orders, fines, and potentially a custodial sentence.

How should it be dealt with?

How to deal with bullying

The main issue in cases of bullying is whether procedure has been followed. As in all areas of law, procedural impropriety leads to appeals and the overturning of verdicts or judgements and can be a *prima facie* reason for a case coming before the court. Employers are required to lay down legal provisions for the protection of their employees against bullying and harassment. Complaint and grievance procedures should be made clear in case that protection should fail. This is a very important point which needs to be explained. However, in order to do so, the term 'constructive dismissal' ought to be defined first.

Constructive dismissal is where either due to the act or omission of the employer the member of staff feels it necessary to resign. For example, if a head teacher of a school was being blanked and ignored by the chair of governors and their staff to the point where they could not do their job and subsequently resigned, they could sue for constructive dismissal. The governors have acted in bad faith causing the resignation of the head. That is illegal.

Points to note

1. If a person makes an allegation of bullying, the employer is legally obliged to investigate and, if necessary, impose sanctions on the bully.
2. Failure to do so by the employer is a breach of a statutory duty.
3. In some cases both the employer *and* the employee who is the bully are liable. Under the principle of vicarious liability, the employer takes the legal consequences of any action brought against employees while acting in the course of their duty as employees. However in order to remedy the loss arising from the action brought against the company, they may dismiss the offending member of staff. In addition, the claimant suing the employer may also seek separate, even criminal, action against the bully.

4. Procedures are vitally important for protection not only of the employee but also the *employer*. Lack of grievance procedures is not only unadvisable, it is illegal.

Most people's first point of contact with these issues is through ACAS, which has an extremely helpful and accessible website[1] with a free e-learning programme to guide people through the relevant issues on harassment and bullying. There are often issues concerning redress. ACAS is able to offer free legal advice in this area. Very often cases relate to some form of sexual harassment and relevant statutory provision will be found in the Sexual Discrimination Act. Before contacting solicitors it is worth checking first with ACAS.

Responses and interventions

Organisations and churches should have clear anti-bullying and anti-harassment policies. However, having the policies is not enough. It is necessary to provide training for managers and employees, to ensure clear procedures for reporting any abusive behaviour. It is also important to train managers in early recognition of bullying behaviours. It is often the case that bullying behaviour is tolerated or even valued within the culture of the organisation. Managers and clergy need actively to create an environment which fosters open communication, respect for employees, clients or members of congregations, and dignity, security and trust in those in authority. Involvement in Employee Assistance Programmes (EAPs) can also help to provide support for those who suffer as a result of bullying.

As well as having good policies, it must be clear that policies will be implemented when necessary and that anyone found to be bullying or harassing an employee will be dealt with appropriately. Having said that, there must be even-handedness, and victims may also be required to change aspects of their behaviour as well. It is essential that victims or managers keep written records detailing any incidents and the attendant circumstances. In larger organisations it is important to make use of the

1. www.acas.org.uk

personnel department and trade union representatives. Small organisations often have no trade union representatives, and if there is an unpleasant work culture, bullies can get away with abusive behaviour. Employees are reluctant to invoke formal mechanisms, as seeking redress can have serious implications for future career and working relationships.

There is evidence to suggest that morale is higher in organisations that have specific anti-bullying policies (see Appendix 2 on page 363 for an example of an anti-bullying policy). This piece of research showed that in eight out of nine cases where the trade union representative was involved the cases were resolved satisfactorily. On the other hand, in six situations where only the employer was informed, only one was resolved satisfactorily.[1]

Can it be treated?

Can bullying be treated? Randall provides a number of case histories but is rather sanguine about the benefits of counselling for bullies.[2] Peyton suggests that it depends on the type of bully. She suggests that bullies who are afraid and vulnerable themselves, who have low self-esteem and who feel that they are being persecuted, can be helped with coaching and training. This also applies to those whose behaviour is based on copying behaviour that has been modelled by other managers. Again, retraining and coaching can be helpful for these people. The bullies who are self-righteous, with antisocial personality features, are less likely to benefit from counselling, coaching or retraining, as they will tend to see victims, rather than themselves, as the source of the problem. Counselling and assertiveness training can, of course, be helpful and sometimes necessary for victims. Peyton[3] has excellent advice and information for counsellors and managers, and the website of the Andrea Adams Trust[4] is also well worth visiting for advice for victims and managers.

Lastly, Professor Cary Cooper of Lancaster University recommends that those who witness bullying should not turn away but should inform the

1. http://workplacebullying.co.uk/aethesis.html
2. Randall, P. (1997). *Adult Bullying: Perpetrators and Victims* (Routledge).
3. Peyton, P. R. (2003). *Dignity at Work: Eliminate bullying and create a positive working environment* (Routledge).
4. www.andreaadamstrust.org

human resources department or a supervisor. They can also help the bullied by expressing concern and support. They should also not be afraid to take action as the whole organisation suffers when bullying is allowed to continue unchecked.[1]

1. Cooper, C. (2007) in Higginbottom, K. (3 November, 2007). 'Innocent bystanders?', *The Guardian,* Work section, p. 2

A Christian response

The Psalms, which were the foundation of Jesus' prayer, regularly invoke God on the side of the poor and oppressed. In Psalm 142, for example, we read:

> Rescue me from persecutors
> stronger than I am.
> Free me from this imprisonment,
> and I will thank your name once more.[1]

The story of Susanna in the book of Daniel (Daniel 13) is a clear example of bullying and sexual harassment. Two judges, who were elders in the community, attempted to have a woman who resisted their sexual demands put to death. The case is brought before Daniel who discovers the dishonesty of the two judges.

Jesus began his ministry by quoting from the prophet Isaiah:

> The spirit of the Lord has been given to me,
> for he has anointed me.
> He has sent me to bring good news to the poor,
> to proclaim liberty to captives
> and to the blind new sight,
> to set the downtrodden free.[2]

Jesus ministered to people from all sections of society, but clearly had care for those who were marginalised, rejected or bullied. The woman taken in adultery, for example, was being bullied by the men who dragged her in front of Jesus (John 8:1-11), and Zacchaeus (Luke 19:1-10), although in a position of power because of his role as a tax collector, was marginalised and considered a sinner. However, Jesus chose to dine at his house.

Christians, when faced with violence of any kind, find themselves challenged to support the weak and vulnerable but not to reject the

1. *Jerusalem Bible* (1966). (Darton, Longman and Todd)
2. Luke 4:18

perpetrator. Jesus' injunctions to 'forgive seventy times seven' and to 'love your enemies, including those who persecute you' have enabled Christians to extend empathy to perpetrators of violence and have provided a basis for rehabilitation of offenders. On the other hand, Jesus also advises his followers, 'If your brother does something wrong, reprove him' (Luke 17:4). Avoidance of conflict and denial of the existence of difficulties are not Christian virtues.

Gerald Arbuckle offers five principles for preventing bullying, which are worth repeating here:

1. Recognise that bullying is an evil and an assault on the dignity of the human person.
2. Acknowledge that everyone is capable of bullying because we are all prone to sin.
3. Understand that God has a preferential love for the victim and so must the followers of Christ.
4. Foster the values and structures of openness in organisations and clearly state that bullying is to have no place in them.
5. Identify and challenge prejudices within oneself, one's workplace and one's community because prejudices lie at the root of bullying.[1]

Perhaps the most important injunction for Christians is to 'do unto others as you would have them do unto you'. If we place ourselves in the position of victims, what would we want from others? As Gerald Arbuckle writes, God is on the side of the victim and the oppressed. A Christian response requires support for the victims, positive interventions to prevent bullying, and active approaches to management to create, disseminate and implement anti-bullying policies in workplaces and churches.

Cardinal Cardijn,[2] who founded the Young Christian Workers' movement, encouraged the use of a simple formula: See – judge – act.[3] Christians are

1. Arbuckle, G. A. (2003). *Confronting the Demon: A Gospel response to adult bullying* (Collegeville, Minnesota: Liturgical Press), p. 20.
2. http://www.ycwimpact.com/page.php?page=7
3. http://www.stpaulstervuren.be/nurture/sermons/14sep03.htm

asked to look carefully at what is happening in their community, church or place of work. This involves an ability to stand back and notice how people are being treated and affected by the behaviour of others. The second stage involves making an evaluation of what is seen. Is this respectful of people? Is it furthering the goals of the organisation? Are the values of the organisation being put into practice or ignored or undermined in some way? Is this consistent with my own values and beliefs?

The third stage involves action.[1] This is undoubtedly the hardest part when it comes to witnessing bullying or harassment. Laws protecting whistle-blowers, for example, would not exist unless there were serious costs to reporting criminal or abusive behaviour. At the same time, it is not difficult to see the cost of looking the other way or passively supporting behaviour which we would not condone. The Church of England, in its report concerning care of vulnerable adults, offers the following reflection:

> Jesus constantly showed himself to be compassionately on the side of the outcast, the marginalised and the stranger, reaching across social barriers with the inclusive love of God . . . The risen Christ's commission to his followers ('As the Father has sent me, so I send you', John 20:21) requires the Christian Church to exercise that same concern for those whom some in society treat as the outsider and the stranger, to reach across barriers of exclusion and demonstrate a love which shows itself in compassionate pastoral care and in the quest for justice in all our relationships.[2]

However, the authors were also aware of the costs of intervening and reporting, and include a recommendation that 'Colleagues should not be penalised for following this guidance or for taking action regarding others and this guidance.'[3] The decision to act requires good judgement and an

1. Graham E., Walton, H. and Ward, F. (2005). *Theological Reflection: Methods*, chapter. 6. Praxis. (SCM)
2. *Promoting a Safer Church* (2006). Policies for safeguarding adults in the Church of England. 1.4, p. 3. Available at http://www.cofe.anglican.org/info/papers/promotingasafechurch.pdf
3. *Promoting a Safer Church* (2006). Policies for safeguarding adults in the Church of England. GP 2.4, p. 15. Available at http://www.cofe.anglican.org/info/papers/promotingasafechurch.pdf

awareness of possible consequences. As has been seen in the Churches and in the professional world of childcare, clerical and other cultures can exert a powerful influence over people to keep silent and conceal malpractice and abuse. While it is easy to encourage intervention, only the person in their circumstances can weigh the various benefits and costs and decide what is right in their situation.

Do's and don'ts

- Do have anti-bullying policies in place.
- Do ensure that policies are implemented where necessary and appropriate.
- Do provide training for employees and managers.
- Do make use of Employee Assistance Programmes.
- Do not pretend that bullying cannot exist in your organisation or church. Caring professions are just as susceptible to bullying as industrial and commercial organisations.
- Do create a work culture that values honesty, open communication, respect, trust and the dignity of all.
- Do maintain an ethos of professionalism, with appropriate professional courtesies and manners.
- Do provide support for victims, and counselling and/or training for bullies.
- Do not walk away from incidents of bullying but report to those who are responsible.
- Do keep written notes of incidents and circumstances.
- Do be informed regarding the law and procedures in your organisation.
- Do avoid racist and sexist language, and humour that offends colleagues.

Conclusion

This chapter began with the story of Joan, who was bullied by one of her bosses. Joan spoke to the other administrative assistants and told them that she would not be helping them with their workloads, as had been their normal practice, as it would lead to the perception that she was under-worked. The senior partner was made aware of the situation and called a practice meeting to say that the current arrangements were not working and a reorganisation of workloads was necessary. Joan kept her job, but Michael was never confronted. Low-level hostile aggression, with sniping and subtle belittling, continued. It would have been gratifying to suggest that he was confronted and his behaviour changed, but sadly that is not the typical outcome of these situations at present.

This chapter has attempted to present information about the incidence and effects of bullying in workplaces and churches. Characteristics of bullies, victims, bystanders and organisational cultures have been explored. Legal issues have been clarified with up-to-date information with respect to the law on bullying and harassment. Recommendations for intervention have been offered and a Christian response has been suggested for those who work in organisations and churches.

Recommended reading

- Peyton, P. R. (2003). *Dignity at Work: Eliminate bullying and create a positive working environment* (Routledge)
- Arbuckle, G. A. (2003). *Confronting the Demon: A Gospel response to adult bullying* (Collegeville, Minnesota: Liturgical Press).
- Randall, P. (1997). *Adult Bullying: Perpetrators and Victims* (Routledge)

Websites

www.andreaadamstrust.org – Committed to preventing workplace bullying

www.workplacebullying.co.uk – Workplace bullying, stress, employment, law and you

www.balmnet.co.uk – Bullied and abused lives in ministry

www.acas.org.uk – Information and free advice

www.hmso.gov.uk – Acts of Parliament

Violence in the Workplace

Michael Fitzsimons

Recently, when disposing of the junk 'mail' which regularly clogs up our office fax machine, one of the papers caught my attention: in-between debt collection and hire car offers there was a crime management firm advertising security services. This is not unusual until you consider its headline, which targeted organisations seemingly at risk from anti-social behaviour. It listed schools and educational establishments, public transport, empty properties, parks and then, perhaps surprisingly, churches. Having worked in the voluntary sector for a number of years, I was accustomed to thinking about these issues but initially I was surprised that now churches would be seen as prime targets for such services. Then almost immediately I began to reflect on how the current church premises I work from have regularly been subjected to vandalism. Groups of young people often gather in or nearby the churches and church houses in the area where I live and cause disturbances. Indeed there has been a growth of violence and violent attacks made on clergy and other church workers in recent years. It was not hard to bring to mind numbers of situations known to me personally where clergy had suffered from intimidation, theft, burglary and, occasionally, violent attacks. Perhaps I shouldn't have been surprised by this fax at all.

The issue of violence and aggression is current in our society and generates much discussion as to its causes and its perceived growth. Acts of violence and aggression directed against caring professionals, including clergy and other pastoral workers, are seemingly more commonplace and often attract significant media attention and wide coverage. This both serves to highlight the issue but also potentially increases fear of such attacks which generally, thankfully, are still not commonplace. However, it should encourage us to think critically about the threat of aggression and violence in our workplaces and pastoral activities, and actively consider steps to promote safety and well-being of employees, clergy, pastoral workers and those who work in the voluntary sector. What can be done to further understand this problem and how can we make an effective response?

What is violence in the workplace?

We often make various assumptions about violence and aggression in terms of both what it actually is and also what causes a person to become violent and aggressive. Some of these assumptions can be helpful but often they do not take the full situation into account. Firstly let us consider defining violence. We may assume that an act of violence is when someone is physically harmed, but what about intimidation or threat, which can be equally debilitating and cause equal fear? We may assume that all violence is intentional, but must we then consider whether sometimes the aggressor is out of control due to the influence of alcohol or drugs or simply at the end of their tether? Maybe we would want to say that all violence is unjust or unfair but how do we define legitimate self-defence?

In reality, violence is a more widespread phenomenon than we might at first imagine. Let us think of the many times when we are asked to offer pastoral care to individuals or groups we would consider to be 'victims' of violence. This may include situations of abuse, domestic violence, neighbour threats and intimidation, violent crime, racial or homophobic harassment, working with asylum seekers or refugees fleeing institutional or political violence to name just a few. Any definition would need to include direct physical violence and threat of violence but also the wider social, structural and cultural aspects of violence. Engage[1] offers one possible definition:

> Violence is any physical, emotional, verbal, institutional, structural or spiritual behaviour, attitude, policy or condition that diminishes, dominates or destroys ourselves or others.[2]

This definition then continues by recognising that violence is motivated by fear, anger, greed or the desire to control and dominate, but also at times can be motivated by frustration in the face of perceived injustice, or used by people with the conviction that they are attempting to overcome past violence directed towards them, and that there is no other way. It also

1. Engage is a study programme and a project of *Pace e Bene* Nonviolence Service, Las Vegas, Nevada, USA.
2. Definition from *Engage* in Slattery, L., Butigan, K., Pelicaric, V., and Preston-Pile, K. (2005). *Engage: Exploring Nonviolent Living; A study program for learning, practicing and experimenting with the power of creative nonviolence to transform our lives and our world* (Oakland, California: Pace e Bene Press).

notes that violence often provokes new and additional violence in a spiral of retaliation.

The reasons why individuals resort, deliberately or otherwise, to aggression, violence, intimidation and threat are myriad and potentially complex. It is possible to identify and summarise up to eight possible groupings of theories about the causes of aggression and violence.[1]

1. Natural or innate theories see aggression as a natural part of every animal and indeed every human being. Humans, as the most dominant species, are the most aggressive of all and are the only group who will fight over an idea or a belief, and furthermore we are continuing this need to dominate by destroying ourselves in warfare. More positively viewed, these theories propose that aggression can be used to survive difficult situations and challenges in life.
2. The frustration theory proposes that people become aggressive when their needs are not met and this is a response to the frustration generated. The frustration is relieved, permanently or at least temporarily, once the aggressive act is over.
3. Behavioural theories suggest that aggression is a learned process. Behaviour is controlled by past experiences and the consequences derived from those experiences. If someone has learnt that the use of aggression and violence achieves their aims and desires, there is no incentive to change.
4. Ecological theories note that people are affected by the conditions in which they live. Some theories identify that people resort to violence when food, air or space is scarce. Environmental factors such as overcrowding, poor lighting, shabby furniture, enforced use of shared or inadequate facilities can all contribute to aggressive behaviour.
5. Sociological theories identify the causes of aggression and violence as being rooted in culture, roles and stereotypes created

1. Braithwaite, R. (2001). *Managing Aggression* (London/New York: Routledge/CommunityCare).

by and within society. The potential for conflict and aggression is increased when society distributes its resources based on stereotypical norms (class, gender, ethnicity, educational achievement, accent) and thus they are distributed unequally.

6. Psychodynamic theories place emphasis on the influence of our past and how others, particularly significant relationships, related to us. Being constantly told as children that we were bad or naughty, or regularly and unfavourably compared with siblings or others, can have a significant impact on our lives. Not having the skills to give this appropriate expression as children or when tired or frustrated, aggressive behaviour is perceived as rebelliousness. The resultant reaction of parents or teacher reinforces the child's sense of 'badness'. Hence anger is bottled up, sometimes over many years, until it explodes in violent temper outbursts or can be triggered by someone, often an authority figure, who reminds us of our childhood protagonist.
7. Interactive theory understands violence as a process influenced by others. If we are hostile to another person, this may lead to hostility and aggression in them. Violent acts may then be perpetrated thus giving our initial aggression validity. This theory sees violence and aggression as a continual vicious circle of hostile acts and responses which deepen the initial hostility and aggression.
8. Finally, chemically induced theories propose that chemicals, be they introduced by use of alcohol or drugs, or certain foods that contain toxins, or produced internally due to physical illness or hormonal imbalance, can give rise to aggressive behaviour.

Added to this are certain behaviour patterns or actions which combine different and various aspects of some or all the theories identified above. However it is understood, most forms of violence and aggression do require a cause of some sort. We can stop and consider ourselves for a moment and think about what can make us angry, upset or nervous, and then ask ourselves what happens when this intensifies or escalates to a certain degree or level. Once we reach a particular threshold, most of us can feel aggressive or even potentially violent. If we are being honest, most of us can think of situations where we would at least be tempted to become aggressive, especially if we felt the aggression was justifiable in the context.

It is also possible to learn that if we use violence, we can get our own way. This can be from a very early age and we can observe the schoolyard bully learning that if you threaten someone with violence, then they may give you their sweets; if as an adult you walk into an advice project, community centre or church and patiently sit and wait your turn, someone will come to you, but if you walk in and start to shout and bang the tables with your fists, you are guaranteed the attention of at least one member of staff. Sadly some people have learnt that resorting to violence can get you what you want.

Violence against professionals

Violence against professionals in the community was the focus of research funded by the Economic and Social Research Council in 2001.[1] This study examined the nature and extent of violence and whether it was socially patterned by the professional's age or gender, and secondly how these professionals responded and managed both the threats and actual incidence of violence. The research focused on GPs, probation officers and Anglican clergy. The most common form of aggression reported was verbal abuse. 71% of clergy indicated that they had been verbally abused at least once over the previous two-year period. In the same period 22% of the Anglican clergy indicated that they had been threatened with violence, with those working in inner-city areas reporting a significantly higher incidence compared to those working in rural areas. Female clergy reported slightly fewer threats than males.

Across all the professional groups 10–12% reported being assaulted, with slightly higher levels of reporting amongst the clergy. For the most part these assaults involved being pushed or shoved without injury. Some

1. www.esrcsocietytoday.ac.uk

key differences emerged for the clergy who reported these assaults. While the majority of assaults on GPs and probation officers occurred in their main place of work, most assaults on clergy were in their homes, on the street or local estates rather than in or near church buildings. Whereas the majority of GPs knew their assailant, almost half the clergy reported being assaulted by someone not known to them. All the professional groups reported that being assaulted affected the way they dealt with clients and made them feel less secure. Given that many of the clergy had experienced assault in their home, there is potential for these feelings of insecurity to be higher.

It is interesting to consider what the research tells us regarding the varied responses from different professional groups to such violence and aggression. The fluidity and elusive nature of some risks, combined with the complex working relationships between professionals and the people they work with and how they understand such relationships, was significant. The clergy, alongside GPs, were the least likely to use formal risk assessment procedures, utilising these measures much more haphazardly and reactively. The increase of women clergy in the past few years may also be a significant factor. Although this research focused on Anglican clergy, there is a growing presence of women working in pastoral care in all the Churches. In fact, the majority of workers in lay-led initiatives tend to be women. The presence of women has challenged conventional working practices such as making late-night home visits alone which perhaps assumed the presence of male clergy. Women in all three professions reported both higher fears of violence and being more likely to take precautions on a regular basis. The reported incidence of threats and assaults was lower for women than for their male colleagues.

A number of commentators within different Churches responded to this research by associating aggression and violence with the alleged decline in respect for clergy, and indeed all professional groups in society. Interestingly, in the ESRC research there was a generational shift in this area, with older clergy and GPs explaining the rise in aggression due to a perceived loss of status. Younger clergy and GPs, on the other hand, were more likely to identify aggression in contextual terms such as the socio-economic or personal circumstances of the communities and individuals they serve, and possibly stressing a more egalitarian relationship between clergy and people.

This research corresponds with other evidence on violence in the workplace and specific research on threats against clergy. In 2006 Nick Tolson of National Churchwatch found that 48% of a sample of 90 clergy had suffered at least one violent assault in the preceding twelve months,[1] and other evidence suggests that certain occupations are at special risk, including nurses, social workers, those providing care and advice, and those who work alone.[2] You are more likely to face direct violence and aggression in the 'care' sector than in retail, banking or even the security sector.

Being aware of the complex nature of violence and aggression and the possible causes of such behaviour enables us to identify the elements over which we have some control. We can then start to formulate effective approaches both to reduce and minimise the risk of having to face such aggression and even strategies to confront and resist violence when it occurs.

1. Nick Tolson, 'The Clergy Lifestyle Theory', at www.nationalchurchwatch.com
2. Chappell, D. and Di Martino, V. (2000). *Violence at Work* (2nd edition) (Geneva: International Labour Office).

How should it be dealt with?

Preventing or minimising the risk

The first response when considering the risk of encountering violence and aggression in our ministry and work is to reflect on how this risk can be prevented or minimised. There are two aspects to prevention: firstly examining the physical security of our buildings and homes (particularly as many clergy use their home as a place of work where they see various people in need); and secondly looking at safer working practices that will reduce the risk of violence or assault. Physical security measures can include considering:

- Security lighting
- Door entry systems
- Perimeter fencing
- CCTV
- Alarms and panic buttons

The use of door entry systems, CCTV, or a simple spyhole in a door can be both effective and relatively inexpensive. Where possible, also consider the layout and use of premises. Keep rooms near to the entrance for interviews, counselling and support, and, where possible, have more than one entry or door to these rooms. Think about the layout and use of furniture in the room – ensure that you can be seated nearest the door.

This also applies to counsellors, nurses or care workers who interview vulnerable adults, some of whom may be violent or under the influence of alcohol or drugs, or be suffering from a personality or organic disorder such as schizophrenia. Furnishings should be warm and welcoming but eradicate any unnecessary risks by the removal of heavy ashtrays or other ornaments that could be thrown or used as a weapon.

Having examined the physical safety of your premises, consider next your work practices and procedures. Are there ways of reducing risk? Firstly consider that you are much more at risk when you are working alone. This cannot always be avoided when offering one-to-one support or confidential services, but having someone else around in the house, church, office or project will significantly reduce your risk. The person does not have to be working directly with you but a colleague, receptionist, secretary, sacristan or church volunteer who may be doing other work will both reduce the risk and ensure that there is someone to raise the alarm if necessary. There is strong evidence that simply having another person present can significantly reduce the possibility of violent or aggressive behaviour, even if they are not trained, experienced or even expected to deal with any violent situation or threat.[1]

Often people in need call unexpectedly or 'out of hours', but do consider whether this should be encouraged and whether it can be avoided. Think carefully about what you are actually able to do. Some organisations which offer 24-hour telephone support, for example, have a policy of not opening the door after a certain time at night. In cases of emergency, the police can be called. If you do allow someone entrance, consider telephoning a colleague or a parishioner, for example, and tell them that you are allowing someone in and ask them to call you back in 30 minutes. Similar arrangements can be put in place where clergy or care workers are 'on call' and asked to attend or visit other people's homes. A few practicalities should be borne in mind. Firstly always carry a mobile telephone and personal attack alarm, even if you know the people you are visiting. Remember, even if you know the person you are visiting, you do not know who else might be present – another family member, for example, or an ex-partner. Again, consider letting someone else know that you are going out to see someone, and tell them to phone you on your mobile phone at an agreed time, or inform them that you will contact them when you return.

These practices may initially seem excessive or overcautious, but they are basic common sense and would be expected of many other professionals working in community settings. Just consider the following scenario. One evening you have allowed someone in to your home who has arrived unexpectedly in a distressed state. You call a parishioner and ask them to call you in 15 minutes. When you return to attend to the visitor, he

1. Nick Tolson, 'The Clergy Lifestyle Theory' at www.nationalchurchwatch.com

has become more agitated and at times aggressive, and you feel uncomfortable and under threat. When the parishioner calls in 15 minutes, it allows you to leave the room to answer the phone. You can then decide if you need to call in extra help, or even contact the police if appropriate.

All this consideration of risk reduction and prevention of violent attack may seem contrary to the purpose of an organisation or the mission and ministry of clergy. Surely we want our places of employment, churches, church houses and projects to be places of welcome, highly accessible and open to all people and especially anyone in need of care or support? Focusing specifically on churches, we could be the safest church, presbytery, or rectory, with the safest work practices and procedures, but end up being distant, removed, inaccessible and entirely irrelevant to the communities we seek to serve and minister to. Equally, though, we also have a duty of care to ourselves and others who work and serve alongside us. We need to be aware of our limitations and feel able to say 'no' at times when we feel vulnerable or unsafe. Safety and risk reduction and accessibility and welcome are not diametrically opposed, but rather need to be in constant dialogue.

A word of warning, though: we can become over-reliant on technology without thinking what it will actually achieve. I remember reflecting once with staff in a local prison after an alarm bell had been triggered, which immediately resulted in radio contact with staff and a number of officers being present at the scene within seconds and minutes, with other specially trained and equipped staff potentially available quickly. I couldn't help but compare this with the homeless drop-in centre where I was then working. The centre also had an alarm bell which set off a loud and usefully distracting siren, but ultimately it still left me and four or five volunteers to deal with any potential incident of violence or aggression. Consideration can be given to the possibility of panic alarms and indeed personal alarms being automatically connected to police or security centres. This will be helpful in some settings, but simple over-reliance on technology, practical security measures and risk assessment is not enough.

Given that you have considered physical security and balanced that with the desire to be accessible and available, there is still the potential of having to deal with an unknown person, or indeed the known aggressive person who has turned up unexpectedly, until help can be summoned. In this section I will attempt to offer some practical, non-violent and realistic responses. I will try to offer ways of directly responding to an incident of violence and aggression directed at an individual.

Defusing the situation

The first task is to attempt to defuse the situation gently, slow things down and hopefully avoid actual violence. In reality, many violent or aggressive incidents occur very rapidly, giving you little time to think through a strategy or response. Here, therefore, I will examine any given violent or potentially violent encounter in 'slow motion', considering the assessment of the situation and those involved, responding, dealing and then managing the incident, and finally attempting to avoid escalating the situation and so bring it to a successful outcome.

When confronted with aggression, threat or actual violence, certain 'automatic' responses can immediately kick in. These can be typified by the fight, flight or freeze responses, which are all natural, biological, physiological responses to situations of fear, violence and aggression. Natural angers, fears, frustrations and panic quickly come to the surface when we are faced with such situations. Before we know it we are thinking and responding: 'How dare he speak to me like that, I'm going to give him a piece of my mind' or 'She has a knife – get out of here' or 'They're coming at me – what should I do?' Each of these responses is natural and understandable, and indeed is controlled by the automatic physiological changes that happen in situations of stress. (These same physiological factors are occurring in the aggressor, and these control and promote their behaviour and reactions.) While these initial responses are all understandable, they may not always be the most appropriate ways of responding to situations of conflict, aggression and violence.

Keeping calm

Initially it is essential to stay calm and to try and relax. This is easier said than done when faced with aggression, but it is achievable and essential to buy you time to make an effective assessment of your situation. The following steps will allow you to attempt to calm yourself and, as much as possible, to relax and stay in control of your mind and your body.

- Say STOP to yourself
- Breath in deeply, breath out slowly
- Drop your shoulders
- Relax your hands
- Do it again!

As has already been stated, we often spring into action when faced with violence. Just stopping ourselves from immediate reaction is the first step. Allowing ourselves to breath deeply and slowly is a powerful relaxation agent. This allows time to make an assessment of both the environment and the aggressor. First consider if there is any avenue of escape. No one should feel under any obligation to remain in a situation of violence or potential violence if they can legitimately remove themselves from it. If you can leave a room, do so, thereby preventing a person's access to you and potentially causing you harm. Remember that no threat to property or resources can be compared to any individual's personal safety and security. A second assessment is needed about whether anyone else is present.

- Who are they and how near are they?
- Are they people you have a responsibility for – service users, parishioners or colleagues? If you left, would they be in danger?
- Are they people who can help or summon assistance from, for example, the police?
- Are they also potential threats?

The presence of another person, whoever they might be, is a significant factor in reducing the threat of violence or assault.

The final factor to consider in your physical environment is whether there are any large objects such as desks or church benches that could serve as barriers. If someone is being verbally threatening from the other end of a large desk or table, I certainly will feel slightly better than if I am in a small room with only chairs, which is isolated from other rooms in the premises and where there is no effective barrier between myself and the aggressor.

The next assessment needed is of the threatening person themselves:

- Who is this person?
- Do you know them?
- What is your relationship?
- How near are they to you?
- What is their emotional state?
- What is being said and how?
- Is there evidence of alcohol or substance use?
- Do they possess any weapons such as a gun or a knife?

All this information is important for you as you try and remain calm and keep control of the situation. Any of the above information will help you make better-informed responses. It is more likely that you will know the aggressive person, as most reported incidents of violence are from people known to the victims. Evidence of alcohol or substance use can indicate that the person is more likely to resort to violence or aggression. But equally if they are highly intoxicated, it may be easier to make an escape if needed. As well as the possession of actual weapons, also consider the availability of any makeshift weapons such as smashed bottles, cutlery or lightweight furniture which could be thrown. Be aware that even objects we do not ordinarily consider as potential weapons, such as candlesticks or lamps, could very easily be used against us.

Communicating with the aggressor

Having made the fullest assessment possible, we now have to try and open communication with the aggressor. The most influential channel of communication will be non-verbal:

- Often it is all we have initially, but it is first and immediate.
- It buys time and can have a powerful calming effect.
- It accounts for approximately 75% of all we communicate!

There is a problem here as fear and violence look similar! Naturally you will feel fear or indeed aggression – you are in fight-or-flight mode, which is how we are 'hard-wired' to deal with threats to our person. Indeed most people would consider it reasonable to be fearful if someone is acting aggressively, especially if they are threatening actual physical harm. Naturally our bodies will want to communicate this fear or even our own aggression and defensiveness. The problem is that we ought not to show this fear but rather signal non-aggression. In other words we must teach our bodies to lie! Yes, we may feel fear but what we will try to display and signal is an attitude and position of non-aggression. Signalling non-aggression is powerful and also puts you in a position of strength, not weakness, while still resisting and confronting the violence. To signal non-violence:

- Create space
- Relax your posture
- Drop and extend your arms
- Open your hands
- Lower your voice
- Slow your movements

Having signalled non-aggression, we can now attempt to calm the situation. In all the following strategies it is worthwhile to note that we cannot solely calm and resolve this aggression and potential violence. This will take two parties – you and the aggressor. Remember all that has been said about non-verbal communication, which is still a primary tactic at this stage. We can, however, now start to encourage talking and use verbal communication ourselves. Offer reassurance where appropriate. While there remains a high potential for violence, at this stage no one has been physically hurt and the situation is not out of control. It has not gone too far and can still be resolved amicably. So often in my experience it has been possible to reassure an aggressor that things can still be managed and at this stage no sanction will need to be imposed. This was particularly the case while working in homeless projects and hostels when people often felt that they had nothing left to lose and they were sure they would be barred or evicted from the project. People engage in high-risk strategies when there is little to lose and a high-risk gamble appears to be worth taking. If people perceive that a change of attitude or behaviour may result in a better outcome, there is a higher likelihood of reducing the emotional temperature.[1] Hearing that, at this stage, it may be possible for them to remain and explain their need, often led to a defusing of tension and a reduction in the threat of violence.

It is essential when dealing with any incident of violence or aggression not to rush to resolve it or run ahead before the aggressor is starting to calm and engage with you. It is better to proceed gradually and surely. I can think of numerous situations when dealing with an incident of violence when I have made assumptions about how someone will respond without allowing them time to calm. This inevitably led to inflaming the situation further. A violent incident can often attract attention from many others present, which is not always helpful – consider a fight in a school yard which will soon attract a good crowd of children to observe, and even encourage, the fight. As a person starts to calm, consideration can be given to moving to a less public space to avoid an audience. Clearly we should never isolate ourselves with an aggressor but perhaps we can ask others present to back off a little or to continue with their normal activities. Finally, at all times continue to anticipate violence and ensure continuing vigilance. People who are aggressive rarely calm down in seconds or minutes and must be given appropriate time to relax and allow their aggression to dissipate.

Once a situation has been calmed, we can move to further stages of relating to the aggressive person and ultimately managing the situation.

1. Leith, K. P. and Baumeister, R. F. (1996). 'Why do bad moods increase self-defeating behavior? Emotion, risk-taking and self-regulation', *Journal of Personality and Social Psychology*, 71, 1250–1267.

We might not particularly feel like relating with someone who has threatened us, let alone dealing with them with understanding and warmth, but if we set it in the context of resolving the situation and protecting ourselves from further violence, it is a worthwhile thing to do. Try to encourage agreement and verbalise this with 'yes' statements that both of you can agree. Remember it takes both you *and* the aggressor to resolve the issue successfully without the use of violence and so use 'we' statements to agree that you can resolve the issue peacefully and that you don't wish to hurt or harm the other person. It is only at this stage that we can move to verbal communication and then continue to try and manage the situation non-violently. Open up channels of communication, thank them and use praise appropriately and sensitively if they start to cooperate. Ask them to sit down and see if there can be any compromise or alternative solution to their problems. Always include the other person in trying to resolve the issue so that they feel included and empowered. As any violent situation seems to be diffused or resolved, one final note of caution is to avoid escalating behaviour. So often violence and aggression can be re-triggered or re-inflamed by the wrong word at the wrong time. Avoid criticising the person or belittling them, especially in front of others. Try to be aware not to use unhelpful gestures like pointing which can appear authoritarian or controlling.

Self-defence

No guide to dealing with violence and aggression would be complete without referring to self-defence. Surely we all have the right to use legitimate force to protect ourselves from violent attack? The answer is yes, but within the limitations of what is deemed to be both necessary and reasonable. Here a sense of proportionality must come into effect. Thus, in considering what force is necessary, we must take into account what is reasonable. For example, it may be considered both necessary and reasonable to use force which may seriously injure or even kill someone when faced with the real possibility that your own life is endangered, but it could hardly be justifiable when responding to verbal insults or spitting, however unpleasant these may be. In order to help define 'necessary' and 'reasonable', a number of factors should be considered: the gravity of the crime being prevented, whether it was possible to prevent it using non-violent methods, whether you were willing to try those means first, and finally the relative strength of the persons involved.[1] Alternatives considered by some organisations, projects and individuals are implementing training in breakaway techniques or developing the use of control and restraint. This is the Home Office-approved technique for the management of violence in the prison system which has also been adapted to many healthcare settings. While each has their uses, they also have significant limitations. Breakaway techniques can be both complex and varied, and in the heightened atmosphere of a physical attack a victim would easily become confused in their application.[2] Would you be able to remember more than a handful of techniques for very specific situations? Control and restraint is only applicable in certain settings and it would be unwise to try to replicate it in church or voluntary settings. It is taught by approved trainers over a period of anything from up to two days to a week with specific follow-up refresher training. Given the disadvantages of its specific training, its potential misuse and even the possibility of escalating violence if applied inappropriately,[3] it is not really a suitable strategy or response by individual workers, clergy, small projects and churches. So, broadly speaking, while it is both desirable and fair to say we all have the right to self-defence and to use physical force to protect ourselves when we are faced with violent, physical attack, this needs to be tempered with the notions of what is both reasonable and necessary, and the inherent difficulties in deciding what falls within the parameters of these terms.

Witnessing an attack on another person

As has been stated above, a key factor in safety or reducing risk of violent attack is working with another person rather than in isolation. Given this, it is worthwhile to consider how to respond if you witness aggressive behaviour or even a violent attack directed at a colleague. The first principle is always to

1. Dawes, M. and Winn, D. (1999). 'Managing the monkey: How to defuse the conflicts that can lead to violence in the workplace' p. 57. (Hailsham, East Sussex: The Therapist Ltd)
2. Dawes, M. and Winn, D. (1999). 'Managing the monkey: How to defuse the conflicts that can lead to violence in the workplace' p. 62 (Hailsham, East Sussex: The Therapist Ltd)
3. Mason, T. and Chandley, M. (1999). *Managing Violence and Aggression: A manual for nurses and health care workers* (Edinburgh: Churchill Livingstone), p. 157.

raise the alarm. Let others know what is happening and either call for the appropriate backup and support (which obviously may include the police) or ensure someone else is doing this. Only then is it helpful to make any direct intervention to support the person being attacked. This can appear to be callous, but it is better to ensure that help is on its way before, in a worst-case scenario, there are two people trapped by a violent aggressor. Any immediate intervention is best taken from a safe distance. Let the aggressor know that you are present and are witnessing the incident. If direct physical harm is being inflicted, or the victim is being physically restrained, repeatedly tell the aggressor to stop or let the person go. Final consideration can be given to physical interventions such as dragging the aggressor off the victim, disarming them or using restraint. Firstly it is essential that any such action and intervention is thought out carefully to ensure there will not simply be two victims rather than one. In addition, notions of reasonable force and proportionality, as discussed above, would come into play. If you intervene physically and your colleague is freed to help you in restraining the initial aggressor, consideration must be given to the relative strength of the two parties involved – it is now two against one. Again what was the severity of the crime being prevented and did you use non-violent means first? It is worthwhile to remember at all times that your physical presence alone is a significant factor in reducing the possibility of violent attack.

The responses outlined above are deliberately non-aggressive but *not* passive or weak. They do not rely on practical security measures. They are simple and don't require physical training or regular practice such as are necessary in self-defence or with breakaway techniques. However, it is worthwhile to consider training in the management of violence and aggression. Numerous courses can be offered both to individuals or bought in to train groups of staff and can be tailored to specific situations and settings. When considering attending or buying in training, *do* check that the training organisation and individual trainers understand the sensitivities of churches or specific voluntary projects and indeed their limitations. The internet, local voluntary sector advisory or umbrella agencies, local authorities and local training providers and consortiums are useful places to start to find appropriate resources.

What to do after a serious incident

My focus here will be in two parts. Firstly I will briefly consider what support and response needs to be given to a victim of violent attack which is experienced in the course of work or ministry. Secondly I will examine what can be done to treat or respond to people who are highly aggressive and who routinely use threat and violence. In considering the aggressive and violent person, by no means do I wish to reduce the importance of responding to the needs of those who are victims of violence: their needs are always paramount. However, in the course of my ministry and working life I have encountered many individuals who regularly become aggressive and even violent, but who deeply regret their violence and would love to find alternative ways of dealing with their feelings and learn different patterns of behaviour.

The victim

Firstly let us consider who might need support or need to take action after an incident of aggression and violence and what needs to happen post-incident. The following people or groups all need to be taken into account:

- The victim
- The victim's family
- Colleagues
- Other people who attend the church or use the services offered
- The wider organisation or church

The primary focus is, of course, the victim. An immediate concern is that they receive any medical or health intervention needed if they have been physically harmed. Secondly it is essential that the victim is debriefed and has an opportunity to talk through what has happened. It is important to do this in the immediate aftermath of the incident so they can calm themselves, but also that at an appropriate time in the future an opportunity is made available for further reflection and, if necessary, counselling. Considerable progress has been made in what is known as Critical Incident

Stress Management. It appears that while people benefit from the opportunity to talk through what has happened, intensive counselling at this stage can be counter-productive as it invites people to loosen their natural defences at a time when they need to maintain them. If, after about six months, the person is still affected by the event, that is the time to offer more thorough therapeutic support.[1] It is also worthwhile to remember the victim's family who can also be very distressed and upset at the news of the incident. Particular concern and intervention is needed if the incident has taken place in the home where the victim and any other family members live.

After a serious violent incident it is important to inform any other people who may work from the same premises such as other employees, ministers, administrators, housekeepers and volunteers. Often such people can also feel vulnerable, even if they were not directly involved in the incident. This is especially the case if the aggressive person has left the premises, not been detained by the police or other authorities, and there is the potential of further threat if they return. Consideration should also be given to alerting neighbouring priests, ministers and projects if it is likely the aggressor may turn up at their homes or premises. (This is also the case with 'con artists' who are skilled at manipulating people who work in the caring professions.)

Remember that all those who use a given project or the whole church community will be affected by a violent incident. Many will simply be concerned; others may be fearful of being vulnerable if they come to the church or the project premises. Church officials in dioceses or other structures and management boards and managers in the voluntary sector also have a responsibility to ensure that appropriate support and any necessary follow-up response is in place after an incident. There should be clear and commonly understood procedures regarding who needs to be informed and what action each person responsible should take. All too often there are no reporting or responding mechanisms in place in church organisations or smaller voluntary projects, which results in incidents of

1. Rothschild, B. (February 2005). 'Applying the brakes', *Counselling and Psychotherapy Journal*, 15, 1. Can be retrieved at http://www.saskworld.com/bodymindspirit/edition21/17_article_rothschild.htm

violence not being recorded appropriately or responded to effectively at a managerial or organisational level.

The aggressor

Secondly, there needs to be a brief discussion on the needs of those who are violent – or use violence – and how they can be helped. The reality is that there is little help or treatment available. This is not considered a worthy cause for help and support. However, I do know of people who have been greatly disturbed and upset by their violent tendencies or their willingness to resort to violence – even extreme violence. These people may be disposed to benefit from help if it were available to them.

As we have seen, there is a wide range of complex and often interacting reasons why people may use violence and aggression, and any treatment response would be highly dependent on any individual's specific needs. Additional to this is the focus of the arena in which the person becomes violent – for example, some use violence in the home, others against children or other vulnerable people, and others when under the influence of alcohol and drugs. Specific treatment and interventions have been described in other chapters of this book. The reality is that a number of people have difficulty with expressing their anger or frustrations. Due to lack of experience of the range of options in dealing with anger, they may resort to violence or other negative ways of expression. We need to ensure that those who are willing to engage constructively with their behaviour are not further disadvantaged and isolated.[1] Working on an individual basis, some people will respond well to befriending and support schemes, particularly where a relationship can develop to explore feelings and emotions and possible strategies can be suggested to deal with these feelings. Additionally, empowerment and advocacy schemes may be of assistance to individuals to help develop alternative strategies to ensure their needs can be met.

Group-work initiatives, such as anger management, would offer a specific treatment response. However, such initiatives are virtually inaccessible until after an offence has been committed! Therapeutic

1. Braithwaite, R. (2001). *Managing Aggression* (London/New York: Routledge/CommunityCare), p. 167.

groups are offered within the criminal justice system by prison and probation services but in one sense they are being offered too late. Group therapy can be particularly effective in these cases, as people explore their beliefs, feelings and behaviour, and learn strategies for managing their anger and how to become more empathic towards others. Sadly, there is little financial support for this kind of group in the community.

The final sanction is incarceration in a mental health facility or imprisonment, hopefully alongside therapeutic help and rehabilitation and medical or psychiatric intervention. Again, this is usually only available after a violent attack or a potentially serious offence, and is usually only initiated in the most serious of cases.

One of the great sources of sadness for those working with these groups is the difficulty in accessing such treatments and interventions where they actually exist. Most treatment and intervention is only offered within the criminal justice system or more secure aspects of mental health services. Being aware of the few services that might be willing to help and support, and how to refer people to them, could be a critical factor in offering pastoral care to those who struggle with violence.

A Christian response

When writing this chapter came up in conversation with other people, including those who work in ministry, many responded that it was interesting and worthwhile. However people often commented, usually towards the end of the conversation, that while non-violence was a nice theory, in the end there were always situations when you would have to use violence or at least physical force. I don't want to criticise those people or even necessarily disagree, but a belief that the use of violence is inevitable saddens me and, more importantly, leaves me with a real sense of disquiet. I can't help but think that we have a new idolatry of violence which deceives us into thinking in destructive and ultimately aggressive terms.

Walter Wink identifies what he has termed the 'myth of redemptive violence',[1] which has been present in religious and literary writings from the earliest times, from early Babylonian myths to contemporary cartoons. Citing the Babylonian creation myth and the modern Popeye cartoons, he shows that violence is seen as a creative force that ultimately liberates us. He argues that this myth is so successful and strong that it hardly seems mythic at all, but rather simply the way things actually are. 'Redemptive violence gives way to violence as an end in itself. It is no longer a religion that uses violence in the pursuit of order and salvation, but one in which violence has become an aphrodisiac, sheer titillation, an addictive high, a substitute for relationships. Violence is no longer the means to a higher good, namely order; violence becomes the end.'[2]

As has been seen in preceding pages, there are various ways we can choose to respond, or sometimes simply instinctively react, to aggression and violence. In short, a number of frameworks can be identified to describe how we often react.[3] We can choose to avoid violence, remove

1 Wink, W. (November 2007). *Facing the Myth of Redemptive Violence.* Retrieved from http://www.ekklesia.co.uk/content/cpt/article_060823wink.shtml

2. Wink, W. (November 2007). *Facing the Myth of Redemptive Violence.* Retrieved from http://www.ekklesia.co.uk/content/cpt/article_060823wink.shtml

3. Slattery, L., Butigan, K., Pelicaric, V. and Preston-Pile, K. (2005). *Engage: Exploring Nonviolent Living; a study program for learning, practicing and experimenting with the power of creative nonviolence to transform our lives and our world* (Oakland, California: Pace e Bene Press).

ourselves from its presence and isolate ourselves from risk; we can accept or accommodate it, seeing it as inevitable; or we can respond with counter-violence, as the ends justify the means or to ensure that through force justice will be achieved. A fourth and more authentic way is to resist the violence through active non-violence.

Christianity has been identified with all these ways of responding, from pacifism to the use of morally justified violence. Sometimes the accusation of passivism has also been levied at Christians – that is, that we simply stand by passively, neither resisting nor defending ourselves against violence. In reality there has also been a long tradition of active resistance through a spirituality of non-violence, but all too often this tradition has been silenced or smothered by the myth of redemptive violence.

Martin Luther King commented on how difficult it was to get his message of non-violent action understood, when so many people had not heard of its methods. Moreover non-violent action simply did not make sense to them – they were so used to avoiding violence or accommodating violence, or they believed that the only other response was violent resistance. 'We had to make it clear that non-violent resistance is not a method of cowardice. It does resist. It is not a method of stagnating passivity and deadening complacency. The non-violent resister is just as opposed to the evil he is standing against as the violent resister but he resists without violence.'[1]

We can turn to the person of Jesus as an ideal role model for nonviolent resistance. There are many who would wish to dismiss Jesus as accommodating violence and oppression, advocating that his followers turn the other cheek and not resist evil. Yet you can see posters and T-shirts depicting Jesus in the image of the revolutionary Che Guevara with the phrase 'Meek. Mild. As if.' Two sides of the same coin, both of which are equally false. Jesus rejected both absolute passivism and violence, and rather promoted a new third way of active non-violent resistance. Walter Wink points out the scriptural translation and contextual problems of Matthew 5:38-41.[2] An alternative translation of 'Resist not the evildoer'

1. King, M. L. quoted in Washington, J. M. (ed.) (1992). *I Have a Dream: Writings and speeches that changed the world* (San Francisco: Harper San Francisco), p. 30.

2. Wink, W. (2003). *Jesus and Non-Violence: A third way* (Minneapolis: Augsburg Fortress) pp. 10–12.

can be rendered 'Don't react violently against the one who is evil'. He further contests that the platitudes that follow of turning the other cheek, giving your cloak and going the extra mile can all be seen in the context of the audience of Jesus in first-century Palestine. These are direct, cultural references which inspire and call the people to take control and to stand as equals with those who would subjugate them, rather than recommend being meek and submissive. This third way of Jesus – the way of non-violent resistance – resonates with his teachings and example. He calls his followers to love their enemies and to bring about the Gospel. He encourages them to acknowledge their own faults and violence, and to take up their cross in solidarity with him to challenge and overcome oppression.[1] We can add to this the profound social and communitarian dimension, and the objective of Jesus' teaching to transcend the individual and transform the community – if not the whole world. Indeed, we can see how Jesus would want to direct us, along with Martin Luther King, to a very different destination to that of violence. 'The end of violence or the aftermath of violence is bitterness. The aftermath of non-violence is reconciliation and the creation of a beloved community.'[2]

1. Wink, W. (November 2007). *Facing the Myth of Redemptive Violence.* Retrieved from http://www.ekklesia.co.uk/content/cpt/article_060823wink.shtml
2. King, M. L. (1957). 'The Power of Non-Violence'. Retrieved from http://teachingamericanhistory.org/library/index.asp?document=1131

Do's and don'ts

- Do consider the risks of violence and aggression.
- Do take practical steps and consider your security.
- Do when faced with a violent person, stay calm.
- Do signal non-aggression.
- Do try to communicate verbally and negotiate.
- Don't let your guard down, even when thr situation seems close to being resolved.
- Do when feeling vulnerable, ask for assistance.
- Don't assume it will never happen to you.
- Do access appropriate training.

Conclusion

I started by reflecting that there are no easy answers. How anyone reacts when faced with direct violence and aggression needs to be understood and accepted. Christians in daily life should be wary not to set themselves up as saints! We would all like to have more ideal responses or be convinced that we could resist resorting to violence, but we can also recognise in ourselves, if we are honest, that we are subject to anger, frustration and irritability which can be expressed destructively and even violently.

> There is so much focus on the distinction between non-violence and violence, between non-violent people and violent people. But in reality it's not easy to take sides like that. One can never be sure that one is completely on the side of non-violence or that the other person is completely on the side of violence. Non-violence is a direction, not a separating line. It has no boundaries.[1]

As Christians, we should not be debating whether we are non-violent, passivist, pacifist or willing to use morally justified violence in certain settings. Rather we can all agree that we are heading in the direction of non-violence – rejecting violence as a preferred mechanism to achieve goals and its seductive power as a solution to our problems, in favour of active peacemaking and becoming agents of love and genuine encounter with others.

Recommended reading

- Davies, W. and Frude, N. (2000). *Preventing Face-To-Face Violence: dealing with anger and aggression at work* (Leicester: The APT Trust).
- Slattery, L., Butigan, K., Pelicaric, V. and Preston-Pile, K. (2005). *Engage: Exploring Nonviolent Living; a study program for learning, practicing and experimenting with the power of creative nonviolence to transform our lives and our world* (Oakland, California: Pace e Bene Press).

Website

www.nationalchurchwatch.com

1. Thich Nhat Hanh in Slattery, L., Butigan, K., Pelicaric, V. and Preston-Pile, K. (2005). *Engage: Exploring Nonviolent Living A study program for learning, practicing and experimenting with the power of creative nonviolence to transform our lives and our world*(Oakland, California: Pace e Bene Press).

Part II

Caring for Yourself

Alison Moore

The subject of 'caring for yourself' is written primarily for those who find themselves in a leadership position and faced with a seriously difficult situation. This could be because someone they have responsibility for is involved in one of the situations described in the first section of this book, or any other situation that is, by definition, testing and not easily resolvable. It is also relevant to any concerned individual who is caught up in this kind of situation, or indeed anyone who is interested in the areas of leadership and self-care. It is written for Christian contexts – for example, churches – and for leaders in other organisations who are Christian.

You might have been attracted to this subject out of a precautionary interest – 'in case I ever need it' – or you might be checking out how it compares with what you have experienced in the past. But it is possible that you are *at this moment* caught up in a difficult situation, and you are the person I have mainly in mind. You will be under pressure to perform in a properly professional manner, quite possibly more in the public eye than normal, and in unusually stressful conditions. Your capacity to do this will be affected by various factors, as will the length of time it takes for you to come through to the other end of the experience and regain your normal balance and perspective. Some of those factors are internal and personal to you: what sort of personality do you have? What sort of previous experiences, professional and personal, do you bring to this situation? Other factors are external: is this difficult situation time-limited though unpleasant, or is it apparently endless and unresolvable? What sort of organisation do you belong to? What kind of procedures and support are available?

If you haven't the energy to read about this subject, then please give it to a colleague or friend who can point you to any parts that might be helpful to you.

The first section describes what self-care looks like, and moves on to look at normal short-term responses to shock and longer-term responses to stress. The second section explores ways of approaching sensible self-care. It invites you to take a step back to assess the bigger picture. This applies both to you (how do I 'tick'?) and to the situation as a whole (what sort of an organisation am I working in?). If you are in the middle of a crisis situation right now, this is the part you will probably be tempted to skip. It is counterintuitive to step back once the adrenalin is flowing and events are unfolding by the minute. However, anyone who needs to do a good job under pressure will still take the time to check that their tools are in good order, knowing that this will pay off later. So I suggest it will be worth reading it. The third section gives a brief defence of the rationale for self-care. In spite of the commandment that all Christians agree on to 'love our neighbour *as ourself*', self-care can still be a contentious area, where people experience considerable discomfort. The final section offers some lists of practical suggestions that might help, gleaned from observation, anecdotes and the experience of people who've been through just such situations.

What does self-care look like?

Should we be leading perfectly balanced lives? In spite of the current popularity of phrases like 'work-life balance', I've rarely encountered anyone who feels they achieve this. Actually we aren't called to be 'balanced', but to be disciples, made in the image of and living the life of our complex vibrant God. Part of this calling is to be thoroughly human. This means that we are subject to our physiological and our psychological makeup. Therefore, when exposed to trauma or stress, we experience the normal physiological and psychological consequences of this. When we sometimes describe ourselves as 'in pieces', this does not mean that God doesn't love us, nor that we have been the wrong sort of Christian. It probably means that we've been subjected to a heavy weight of one sort or another. I've sometimes gone to the kitchen cupboard for a particular plate only to find that it's mysteriously cracked. Then I see that it has been at the bottom of a great stack of assorted plates since last year. It was not a faulty plate. It was simply subjected to too much pressure. Like the plate, we can be broken by prolonged stress; unlike the inanimate plate, we have the possibility of regeneration and repair.

What is self-care?

Care of self is to do with the whole self

In other words, self-care applies to our physical, mental, emotional, behavioural and spiritual experiences, which are interrelated. If you doubt this, think about these examples:

- If you feel excited *(emotional)*, your heart beats faster *(physical)*.
- If you have flu *(physical)*, you feel miserable *(emotional)*.
- If you think you cannot speak in public *(mental)*, you probably won't be able to do it *(behavioural)*.
- If you eat too much sugar *(behavioural)*, you will crave more *(physical)*, and you will think you cannot function without another chocolate bar *(mental)* so you will eat another *(behavioural)* and feel guilty *(mental / emotional / spiritual)*.
- If you receive through the Eucharist (or other religious service) a sense of God's love and purpose for you *(spiritual)*, your anxiety decreases *(emotional)* and your knotted stomach relaxes *(physical)*.

Sensible self-care recognises that these are linked and makes allowances.

Care of self is to do with long-term ways of living

We are physically designed to alternate between stress and rest, tension and relaxation. People who do only one or the other lose touch with their humanity. The purpose of a rubber band is to hold something together by being stretched in tension. However, if it is left permanently in the stretched position, it will stop functioning and need to be thrown away. Rubber bands last longest if they are put back in the drawer in relaxed mode until needed again. Like rubber bands, most people can stretch to function well under stress, and our bodies are designed to do just that. However, when we habitually override the instinct to rest, we reach a point where we can no longer relax, mentally, emotionally, spiritually, behaviourally or physically.[1]

1. See Sarah Horsman's helpful work on stress reactions described in Litchfield, K. (2006). *Tend My Flock* (Canterbury Press). See particularly chapter 4 sections 4.28–4.31.

Care of self is essential for good leadership and management

You may agree with what has been written so far, but still see that the world (including the Christian world) is full of people who seem to succeed without taking any notice of the principles of self-care. So many people do push themselves hard, by choice or circumstance, and make a success of it, that we may well wonder what's wrong with this. What *is* the point of 'self-care'? Remember the rubber band: we too can become useless if we habitually overextend ourselves.

'Becoming useless' might include:

- *physically* – exhaustion, sleeplessness, appetite change, minor or major illness
- *emotionally* – numbness, incapacity to see or respond to others, or to receive feedback from others, overreactions, inappropriate reactions
- *mentally* – skewed thought patterns and illogical approaches, inability to assess situations, inability to realise this
- *behaviourally* – excessive drinking, caffeine intake, extremes of sexual activity, obsession with detail, longer but less productive hours, anger outbursts, irregular eating patterns
- *spiritually* – avoidance of prayer or only praying for miracles, superficial external religious compliance, skewed sense of responsibility and therefore guilt that blocks receiving compassion, emphasising some Christian themes more than others, ignoring failure as a route to new possibilities, acting out of pride disguised as responsibility.

Looking at this list, it becomes clear why the overstressed leader is not good for their organisation or those they are responsible for. The likelihood of serious errors of judgement is increased, as well as serious breakdown in relationships, illness or self-harming behaviour.

A certain level of self-knowledge and awareness is simply sensible, particularly in our twenty-first-century Western society where compliance with legal and good practice guidelines is essential.

Care of self will look different in different people

Our personalities really do make a difference here: the introvert will sometimes need to withdraw from others in order to function well; the extrovert is more likely to seek people out; some people are energised by activity, others by quiet; some need regular strenuous physical exercise to be able to think straight; some need more sleep than others. We often forget this and feel we must follow someone else's good advice, rather than trust our own instinct about what *we* need; or we become worried about someone's apparently odd behaviour, when in fact they are looking after themselves in their own way.

Normal responses when a difficult situation arises

Normal initial responses to shock[1]

When we are faced with a seriously difficult situation, we are likely to experience at first the sort of reactions common to any significant loss. If nothing else, we will have lost our normal routine. There are various ways of describing the pattern of reactions after such a loss, but common to them all is the idea of *shock* to sum up the collection of reactions in the first instance. Remember that the whole self will be affected. So physical sensations, behaviours, thoughts and feelings are likely to be different from normal. People typically report signs like these:

- *physical* – feeling sick, tight chest, weight in stomach, losing appetite, adrenalin flow
- *behaviours* – sleep disturbed, extra alert and energetic, complete loss of energy, inability to concentrate
- *thoughts* – questions ('Why me/us? What should I do?'); going back over conversations, images, situations; denial ('I don't believe this is happening', 'This happens to other people, not me'); clear thinking
- *feelings* – depending on the nature of what is happening, initial feelings can include anger, fear, pity, revulsion, excitement. Or there might be an absence of emotion.

1. There are many good descriptions of responses to sudden loss. Any book on bereavement will cover this – for example, Worden, J. W. (2001). *Grief Counselling and Grief Therapy* (3rd edition) (Bruner-Routledge).

Of course, a feature of shock is that any of these can change dramatically and without warning, as vacillation of feelings and thoughts is very normal. In the morning, there is a sense of calm and of handing it over to God; by the afternoon, only a sense of despair that it's all out of control.

Shock reactions are normal and there for good reason. Physiologically we need to survive, and it is as if, with a limited amount of energy available, parts of us shut down temporarily so that other parts can function well. For example, sadness is likely to follow a close friend's move to another country, but it can be some months before this is felt, because at the time you were sharing their excitement, joy and anticipation. Many people find that when they are bereaved they cannot do their own grieving because of the normal demands of life – young children, vulnerable parents or simply work. Some of the reactions that were not able to happen at the time will rise to the surface later when there is opportunity. In my counselling work, I've met many who are distressed and astonished to find themselves 'cracking up' or 'in pieces' when they are at last settled, secure and happy having survived prolonged difficult spells. It's as if something inside us knows when it's time for the difficult or painful thoughts and feelings to be allowed to the surface. It's been described as 'putting them in the freezer' – they don't go away, but thaw much later. Unlike a cook, the person doesn't usually even know that this stuff is in the freezer, and is surprised when it emerges and thaws on the carpet of their new and happier life.

Many people in a leadership position experience the positive aspect of shock reactions – adrenalin leads to clarity, decisiveness and more energy than normal. 'I am energised in a crisis', said one manager, and another, 'I operate very clearly and well under stress.'

However, there is a downside: too much adrenalin can paralyse thinking processes. Worst of all, you can be completely confident that you are functioning clearly, when actually you are unaware that you are *not* seeing the broad picture in a way that you would normally. If others normally see you as a competent leader, they are unlikely to question your decisions now. This can lead to unwise decisions and actions that can create difficulties for later.

'Looking back on that time, I think the staff would say that my judgement was affected sometimes.'

So it is clear that in the early days of a difficult situation there will be an impact on your *role*. People will have added expectations of you as a leader or manager: you will be expected to function competently as normal, and manage the unfolding situation in a wise way, and anticipate and meet the needs of those you are responsible for. You are unlikely to succeed in meeting these expectations, or certainly not for long.

Equally, your relationships, at work and personally, will be affected. As leader/manager, how you perform is going to be the focus of other people's interest, advice and, quite possibly, criticism. A difficult situation is likely to bring with it certain delicacies which mean that the whole truth cannot be revealed to all the people all the time. So misunderstandings can flourish and relationships suffer. Sometimes criticism or advice will be offered directly, sometimes not. 'When people gave me their opinion or advice, all I could say was "thank you for that", although I knew they only knew one side of the story.'

By being unable either to explain or defend yourself, you can find yourself becoming a different sort of leader from the sort you thought you were. People who had trusted you may trust you no longer.

In church contexts, the divide between work and personal relationships can be much less clear than in other work situations, and church members may well not be conscious of the need for different roles in different circumstances. If the difficult situation is open knowledge, there might be much warm personal support for you. If not, the confusion and hurt of not knowing why the minister 'has no time for me at the moment' can cause problems.

At home, family relationships are inevitably affected. The difficult situation may take a lot of time and will certainly drain your energy. Relationships at home might be robust enough to accommodate a period when you are preoccupied, but if there are ongoing demands there too (young baby, elderly parents, family bereavement, teenagers . . .), it can be challenging to keep functioning well, particularly when your energies are already depleted.

Normal mid- to longer-term responses to shock

One manager who faced two unrelated major difficult situations in his firm within a short space of time described how the cumulative exhaustion from the first incident was still very much around when the second broke. He found himself thinking, 'Not again,' but at the same time, 'Oh, OK – I know I can do this.'

His experience that emotional exhaustion was still present months after a difficult situation is over is very realistic. Once a situation has been dealt with and things are pretty much back to normal, or some way has been found to deal with them, the relief can lead to a belief that we are quite back to normal ourselves. At this point we don't realise that our perception is distorted so we are unable to see our own dysfunction. We might continue with excessive leaning on stimulants to get us through, and still experience disturbed sleep patterns.

Also at this stage the delayed emotional and physical reactions from the initial 'shock' phase can kick in, bringing waves of tiredness. 'I felt "dead"' was how one man described it.

Even two or three years after a seriously difficult situation, a loss of confidence can still be felt. I listened recently to two competent and self-aware professional women comparing notes. They had each gone through quite separate prolonged difficult situations, in both cases involving sustained personal criticism. One commented, 'I know that I am not as confident as I used to be when I'm speaking in public, though it's gradually coming back.' The other agreed, 'I'm aware that I'm not putting myself forward in the way that I used to.'

At this stage, the impact on *role* and *relationships* is going to be just as strong, but possibly less obvious. David's approach to management was goal-oriented: 'When a situation arose, I would sort out how to deal with it and move on.' Faced with an ongoing situation involving someone who frequently exhibited difficult behaviour, he had to come to terms with the fact that a different role was demanded of him – containing rather than solving.

> When it started I hoped that once we understood the problem properly, we could solve it. Later it was clear that it was not going to be solved, so my role was to manage and contain the ongoing difficult situation. It was depressing to think that it would probably go on for ever.

As manager or leader in an organisation, the ongoing effects will still be with you, but others are likely to forget this. Relationships can change as a result.

> Wendy was a highly approachable tea-shop manager, who ran her small team in a friendly and co-operative manner. Her difficult situation emerged when she became suspicious that one of the staff was molesting children. After agonising, she contacted the police whose investigations finally led to a prison sentence. However, the other staff, as well as the customers, had not believed the allegations to be true, with the result that some regular customers stopped coming in and a couple of staff left for other jobs. A year later, Wendy found herself wondering what was wrong because she had ongoing anxiety, and her husband had difficulty persuading her to go out at the weekend with him because she felt people didn't like her.

Relationships can also be affected where there are long-term complicated confidentiality issues. As leader/manager you will need to go on keeping your guard and monitoring how you respond to enquiries, comments or criticisms.

What does 'normal' mean for me?

So far, I have described some recognised 'normal' responses to shock and stress. However, our individual reactions will differ depending on our personality and usual way of functioning. My 'normal' is likely to be different from yours. We can be surprised by reactions, our own or other people's because under stress some people become *more* like their usual self while others become *less* so. It can be helpful for you and those around you if you are familiar with your own tendencies.[1]

1. The Gilmore Fraleigh 'Style Profile' work is easily accessible and makes a useful distinction between typical reactions when life is calm and when it is stormy. See, for example, Gilmore, S. K. and Fraleigh, P. W. (2004), *Style Profile for Communication at Work* (USA: Friendly Press). The Mennonite Centre in London has a good book service. www.metanoiabooks.org.uk

Approaching self-care

Seeing the wood for the trees

Whatever the difficult situation that now faces you as manager/leader, some of the following are likely to be true:

The difficult situation . . .	*. . . the consequence*
You have neither chosen nor planned this. Any plans you had for this week/ month/period are now up in the air. So . . .	. . . you experience a loss of control.
Your sphere of contact is suddenly bigger. This might be your first experience of dealing with police, social workers and the media as well as church authorities, senior colleagues, your organisation's hierarchy. So . . .	. . . you are on a steep learning curve.
Your 'day job' responsibilities continue. There might be no immediate colleague to share with or delegate to. In organisations with a strong culture of self-sufficiency, like the Church, it can be difficult to hand over responsibilities. Also you will need to respond to others, who will want to talk about what is going on. So . . .	. . . your overall workload increases, while the time available to do it decreases.
Because the difficult situation is by definition unusual and serious, you are likely to be operating at the edge of or just outside your competency zone. So . . .	. . . you need to be extra alert.
As leader, you are expected to pick your way wisely through complexity. So . . .	. . . you need time for reflection when there probably isn't any.
As leader, you are expected to make the *right* decisions, in the *right* way for everyone, at the *right* time. So . . .	. . . you are bound to fail.

Some people thrive on the roller-coaster experience of a crisis, shown in the right-hand column; others don't. Whichever category you come into, if you want to do as good a job as possible, while keeping an eye on your sanity and health, it makes sense to take time to assess, or 'map' both the situation and yourself.

Mapping the situation

Assessing the demands of the difficult situation and the resources available

Different people will be caught up in the difficult situation, not necessarily all part of your organisation. It helps to be clear where the lines of responsibility lie between these people, and what the roles are. You might need to have different roles at different times and in different relationships. Some of these will be incompatible.

'I offered pastoral support,' (to the church member and her husband, who had been accused of an offence), 'but later they didn't want to talk to me' (the minister was asked to give evidence in court). Churches are often unclear organisations, with a volunteering culture that can take good practice for granted rather than setting out clear guidelines.

What follows are suggestions for structured ways of making sure you are clear about the elements of the difficult situation. It is sensible to look at these with someone else, or to ask someone else to look at your answers. Two heads really are better than one once a difficult situation is underway. If you can make yourself do some of this, so that you are reasonably confident that you have considered most aspects, it will help you channel your energy where it is needed; for example, by clarifying priorities and deciding what interventions *you* should make.

Try answering these questions:

- *Who* and *what* are being affected by this difficult situation? List these. For example: the victim, the perpetrator, colleagues of either – senior or junior, families, neighbours, church members, yourself, any children, the domestic situation, the project, the rota, the corner shop . . . think beyond the obvious.

- What are the *needs* of each person or project? This can be set out in a new column or in a different colour.
- *Whose responsibility* is it to meet each of these? Use a third column or colour.

You should now be able to see two things clearly: firstly, which needs are not being met; secondly, where *your* responsibilities lie. Now you can make some decisions. If your name appears in the third column as being responsible for meeting all the needs, your first decisions will be about priorities, support and delegation; if it appears against some but not others, you can focus just where you need to and point people in other directions if they come to you inappropriately.

> When tragedy struck a retired Anglican priest and his wife, the local vicar visited and the bishop kept in touch. It was the churchwarden who realised after a few days that the couple's niece was the one who was bearing the brunt of the situation, but no one had been in touch with her.

Which legal or organisational policies or guidelines, if any, require compliance?

- Child protection policy
- Vulnerable adults
- Health and safety
- Good practice guidelines
- Grievance and disciplinary procedures
- Staff handbook
- Any other

If you are not sure, then consult with any designated advisers in these areas, or your human resources department or equivalent.

> 'We had a good child protection policy, which I followed, and I consulted with independent advisers recommended by my organisation. My main advice to others is to make sure you have a robust child protection policy.'

What resources are available through your organisation?

These might be designated officers like the child protection officer, someone in the legal or human resources department, specialist advisers in pastoral care or communications, mental health or a particular chaplaincy.

Perhaps you have an in-house peer supervision scheme or mentor who can provide a sounding board. A senior colleague might know of others who have been through something similar.

Your organisation might have an arrangement with a counselling agency.

Which outside agencies and experts are involved? What is your role with them? How can you check this out?

> 'Some of the "experts" were actually pretty unhelpful, and at the start there was a lot of disorganisation.'
>
> 'Whenever the media contacted I made sure I took a brief thinking space and rang them back with my response.'
>
> 'At times my role was very clear, for example at the funeral *(this is a minister speaking)*. At other times it was much less so, and I had to work out what I was offering. I checked with the police to make sure my responses wouldn't get in their way. For some of the time my role was providing a place for the other professionals to meet over coffee.'

What are the lines of responsibility and accountability inside your organisation?

Identify the person to whom you are accountable, and/or the person who acts as your line manager or equivalent. Next, identify who is accountable to you and who you are responsible for. In the current difficult situation, can you work out what each of these people should know, and what each should be doing? This will remind you who needs briefing about what, and might help you ask for what you need from senior management.

> 'I sent the bishop all the relevant papers *(an Anglican priest is talking about a situation that had been going on for many months)* but he hadn't read them before our meeting. He expressed no concern about my well-being, nor did he express his confidence in me or the way I was handling the situation.

This quotation demonstrates how simple it can be to offer support to junior colleagues or staff members, if you remember to do it: express concern about their well-being, and (if you can) express your confidence in them.

The drama triangle

This schematic way of analysing situations can be very helpful when you are trying to map a difficult situation, particularly when things seem stuck, or you find yourself responding in ways you are not happy with. As its name suggests, the 'drama triangle' looks at the role people *actually* find themselves playing. This will probably be different from the role they *think* they are taking.

Without realising it, people can slip into one of the three positions shown in the drama triangle, '**persecutor**', '**rescuer**' or '**victim**'. They then find that they are thinking and feeling just what the named role suggests. The added difficulty is that the roles can quickly swap round. If you can spot which role you are playing, you are well on the way to being able to do something positive about it.

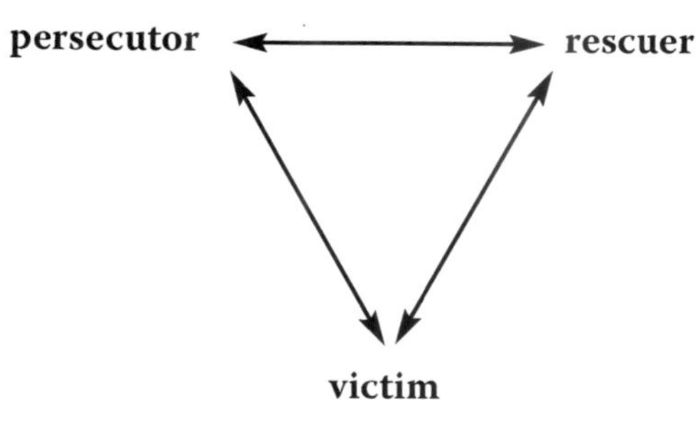

The best way to explain how the triangle can form and the havoc it then causes is with an example where there is an ongoing difficult situation.

I have chosen a church context here, but you will see how it could occur in any organisation:

> Alan is a difficult person in the church. He is latching on to Mary, your friendly pastoral assistant, who is starting to feel hounded. Others are worried about her. You need to take some action.

Here the roles are Alan – **persecutor**; Mary – **victim**; you – **rescuer.**

> You have a quiet word with Alan, who takes offence and complains about you to Mary, who reassures him.

Now you are **persecutor**, Alan is **victim** and Mary is **rescuer**.

> When others in the congregation see that the situation hasn't changed, they berate you and Mary defends you.

Here is a new triangle: you are now **victim**, Mary remains **rescuer** and the congregation becomes **persecutor**.

> You feel depressed and misunderstood and start to think about a change of job.

You have by now behaved, thought, felt or been seen as, in turn, a **rescuer**, a **persecutor** and a **victim**. You've paid a pretty high emotional cost, but the difficult situation remains exactly what it was.

How can you change this into a 'winners triangle'? One of the three players must stop trying to change the others and concentrate on changing their own behaviour. In the drama triangle the **victim** acts as if she does not have the resources to solve the problem – she feels without thinking; the **rescuer** takes too much responsibility for someone else and ignores his own needs; the **persecutor** is absorbed in his own needs and disregards others.

The 'winners triangle' shows how each player *can* make a change:

- the **victim** can become **vulnerable** – recognise his bad feelings – but think sensibly about how to get help to do something about it;
- the **rescuer** can become **caring** – show concern and offer help – but within her own limits and without taking over;
- the **persecutor** can become **assertive** – find ways of getting his needs met – but without bullying or punishing others.

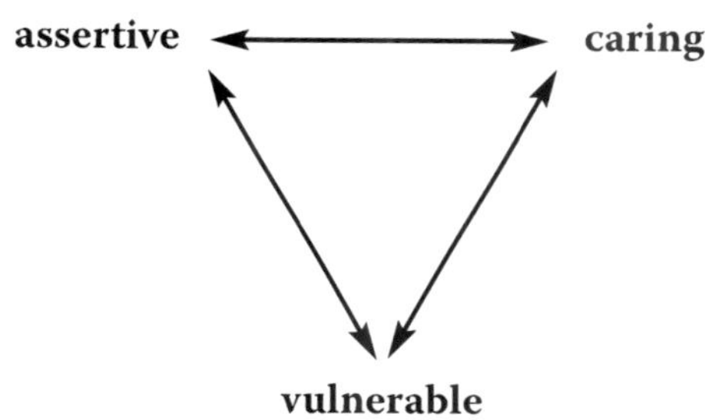

In our scenario, we can rerun the events like this, showing how you can make changes:

> Alan is a difficult person in the congregation; he is latching on (**persecuting**) to Mary, your friendly pastoral assistant, who is starting to feel hounded (**victim**). You need to take some action (**rescue**).

Rerun:

> You spend time with Mary, listening carefully to her predicament but not solving the problem for her; thus she is enabled to think clearly (as well as feel strongly) and she discovers she has some ideas about what to do.

You've become **caring** instead of the **rescuer**; Mary is **vulnerable** but not **victim.**

or this:

> You have a quiet word with Alan, who takes offence and complains about you to Mary, who reassures him. Now you are **persecutor**, Alan is **victim** and Mary is **rescuer**.

Rerun:

> You go back to Alan, and explain clearly and calmly what your concerns are about his behaviour and why you have spoken with him. You understand that he is angered by your earlier conversation. You wonder what ideas he has about how you both can address the situation.

You've become **assertive** instead of **persecutor**; Alan has the opportunity to solve his own problems, rather than become **victim**.

or this:

> When others in the congregation see that the situation hasn't changed, they berate you and Mary defends you. Here is a new triangle: you are now **victim**, Mary remains **rescuer** and the congregation becomes **persecutor**.

Rerun:

> You realise you're feeling helpless and phone your peer supervisor to help you think through what's happened. As the conversation progresses, you can see what's been happening, and you recognise how your role has changed. You decide this is not as serious as you first thought, that you are actually competent in ministry, and that you will take your time to decide how or whether to respond to the critics.

You've become **vulnerable** not **victim.**

Mapping yourself

Suggestions for assessing how you function

This is not the moment to go in for prolonged self-awareness exercises. If you are interested in that, you are likely to have done this already on other occasions; if you are not, you will be tempted to skip this part. However, this section should be helpful whatever you are like: if you are already familiar with this material, it will give you a quick route to remind yourself of what is currently relevant; if this is new to you, it should give you some pointers that you can use fairly easily to help in the current difficult situation.

There are three areas it is worth mapping here: personality, past experiences and current events in your personal life.

Personality

There are various personality typing theories, which give you some sense of how you 'tick'.[1] If you are familiar with one of these, take a moment to revisit its insights, to remind yourself how you function under normal conditions, what sort of behaviours you are likely to exhibit under duress and what resources you need to draw on to thrive. But you don't need to know the theories to think about what you are like when you are in leadership role. Calm? Organised? Focused? Chaotic? Dominating? If in doubt, just ask a friend or colleague how they would describe you. Then consider what you are like when under stress. The same or different? More organised? Anxious? Deadpan? Like a headless chicken?

Even a small amount of awareness can help you and those around you make sure that you access the right sort of resources in a difficult situation. What is right for you might not be obvious to you or those around you.

> As head teacher, Jill likes to know precisely what is going on in her primary school and has a tendency to micromanage. Under duress, she does this even more. When the difficult situation erupted, her colleagues tried to help by protecting her from routine school issues. However, this only made her more

1. Most familiar are Myers-Briggs Type Indicator and the Enneagram. Gilmore Fraleigh, mentioned before, is more concerned with communication styles than personality.

> stressed. Jill also likes to think things through alone first rather than talk with others. Her deputy head now recognises that the best way she can support Jill is by keeping her fully briefed on the day-to-day school issues and by asking her when she would like to discuss things.

It is useful to know whether you would normally change behaviour under stress or remain the same. If you are not sure what you do, ask someone who lives with you or has worked with you for a while.

> 'I am normally a focused achiever at work. But I become an indecisive procrastinator under stress. My husband, in contrast, simply becomes even more of a focused achiever when under stress, and works determinedly through what needs to be done.'

It's also worth being clear about how others can help you when you are in stress conditions. The 'focused achiever' just quoted went on to explain that under stress:

> 'What I need from others is affirmation. I want someone to ask me how I am and tell me that I can do it. What he needs is to be left alone, free to ignore everyone, until things are back under control. For some years, when either of us was under stress, I offered him encouragement and he left me alone – exactly the opposite of what was helpful. The resulting mutual incomprehension simply added to the difficulties.'

Knowing what your likely behaviour is – and also what you most need from the people around you – can help. If you and those you live or work with can recognise this, expectations are realistic and many crossed wires (and cross exchanges) can be avoided.

Relevant past experiences

Our past experience is bound to be relevant to our current situation in ways that we will be more or less conscious of. If you have gone through difficult situations before, you will bring the learning from that into the present. However, there might well be previous experiences which although entirely dissimilar from what is happening now, will still affect how you are currently responding.

Experiences of being under pressure

Cast your mind back – there are probably times in your life when you have had to find extra resilience under pressure. When you have remembered one, answer these questions:

- How did I behave during that time? Was this helpful?
- What and/or who helped me get through that time?
- In what ways was I strong in that situation?
- In what ways was I vulnerable?

It is likely that your answers will give you guidance about how to approach the current difficult situation so that you can maintain your sanity and perform as well as possible.

> 'I was determined not to give in to depression, so I didn't tell anyone. I just made myself get on with each day's work and read funny novels to take my mind off what was happening.'

This person worked through the emotional demands on her own, and this drew from her strengths. So she can probably trust her instincts to do the same this time. However, someone else said:

> 'I was determined not to give in to depression, so I didn't tell anyone. But I just felt worse and worse because I was so isolated and lonely and in the end I couldn't get out of bed and had to see the doctor. I felt really stupid.'

When a new stressful situation arises, this person needs to recognise her vulnerability and make it a priority to identify trustworthy others with whom she can share.

Other previous experiences

Our present is inevitably affected by our past experiences. You don't need to sign up to psychoanalytic theory to see the truth in this. We are often quite unaware that we are reacting to people or situations in an inconsistent way. The phrase 'learned behaviour' is useful here. This simply describes the way that when the *dynamic* is the same or similar to something we have experienced previously, we will *react* in a way similar to our previous behaviour. The familiar phrase 'that pushes my button' describes how each of us has our own sensitive spots that are unrelated to the person who we are with.

Sometimes these are superficial: for example, I will react strongly to a tone of voice that sounds like a frightening teacher from my past; you won't even notice. Others are more engrained.

> Andy, a Baptist minister, has a current long-term difficult situation: someone with a borderline personality disorder[1] has joined every church group and attends every meeting, causing anxiety and distress. Andy makes excuses, ignoring evidence of distress and not wanting to talk about it when colleagues try to raise the issue. He is usually assertive and decisive. Andy grew up in a family which dealt with the alcoholism of the uncle who lived with them by trying to ignore it. Excuses were made, evidence was covered up, no one talked about it and everyone lived as if it wasn't happening.

Under stress, Andy's unconsciously 'learned behaviour' predominates.

Relevant current experiences

Sometimes our personal and professional lives can experience a kind of subterranean crossover, which we experience emotionally rather than rationally.

1. People with borderline personality disorder have difficulties with emotion regulation. They also have difficulties with boundaries, are prone to addictive and self-defeating behaviours, and have a tendency to idealise and then reject significant people in their lives. They fear abandonment, and have often been victims of abuse or disorganised parenting in their childhood. They have a fragile sense of self and can have destabilising or destructive effects in churches or organisations.

> Tim Basker is senior partner in a small firm of solicitors which retains the sense of a family-run business. One autumn, three colleagues leave, all for good reasons (move to another area, maternity leave, retirement). Tim's been in the legal business for 25 years, has seen colleagues come and go many times and can't understand why he feels so hollow and depressed. He's even snapping uncharacteristically at everyone. A friend points out that during the summer Tim's son has emigrated to Canada and his daughter has left home to work in Scotland after finishing her college course.

The hollow sensations have crossed over from home to work.

Take a moment to scan what's going on in your life at the moment. Are you or members of your family in a significant transition stage (for example, children leaving home, important anniversaries, retirements, new jobs, marriages, new generations being born, parents dying)? Or perhaps other members of the family or close friends have just been through restructuring at work, or redundancy, or financial difficulties. Perhaps someone you care about has experienced something traumatic. If any of these is part of your 'wallpaper' at the moment, this could impact on how you are experiencing the current difficult situation, with crossover feelings and reactions.

Seeking outside help

The goal of self-care is to manage our lives and work in such a way that seeking appropriate outside help is simply a normal part of how we live. It makes good sense to have someone you can talk to, especially in difficult situations. Sometimes a good friend, line manager, supervisor or spiritual director can be helpful, when we need to vent, explore options, or reflect on how we have handled a problem. Booking some sessions with a counsellor can offer similar help. Given the stresses and the range of demands made on professionals today, a number of roles have been developed which can be a support for people in management.

Non-managerial supervision

Many healthcare professionals make use of 'non-managerial supervision'. Non-managerial supervision is a relationship entered into between someone in work or ministry and another professional with (usually) more experience, whose role is to help the supervisee to reflect on their work and to explore areas of conflict, tension, stress or difficulty.[1] It provides a level of professional accountability and support, which is not confused with the managerial accountability that is owed to your boss or employee. It is preferable that the person who is invited to be the supervisor does not have another relationship with the person seeking supervision – for example, as friend, manager, priest – as this will result in a dual relationship, which can cloud judgements and interfere with the primary task of helping the professional development of the person seeking supervision. Freedom is required on both sides so that the supervisee can be transparent in what he or she chooses to share or reveal, the supervisor can be appropriately challenging, and the supervisee can risk being vulnerable. This is a requirement in some professions – for example, counselling – and is increasingly made use of by people in ministry. 'Peer review' or 'ministerial review' is a modified version of this that has been introduced in some church contexts.

Coaching

Coaching is a relatively new area. Ilona Boniwell writes, 'Coaching aims to produce fast personality changes through the setting and acquisition of goals. It is explicitly concerned with the promotion of well-being and performance.'[2] Working with a coach may help to improve work-life balance, to identify goals for personal and professional development, and explore aspects of personality and behaviour that are preventing goals being achieved.

1. http://www.infed.org/biblio/functions_of_supervision.htm
2. Boniwell, I. (2006). *Positive Psychology in a Nut-Shell* (London: Personal Well-Being Centre).

Burnout

Unfortunately many individuals who work in the caring professions, especially those with responsibility for management, can suffer from what is known as burnout. Burnout has been identified as a syndrome that involves emotional exhaustion, a loss of a sense of self and reduced personal accomplishment. It tends to develop over time, with a slow erosion of spirit, loss of idealism, possibly cynicism and lack of a sense of efficacy or agency (a belief that my work is making a difference). Burnout has been seen as a maladaptive response to stress. Once stress becomes overwhelming, one way of coping is to 'switch off'.

Burnout is a serious psychological condition, with one study showing that 14% of the Catholic priests who responded to a survey saying that they felt burned out from their parish ministry and a further 16% saying they were uncertain.[1] In a study of Australian, New Zealand and English clergy it was noted that 7% reported feeling filled with sadness they could not explain.[2] This represents a significant number of clergy who are at the very least unhappy, and possibly suffering from some kind of mental health problem. Burnout also affects doctors, nurses, teachers, social workers and other people in the caring professions. When someone reaches the stage of burnout, an intervention from a line manager may be necessary. It is often difficult for people to realise how far they have slipped into the state of burnout, as they may continue to function, but at considerable personal cost and with reduced effectiveness. Treatment for someone in this situation will probably involve time off from work or ministry and individual and/or group therapy. Employers may be able to make use of Employee Assistance Programmes, or organisations such as the College of Counsellors in Durham Diocese, which was set up to provide counselling support for clergy, clergy families and other church members.

1. Loudon, S. H. and Francis, L. J. (2003). *The Naked Parish Priest* (London: Continuum).
2. Francis, L. J., Kaldor, P., Robbins, M. and Castle, K. (2005). 'Happy but exhausted? Work-related psychological health among clergy', *Pastoral Sciences*, 24, 2 pp. 101–120.

A Christian response

Christians have mixed reactions to the idea of 'self-care'.

Surely, we say, we are meant to 'take up our cross, lay down our life, turn the other cheek, go the extra mile'? Don't we believe 'it is more blessed to give than to receive'? Isn't 'caring for self' just pandering to selfishness, which is rampant in our individualist, hedonist Western society? The Protestant work ethic still seems to be in our bloodstreams, ensuring niggling guilt when we remove our noses from the grindstone. Over and over again I've witnessed wise and pastoral people encouraging others to care for self, while patently not applying this to themselves. Even those who really believe in self-care inhabit a world (in and out of the Church) that is so busy, complex and demanding that finding ways to look after themselves seems quite unrealistic.

While acknowledging the truth that self-denial is an important part of Christian discipleship, it is also important to remember how at the centre of the Christian faith is the idea of wholeness of life: life lived in proper perspective, acknowledging that power, wisdom and love are sourced in God, seen in Christ and experienced through the Spirit. Life lived in joy and hope of new beginnings. Life lived with energy, against the odds. Life created in the image of God, and therefore complex and always re-patterning. Life full of surprises, but also carrying responsibility. Life that takes in as well as gives out. Life that reflects as well as acts. The second commandment is 'Love your neighbour *as yourself*'. This carries a profound psychological insight, that how we treat ourselves is linked with how we are able to treat others. The need to have some rhythm to life is central to the Jewish-Christian understanding in the commandment to keep the Sabbath holy, in order to regain energy and perspective and savour life. 'Even the horses need to rest on a Sunday,' my farming grandfather used to say.

In other words 'self-care' is *not* the same as 'selfish'.

Practical suggestions

This section is set out as lists, with quotes where people have made suggestions from their own experience. This is to encourage you to glance quickly through the headings and see what catches your attention that might be relevant to you or someone you know. There is some overlap between the sections.

For general health

- Be realistic about life being different for a while. Cancel unimportant engagements but keep some fun or social engagements.
- Be realistic about sleep and tiredness. It is normal to have disturbed sleep and easier if you don't try to fight it. The cumulative tiredness is likely to be debilitating.
- Be realistic about eating patterns and using stimulants. It is not a major sin to use stimulants – 'my evening whisky was probably a little bigger than usual'; strong coffee keeps you alert; chocolate has a proven 'feel-good' effect; energy dips are staved off with cake. However, you might not notice that you are becoming dependent on the quick-fix effects of sugar or the relaxing effects of alcohol.
- Be realistic about emotions. They might well go higher and lower than is normal for you. 'Sometimes I got very angry, but couldn't put it anywhere. So I would ring a friend who lived far enough away from us to be safe.' Don't be surprised by your own murderous capacity!
- Be realistic about prayer. If you can, keep the regular rhythms of your spiritual life. If you can't do this, don't waste energy on guilt. Ask someone else to undertake to pray on your behalf over this period. They don't need to know the details of what's going on, so long as they will carry you while you're carrying the weight of this difficult situation.

For general sanity

- Remember the big picture. Who are you? A person loved by God. What is the point of your life? To live life, glorify God, love others and savour the world.

  A concentration-camp survivor described how he found something that the guards could never take away from him – the sun. This helped him survive and kept him sane.
- Remember what normally helps to keep you sane. Do this, at least sometimes.
- Remember to stay in touch with writings, projects and people that are good. This is particularly important if your difficult situation involves violence and evil. 'Whatever is true . . . noble . . . pure . . . lovely . . . admirable . . . etc., think about such things.' (Philippians 4:8)
- Remember to keep your world bigger than the difficult situation.[1] If you have young children, spend time with them; if you don't, at least spend time with friends' children or any people who have no connection with your circumstances.
- Remember to be creative. Play football, write a poem, go for a run, play the piano, tidy the office, buy a potted plant, go into the garden, take a short walk at lunchtime, have a haircut or a manicure . . .
- Remember humour. The power of venting difficult emotions through laughter is well known by those who work in demanding jobs. It can make a difference in short-term difficult situations too.

'Our small voluntary organisation was in chaos – it looked as if it could all close down. When we volunteers met, we told each other the worst stories we'd heard that week, criticised everyone

1. Jerusha Hull McCormack describes this in her book *Grieving – A Beginner's Guide* (Darton, Longman and Todd, 2006). Instead of waiting for the grief – or, in this case, the difficult situation – to diminish in order to have space in life for other things, she suggests deliberately enlarging your world so that the grief or difficult situation does not completely fill it.

in the organisation shamelessly, indulged in outrageous joking, laughed till we were exhausted. But then, after the meeting, we got on with our jobs with the public, who never knew what was happening.'

- Remember the power of routine. 'Keeping going, getting on with the job. We had plenty of services. And being of my tradition *(this was a High Churchman speaking)* really helped, because the daily liturgy gave me a routine.'
- Remember 'the inevitability of invasiveness'. If you are feeling contaminated, with your difficult situation getting under your skin, taking over your life, involving distressing, abusive, violent and evil behaviour, make symbolic separations or 'cut off' points in your life.

  'I used to shower and change my clothes when I got home. It was a sign that my family and I were separate from all that was going on.'

  'When we realised that we were talking about it all the time, even last thing at night before we went to sleep, we knew we had to do something. So we decided we would only talk about it up to supper time. Then the subject was banned.'

For general safety

- Avoid email communication where possible. Once the send button has been clicked, it is uncontrollable.

  'It made the whole thing so much more complicated. Everyone in the organisation suddenly knew something was going on. And the person who was critical of how I was handling the situation used it to lobby support – I decided not to email my responses but to go round and have conversations with people directly.'

- Delegate. Ask someone else to act as go-between.

  'When our daughter was so ill, some close friends took on being our mouthpiece to let people know how things were going. It helped us because we didn't have to tell the story over and over again and keep answering the phone, and it helped other people because they didn't have to worry about disturbing us.'

  'When the situation broke, I rang my colleague and asked him to take over the evening service. He didn't need to know why.'

- Prioritise. Others around you might see more clearly than you how you can do this.
- Listen to someone whose judgement you trust. When your adrenalin is flowing, your own judgement can become skewed. So check your decisions or opinions from time to time.
- Find allies. These are people who can help you protect yourself and others from your limitations.

Personal support

- Support from whom? Identifying and using personal support is a sign of wisdom and strength, not weakness.

  'Use all the resources that are available to you.'

  'The regional minister put me in touch with someone who had been through a similar experience.'

  'I was glad of the peer supervision arrangement I had. He gave me valuable advice and provided a sounding board.'

  'I found someone outside the situation who didn't give me advice. I could just use her as a sounding board. This helped to generate ideas that helped me through the situation.'

  'There were one or two friends, who were far enough away for me to be able to swear, relax, laugh, and share my anger with.'

- Support from senior personnel. The response of the senior person in your organisation who has authority is really important. If there is little support from senior management, take the initiative by requesting support or explore alternative options, rather than wait in frustration.

'It made a big difference when my boss asked me not just about the facts but also "how are you in all this?"'

'The project leader was really on my side . . . he felt genuine concern and understanding.'

- Support from colleagues and staff. Supportive personal encouragement is likely to be lacking, but it boosts energy levels and outlook if it comes.

'My staff team were consistently even-handed in their approach to me and the person who was causing me so much grief. They were right to take this line, but it felt irrationally unfair and I felt unsupported. I wanted them to acknowledge how awful it was for me.

'However, *(the same minister continued)* at a meeting, when the subject was being discussed again, one person articulated their confidence in my leadership through this period. It was very important to me to hear this.'

- Support from family and friends. Experience and expectations are very different when it comes to family support. Responses varied from:

'I deliberately said very little about the situation to my wife and nothing at all to the kids. They all had their own life in the church. They didn't need their church relationships to be confused by knowing about this.'

to:

> 'I could not have got through that period without being able to offload on my wife.'

It's worth asking yourself, 'In what way do I look to my husband/wife/family/friends for support?' And where possible check whether they agree with you.

When the difficult situation is in the public arena

- Be sure to use all the resources that are available to you. Double-check that you have thought of all those within and outside your organisation who can give professional support.
- Be on your guard when connecting with other professionals. A group adrenalin can foster a false sense of importance; the salacious details of a difficult situation can be unnecessarily repeated in the disguise of briefing; 'experts' aren't always helpful; crisis managers don't prevent a lot of disorganisation; professional carers can be competitive in their caring for those at the centre of a difficult situation.
- Be sensible – take advice before responding to the media. At least say, 'I'll ring you back in ten minutes.'
- Be resigned to the fact that you can't exit from the public arena.
- Be clear about your particular roles and responsibilities – and stick to them. Consult with someone you trust before changing your mind, no matter what others say.
- Be able to answer these questions: Who is responsible for: the perpetrator? the victim? the organisation? the other people in the organisation?
- Be expecting misunderstanding and criticism. Difficult situations can lead to opposing reactions in organisations.

'Some people thought he was innocent and others believed he was guilty. Everyone wanted me to talk about it, which I wouldn't. So I was in the wrong with most people.'

'There were different reactions when he came out of prison – some left the church, others were in denial, and others expected a public statement of remorse. I had to find a way of managing the different attitudes.'

(*Two different ministers who had sex offenders in their congregations.*)

- Be aware of your role in any drama triangles (see page 291). To see what roles you are playing, draw out some triangles and discuss it with a colleague.

Talking about it

- Essential talk. It is essential to find someone who can act as a sounding board for thinking straight and making good decisions.
- Essential talk. It is essential to make good decisions about communication, within the organisation and publicly; use the answerphone as a way of keeping control of the process and not being bounced into a decision or a reaction that you might regret.
- Optional talk. It is optional to find someone who can let you unload, without needing to edit what you say.
- Random talk. It is likely that you will be approached at any time by people who will ask you (nosily or caringly) about what's happening. Use honest but general phrases ('It's being hard work – it's very challenging – thank you for your concern – please pray for everyone involved – I am fairly exhausted,' etc.). If you give too much detail, you will use up precious emotional energy.
- Talk with your partner. If you are going to talk with someone you live with, decide when and even where you are going to discuss it. Don't talk late at night or in your bedroom – having

your bedroom 'invaded' by the perpetrators or victims of the situation is probably not a good idea.

In church contexts

- Remember that although you are the minister, you are not God.
- Remember that although you are not God, others will expect you to be. You see yourself as 'just an ordinary person', but others probably don't see you like this. As minister, you will already be on the receiving end of others' expectations, projections and assumptions, for good and ill. Sometimes this is right – for example, a leader needs to take a certain amount of unfair criticism without cracking. Sometimes this is disabling – for example, when the congregation members leave responsibility for each other's well-being entirely to the minister and blame them when they fail to deliver.
- Remember self-awareness and self-regulation will stand you in good stead.
- Remember normal habits might not work – for example, regular time off, transparency in management, keeping the peace between groups.

Paying attention to the whole person

As a leader during a difficult situation, you will be maintaining a 'non-anxious presence'[1] which helps to reduce other people's anxiety. This is demanding work. These tips for paying attention to yourself can help.

- Notice what you are thinking *and* what you are feeling. These can help you understand and respond to the situation.
- Stay in your body – listen to it. Aches in head, stomach or back will give you clues about the stress you are carrying. Don't ignore these – even acknowledging that they are there will help.

1. This phrase is used to describe what a mediator offers in conflict transformation work. It provides a succinct summary of what a good leader can offer during a difficult situation.

- Acknowledge the discomfort of experiencing conflicting emotions and thoughts.
- Be kind to yourself.
- Stay connected – with yourself and with others.
- Take account of just how much the emotional energy you are expending is taking out of you. The incident is likely to take its toll. Remember how teachers are often ill in the first week of their holidays!

  'It was still very vivid long afterwards.'

  'I couldn't understand why I felt so low the summer after it had all happened.'

- Be prepared for the long haul. Whatever your difficult situation, it is likely to take much longer to resolve than you anticipate.
- Look for a way of processing the experience later when there's opportunity.

  'Writing about it was very helpful.'

Conclusion

I have written about several principles of self-care. Far from being self-indulgence, self-care is both necessary and godly. A certain amount of self-awareness is helpful. Even under time pressure, it is worth taking a step back, probably with the help of someone else, to assess both the situation and yourself before you make swift decisions. Dealing with a difficult situation will probably take more out of you than you would think possible – emotionally, physically, mentally and spiritually. Make allowances for a recovery period when the repercussions of your exhaustion will go on making an impact.

Much of this applies anyway to us all as we face the normal challenge of finding a sane and deep Christian path in our multi-demanding organisations. When you hold a managerial or leadership role you owe it to your staff, colleagues or congregations as well as to yourself, your family and friends, to be as fit as you can be to deal with these demands competently and safely. So it is particularly important to find a way of applying some of these principles when an out-of-the-ordinary difficult situation arises.

Recommended reading

- Dr Ruth Fowke has written very accessible short books that look at the issues of stress and Christian faith – for example, *The Last Straw* (Eagle, 2000).
- Daniel Goleman's *Emotional Intelligence* (Bloomsbury, 1996) is the classic on the importance of taking whole-person responses seriously.
- Robert J. Wicks has written a book for counsellors and mental health professionals entitled *The Resilient Counsellor* (Oxford University Press, 2008). It contains wise advice for all managers and clergy who find themselves in stressful situations.

Website

www.alban.org – For those working in churches and other Christian organisations, the Alban Institute, an American publisher, has an excellent range of books on 'practical knowledge in leadership and congregational life'.

Practical Theology

Alan Bartlett

What is 'theology'?

I recently found myself listening to a political discussion on the radio, and one of the speakers said, 'We must not get lost in the theology of this issue.' The speaker was not talking about real theology – the relationship of God to the issue in question. Rather he meant that we must not get lost in minutiae or fantasy, inward-looking conversation or obsession with fine judgements of right and wrong. In other words, 'theology' has become a metaphor for irrelevant, introverted and inappropriate talk – as opposed to mature, well-grounded, proportionate and action-creating discussion.

Laurie Green, in his classic book *Let's Do Theology*, opens with a lament which is heard again and again in the life of the Church, from surveys of preaching to responses to official church reports:

> I am often struck by the church notice board slogan which reads, 'Christ is the Answer.' I suspect that many would be prompted to respond, 'Yes, but does the Church know what the question is?'[1]

This is a tragedy. It is partly, of course, a product of the Church's obsession with internal arguments – and the obsessive nature of these arguments – but it also results from the Church's amateurism when talking about real life. The Church (and I write this chapter as an English Anglican priest) is heard as not just believing impossible things but trying to connect them to real life in crass ways. I hope this book is a good example of how the

1. Green, L. (2002). *Let's Do Theology* (London and New York: Continuum), p. 1.

Church can reclaim the language of 'theology', so that it becomes what it should always have meant: serious conversation about the relationship between God and the real lives of 'ordinary' human beings. And this is purposeful serious conversation, because it is about helping people to find methods and resources which will enable genuine encounters with God in the midst of the reality of everyday living, and further, to reflect on real life and these divine encounters so as to enable wiser living. This is Practical Theology. This book is Practical Theology.[1]

1. My specific debts to colleagues and students are acknowledged below, but it is crucial to say at this stage, that any of my insights into Practical Theology owe everything to my work on the master's and doctoral programmes delivered in Durham by the theological colleges – Cranmer Hall, Ushaw College and the Wesley Study Centre – in collaboration with the University Department of Theology and Religion. Two particular colleagues, Fr Chris Hughes and the Revd Dr Roger Walton have been very influential in this work and in my education. I am also very grateful to my colleagues Dr Jocelyn Bryan and Dr Brendan Geary, FMS, for their own rich contributions to my education and for inviting me to contribute a chapter to this book.

What is Practical Theology?

You will have noticed common patterns in the chapters in this book. They all begin with careful professional attention to the reality of human experience. (By 'professional' I mean disciplined, accountable to some set of objective standards – both academic and corporate – and reliable.) We might be personally unused to starting theological conversation with experience, but it has become a mainstream way of doing theology. We might also be unused to this sort of professional human sciences discussion in church documents, though it exists quite widely.[1] I want to suggest that this way of doing theology is just as theological as the classic way, of beginning with Scripture and Tradition and then 'applying' it to our lives, and, more strongly, that it is in fact essential for the life and mission of the modern Church and the society in which we are set. Christians cannot comment on the relationship of God to human situations unless they have informed themselves about the reality of these situations.

Often the reality of these situations is part of the experience of Christians themselves. Whilst it might be possible to read this book as if difficult experiences happen to people outside the Church, the truth is that Christians are not immune, for example, from addictive problems. Part of the difficulty when doing this sort of theological work is enabling Christians to talk about, in appropriate contexts, of course, their real experiences as opposed to the Christian image.

But even if the experience is not something which I, as a Christian, have experienced myself, I can still be enabled to understand it, when it is empathetically presented in a disciplined way. I wonder, where were you surprised as you read this book? Were you surprised by the description of gambling? Not just by the extent of gambling, but by the way gambling addictions can be related to other experiences in a person's life? By the way in which gambling becomes a mechanism for finding psychological relief and so by the way in which gambling becomes addictive? Or were you shaken by the description of the extent of domestic violence and how it

1. Note, for example, the careful research which is included within the recent ecumenical report *Faithful Cities* (Peterborough: Methodist Publishing House; London: Church House Publishing, 2006).

needs to be understood against the background of the long history of unequal gendered relationships between men and women; or, to look at that from another angle, were you surprised by the way Christian theology has often been used to justify what now seems utterly abhorrent behaviour? Coming to understand that sad fact is part of our Christian task of coming to understand this very painful human experience.

One of my own frequent experiences, when working with students in Practical Theology, is that the first deep point of learning comes from beginning to understand an issue in all its reality and complexity. 'So that's what it's really like!' This comes not just from hearing about the experiences but also from beginning to analyse them and place them in a conceptual framework.

The Pastoral Cycle

A frequently used model for this way of doing theology is the 'Pastoral Cycle'.

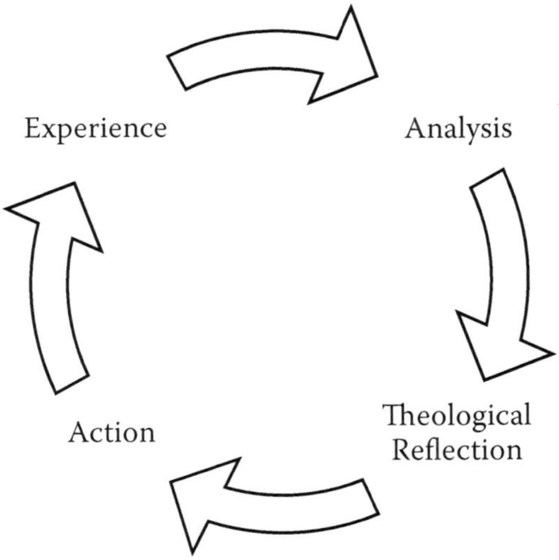

Diagram 1: The Pastoral Cycle

We start with an experience. It can be a crisis experience when something has gone wrong or it can be a routine experience which we want to understand better. Often it is an experience which feels slightly at odds with our understanding of how the world, and God, ought to be. In Practical Theology, we pay careful attention to this experience, to make sure that we have really seen and heard what happened, and then we try to understand it by putting it in a wider framework. For example, in the chapter on 'difficult people', we first see what such people do and how they impact on others. Then we try to understand this behaviour. Here we normally use tools from other disciplines – in this case, psychology – to help us to understand that these are not just individual or random behaviours but can be 'explained' in terms of people's life experiences or the pattern of their personalities and relationships. This is the 'analysis' section of the Pastoral Cycle.

We then find ourselves trying to make sense of this theologically, and exploring our Christian beliefs and values to help guide our actions. At this point, there is often a dialogue. Our response to, for example, a 'difficult person' may be either to try to love them out of their wounded-ness – because Jesus taught us to 'love our neighbour' and even our 'enemy' – or to try to help them to change by telling them the 'truth in love'. As you will see from the chapter, either of these actions could produce the opposite reaction to the one intended by the caring Christian. And then we may find ourselves slipping back into being just pragmatic: we ignore, sideline or sack the 'difficult person' because they are a nuisance. Or we may find ourselves being 'super-spiritual' and praying for certain forms of miraculous healing and behaving unrealistically while we wait for this prayer to be 'answered'. Whereas the question we ought really to be asking ourselves is: 'What would it mean to care Christianly for such a person, with wise and professional insight?' For example, as Christian Practical Theologians, we might ask, 'What can we honestly and realistically hope for as "redemption" for such a person?'

I need to stress here that the theological section of the Pastoral Cycle is very demanding: it is demanding because we are firing questions at Scripture and Tradition and not wanting to get simplistic answers – because that would be at odds both with real life but also with the professionalism with which the rest of our Practical Theology work has been done. But it is also demanding because whilst we are trusting that Scripture and Tradition will have true and wise things to say about real human beings, it is not always easy to discern this wisdom. For example, as part of our answer to the question about 'difficult people', we would have to ask both what Scripture and Tradition say about caring for deeply wounded or even mentally unwell people, and also how do these ideas make sense in the twenty-first century when our understanding of human nature has moved on beyond, say, ancient beliefs in demon possession or the four 'humours'?

Finally we resolve on the action we will take in the situation. But, of course, once we begin to plan the action, and even more as we implement it, we will have new experiences to analyse and reflect on, so the process kicks on again. (In fact, the Pastoral Cycle is better described as the Pastoral Spiral but we will stick to the original phrase because it is so widely used.) This cycle is used by Practical Theologians. But it is also used by all sorts of other professionals and carers.[1] Its objective is to train 'reflective practitioners' – that is, people who have learned to look carefully at a situation and then to analyse it before taking action, and then to review their action.

Good Practical Theology

But how do we do good – that is, reliable and wise – Practical Theology? I often find myself saying to students, 'Keep your theology on hold until you have some understanding of the issue in question.' This sounds strange to, for example, young ordinands but it is crucial, though it needs careful explanation. Any one of us can fall into the bad habit of making snap judgements. But we can be particularly prone to this if we have strong opinions in an area or if it is an area of human experience about which we are ignorant or indifferent. For a variety of reasons, I have no understanding of the excitement of gambling. Therefore I need to be alert to my tendency to make simplistic moral judgements – 'just tell them to stop!' A sharper example is in the area of our response to those who commit child abuse. We assume that we know what we are talking about and that the explanation (and remedy) is clear and simple. This is hugely reinforced if we have strong theological convictions – for example, about the nature of

1. See the classic book Schon, D. A. (1991). *The Reflective Practitioner: How Professionals think in action* (Aldershot: Ashgate).

sin and of God's response to it. Therefore, we 'see' the people involved and the issue in a certain way, because we come to it, to use a familiar metaphor, with a strong set of spectacles. But we may be wrong. We may be at risk of misinterpreting actions or words because we are so sure of our interpretation. Therefore, we need to be careful to stop and check. As my father-in-law, who had worked in industry as well as in the Church, said often, 'There are always simple answers to complex questions. They're just normally wrong!'

A good metaphor for Practical Theology is a set of traffic lights.[1] The first light is red. It warns us to stop and look. 'Do not proceed until you have looked, because you may have an accident.' Each of the chapters in this book asks you to stop and look first, before you come to a judgement. Again, this may feel unnatural, especially if we are 'people of action' or if the situation is pressing. The red light requires us to stop the forward motion until we are safe to proceed. This is a spiritual as well as an intellectual discipline.

Another way of describing this is to use a long-standing Catholic model of Practical Theology, whose origins lay in the difficult context of struggles in post-First World War Belgian industry. It is: 'See. Judge. Act.'[2] Cardinal Cardijn trained his Young Christian Workers to learn to look first. What are the economics of this industry? What are the causes of the high numbers of industrial injuries or the endemic unemployment? This will lead us on to asking deeper questions. Where does the power lie in this situation? Why does the power lie there? Is this balance of power unchangeable (as we are often told)? Are there alternatives? I believe very strongly that we must see and understand first, and then the theological thinking will be talking directly to the world as it is, not to some idealised or sanitised version. The best examples of Practical Theology are those which have thought with such clarity about the human experiences that they have crystallised the issues which are at stake. What is the 'what-is-

1. I am deeply indebted to my colleague, the Revd Dr Stephen Cherry, Director of Training in the Diocese of Durham, for sharing this image with me and for giving me permission to share it in print.

2. See Hughes, C. 'The Roman Catholic Church and its practices: Some aspects of a Roman Catholic approach to Practical Theology' in Bartlett, A., Hughes, C. and Walton, R. (forthcoming) (Eds.). *Real God, Real World* (London: SPCK.

ness' in this situation? Then we can take these issues to our theology and begin the search for insight. Notice how the chapters on addiction have to wrestle with the question of what addiction is, before they can find the best theology to illuminate the issue. This is good Practical Theology.

I need to make two important qualifications to my argument at this point. First, whilst we restrain the introduction of theological insights at the beginning of a Practical Theology process, we acknowledge that the reason we care about an issue in the first place is because of the love of God in Christ embodied in who we already are as Christian human beings within the Church. I am shaken by the stories of abuse because my conscience has already been sensitised by God in my creation and in the Church. Second, we must recognise that even 'objective' analyses of human situations have values embedded deep within them. When we, as Christians, draw on the insights of, for example, psychology when understanding a situation, we need to do so alert to the values which are assumed in that discipline. Psychology is a huge and varied discipline but some elements within it have been critical of or even hostile to religious belief and, at its worst, there can be a sort of reductionism which 'explains away' theological understandings.[1] How do we as Christian theologians evaluate the account being given of the human beings in this situation by this other discipline? Therefore, even at the analysis stage in the process of Practical Theology, we find the flow of questions flowing in both directions.

An improved version of the Pastoral Cycle has been developed by Emmanuel Lartey which includes these insights.[2] Notice the way that there is a real dialogue between the experiences, the analysis with the human sciences and the theological values and insights.

1. For a good way into this particular area see Watts, F., Nye, R. and Savage, S. (2001). *Psychology for Christian Ministry.* (London: Routledge).
2. Lartey, E. (2000). 'Practical Theology as a theological form' in Woodward, J. and Pattison, S. *The Blackwell Reader in Pastoral and Practical Theology* (Oxford: Blackwell), p. 132. I have simplified Lartey's version by omitting his 'situational analysis of theology' and by using my own terminology.

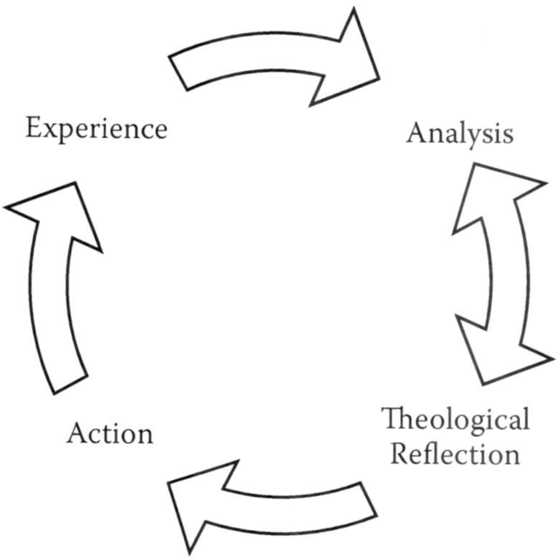

Diagram 2: Two-directional Pastoral Cycle

Nonetheless, I need to repeat my warning to be wary of importing explicit theology too early into the process because of the risk of seeing real life through rose-tinted or indeed grey-tinted spectacles, depending on our own theological presuppositions!

Theology in Practical Theology

So what, then, is the role of 'theology' in this Practical Theology? We have already noted that the reason we wish to think about an issue may be that, because of our Christian faith, we care about those being damaged. Or it may be that the real-life experiences are jarring with our sense of how things 'ought to be' in our God-made world. This is the point in the cycle when we work most explicitly in theological terms. And here the traffic light is on amber, warning us to stop and think, to ponder actively, and then to get ready, to prepare to engage the clutch so that we can move on. It is a good metaphor for this phase in Practical Theology because it is about an anticipation to move – it is not waiting and watching for its own sake – but it still requires patient attention. It remains a spiritual as well as an intellectual discipline.

Another question. One of our former students in Durham was a Professor of Economics before he trained to be an Anglican priest. He approached Practical Theology with a degree of caution, perhaps used to hearing church leaders utter platitudes about complex economic issues. So he used to ask us, regularly, 'What added value is theology bringing to this conversation?' As I might put it, 'Do we need to say something specifically Christian about this issue – or not?' And the chapters in this book may have made you ask that question. Several of them provide clear and reliable accounts of the human experiences and offer wise practical responses, without having to draw much on overt Christian values. We might wish to say, theologically, that this reflects the presence of the Wisdom of God in the world[1] and that some of the values of care for the other and of justice, which are now so deeply rooted in Western society, have their own deep roots in the Christian faith. But it remains the case that we may be asking ourselves, a little anxiously, 'But do Christians have something distinctive to say about this issue?'

I think they have, but these insights are often at the 'big picture' level rather than in the detail. Reading these chapters, I noted again and again reference to the *values* which Christians bring to discussion of human life. For example, in the chapter on sexual addiction, we were reminded that it is *not* the Christian way to fear or despise human sexual activity. Part of the sub-discipline of theology which is called theological anthropology is the study of what it is to be a human being as understood within a Christian framework. The authors of this chapter, and I agree with them, argue that loving and pleasurable sexual activity can be part of the God-givenness of human nature. Therefore, there is an assumption that it is worth the effort to redeem human sexual activity, when it has become distorted, because it is part of God's good creation. We will return to the discussion about the 'cash value' of theological convictions such as 'Creation' shortly.

1. This opens up a rich theological theme. As the *Logos* (Word) of God Christ is present in the work of creation (John 1:3, Colossians 1:15); as is the Spirit of God (Genesis 1:2). Both *Logos* and Spirit shape human beings into the image of God (Genesis 1:27). Part of the expression of this is human conscience (Romans 2:14-16). For examples of how this is explored and justified theologically and then related to human life see Barton, S. (Ed.) (1999). *Where Shall Wisdom Be Found?* (Edinburgh: T & T Clark), especially the essay by Colin Gunton.

I can imagine a thoughtful reader beginning to furrow their brow at this point. Because it has not always been the case that Christian theologians have argued for the positive value of human sexuality. Indeed, for hundreds of years it seems to be the case that human sexual desire was treated as inherently dangerous by the Church. One of the main consequences of the Fall – so it was argued – was that human desire became corrupted and human sexual desire most of all. It was always tainted with concupiscence[1] that is, the power of the senses – in traditional language, the 'flesh' – was out of the control of the mind and of the spirit and so *certain* to lead human beings into actual sin.[2] Whilst modern study of human psychology has reinforced our awareness of the potential for human sexuality to become distorted, it has sharply warned us that inappropriate language of 'sin' can be one of the most potent sources of distortion. In other words, what happens at this stage in the Practical Theology process is that the questions which real-life experiences, and the analysis of them, have thrown up are taken to Scripture and Tradition and often trigger new insights. This can feel challenging, even disturbing and subversive. Certainly, part of the experience of the Church in the last 200 years has been that many of its long-accepted tenets about human beings have been challenged by allowing previously unheard voices to speak – for example, the voices of abused women.

I want to explore this issue of the challenge of Practical Theology a little further, before turning to a more positive account of the value of the classic Christian theological disciplines.

Practical Theology as challenge

Several years ago, one of our younger single male Anglican ordinands had been very moved by his experiences during a hospital placement about the pastoral care of parents who had suffered a stillbirth or neonatal death.

1. When confronted by a technical theological term like this, it is very helpful to use a good theological dictionary, such as the *Oxford Dictionary of the Christian Church* (3rd edition) (Oxford: Oxford University Press, 1997) or a reliable website, such as www.anglicansonline.org/resources/history or www.silk.net/RelEd/churchhist. Theological terms such as this are excellent ways of both summarising and also opening up complex theological discussions. It is good to become familiar with them because – contrary to our wariness of jargon – they enable us to talk with clarity about the variety of Christian understandings.

2. See chapter 3 of Bartlett, A. (2004). *Humane Christianity* (London: Darton, Longman and Todd).

Whilst this was outside his own personal experience, he had researched the issue carefully. He had developed some knowledge of the background medical and psychological realities; the extent of the problem (through some statistical work) and also its social reality (for example, which sort or type or class of person is most likely to suffer this trauma); and, crucially, what it feels like to go through this experience (through conversation and wider reading). In so far as it was possible, he had developed a good empathetic understanding of this experience.

He was then confronted with the problem of understanding it theologically. This raised huge issues about the providence of God. But the point at which he was most 'stuck' was when he turned to the Bible for insight and in particular for resources to use in the liturgical pastoral care of people caught up in these circumstances. He was attempting this in a seminar with fellow students. After some increasingly frustrated conversation, one of the group blurted out, 'The Bible is not much help in this area.' By this, the person meant that biblical texts about the death of neonatal babies often expressed very different understandings about the meaning to be given to such tragic events. They might, for example, be seen as a divine judgement, as in the account of the death of David and Bathsheba's first child.[1] In this interpretation the child had no rights of its own; its fate was entirely determined by the sins of its parents, and especially its father. Crudely speaking – and it is a simplistic stereotype – children in the Old Testament were seen as the property of their parents, especially their fathers. This is a deeply patriarchal account of human life, written in a deeply patriarchal society.[2] So the group had to confront the challenge posed both to classic Judaeo-Christian faith in the providence of God by the tragic death of these babies, but also to some ancient Judaeo-Christian

1. See 2 Samuel 12.

2. This is not the place for an extended study of this issue but interested readers might explore: Trible, P. (1984). *Texts of Terror* (Philadelphia: Fortress); or Countryman, L. W. (1988). *Dirt, Greed and Sex* (Philadelphia: Fortress); or Hays, R. B. (1997). *The Moral Vision of the New Testament* (Edinburgh: T & T Clark). For examples of creative use of biblical materials with people who have experienced a stillbirth or neonatal death, see The Compassionate Friends: Support for bereaved parents and their families. www.tcf.org.uk and also the Stillbirth and Neonatal Death Society (SANDS) www.uk-sands.org. Psalm 139 is one of the most popular and beautiful passages read, for example, at memorial services but it is just worth noting the double-edged nature of this psalm. The baby in the womb is 'wonderfully made' and is known by God but the real baby is, of course, not so wonderfully made as to survive. And the psalm is about God's omniscience, omnipresence and indeed judgement. It surely needs careful handling in this very painful situation.

understandings of the status of the neonatal. These are different sorts of challenge, but both are important. The question of suffering and a God of love remains one of the main causes of disbelief in our society. But the latter perception – that our scriptures are archaic and unhelpful – is increasingly common and is raised precisely by exploration of this sort of human experience in dialogue with our scriptures.

We will return to the issue of hermeneutics – that is, the study of how a text is interpreted – in a moment, but here I want to pause on the challenge to the Church raised by Practical Theology. Especially when Practical Theology is done in a Western theological context, it can feel is if the agenda is entirely one of challenge. So Bible and Church are portrayed as hierarchical, patriarchal, homophobic and so on. These debates need to be handled with care, of course, and crass sloganeering is often insensitive to the complexities and surprises in Scripture and Tradition. There is much good news in both, as we will describe soon. But it remains the case that modern (postmodern?) critiques of Scripture and Tradition are exposing deep problems in the life of the Church.

I will give an example by making a personal comment on the impact of Practical Theology on my doctrine of the Church. Much ecclesiology – the study of the doctrines about the Church – is highly conceptual. It portrays an idealised Church essentially defined by its relationship to selected theological norms. So the Church is 'the Body of Christ'. Such language can disguise the reality of local and wider church life and give a spurious cover to, for example, oppressive actions by the Church done in the name of Christ. Part of the gift of Practical Theology to the Church is to help the Church to look at itself honestly. The Church is both a supernatural and also an all-too-human institution. I believe in the practical fallibility of the Church.[1] Thus, at a micro-level, I have seen Practical Theologians deploy to great effect the tools of group dynamics and social psychology to analyse the reality of local congregational life.[2] It is all very well to believe in, for

1. This is *not* a comment on the nature of the Church's authority or of any of the organs of the Church's life. For discussion of that in an Anglican-Catholic perspective, the reader is referred to ARCIC (1999). *The Gift of Authority: Authority in the Church III* (London: Catholic Truth Society).

2. See Savage, S. (2006). 'On the analyst's couch: Psychological perspectives on congregations and clergy' in Croft, S. (Ed.). *The Future of the Parish System* (London: Church House Publishing).

example, the central importance of either the local congregational meeting (for Baptists) or the role of the local 'vicar' (for Anglicans) in church life, but unless we understand how these institutions and people actually work, then we will make plans based on fantasies. And on a broader scale, it is, I fear, simply the case that serious study of the Churches' history reveals not just occasional problems but rather *systematic* error and abuse. History and Practical Theology force Christians to take account of these ugly realities when doing their ecclesiology and when imagining and planning the life of the modern Church. In other words, and to go back to the version of the Pastoral Cycle offered by Lartey, Practical Theology changes our theology.

Practical Theology and the Bible

We have already explored some of the complexities of using the Bible in Practical Theology, but in this section I would like to push the questions further. (What is said of the Bible in this section, could, with some changes, also be said of how Tradition can be used within Practical Theology.) You may already have noticed how often the Bible is cited in the chapters in this book and how some texts have become dominant in how we conceive of modern Christian mission, for example Luke 4:18, 19. There are two important issues to be addressed when we bring the Bible explicitly into the theological element of Practical Theology: hermeneutics and purpose. We will look at them in turn.

Hermeneutics is the discipline of thinking about how we read any text, especially any ancient text and in particular the Bible.[1] To summarise a very extensive and complex discussion, hermeneutics teaches us that the first step in the process of reading the Bible is to enter as fully as possible into the world of the biblical text. This requires us to do textual study (what is the text?), and historical-critical study (how does our understanding of the history of the text help us to understand its meaning?), as well as linguistic study (what do the words mean and what is the *genre* of the text and so how should we hear it?), and thus what is the overall meaning of the text – its exegesis. But this is only the first part of the task.

1. An excellent way into this complex discussion is Briggs, R. (2003). *Reading the Bible Wisely* (London: SPCK). Also Davis, E. F. and Hays, R. B. (Eds) (2003). *The Art of Reading Scripture* (Grand Rapids, Michigan, and Cambridge: Eerdmans).

The second part is to recognise our own assumptions, conscious and unconscious, about what is true and thus about what is true in any given passage of Scripture. For example, modern people do not believe in a three-decker universe (this could be variously described but one version of this belief is that there is an underworld below us, the world of planet earth which we inhabit, and a further heavenly world above this). We so clearly do not believe this that we do not even notice that we are editing it out of our reading of Scripture. This is a simple example but there are many more weighty examples which bear much more sharply on the issues raised in Practical Theology: the relationship of mind, body and spirit in a human being; the nature of sin; the character of God. Good biblical study will enable us to see more clearly where our world overlaps with the world of Scripture and where it is different.

This, then, leaves the most difficult task, which is to answer the question of how our world *should* relate to the world of Scripture. Christians have always lived with this tension because the Christian version of the Bible includes material explicitly setting aside significant sections of the Hebrew Scriptures (the 'Old' Testament). Crudely speaking, for example, Christians do not accept the food laws in the Torah as still being relevant and to be obeyed. So Christians always operate with a strong hermeneutic when reading the Bible. Often, we only realise this when we are confronted by those who interpret the Bible differently.

A simple example: during my theological training my wife and I went to Nigeria. Helen does not wear a hat to attend church.[1] This scandalised some of our Nigerian hosts and, try as I might, I could not convince them that the command for women to cover their heads was a culturally specific command only relevant to first-century Corinth (if that is indeed what it was . . .). We were clearly liberalising and back-sliding Westerners – though this was implied with great graciousness! But what was more intriguing were the questions from the younger wives in the women's fellowships asking how we had been married for six years but had no children. It was a birth-control question and sprang from an incipient rebellion against the older tradition (hermeneutic) which regarded regular

1. 1 Corinthians 11.

child-bearing as an inevitable and divinely-ordained part of married life. This was practical hermeneutics.

So, when we bring the Bible into conversation with real life, we must do so alert to the meaning of Scripture (and how we ascertain that) but also to the potential gap between the scriptural world and ours, and how we bridge that gap.

This opens up a further area of discussion: the purpose with which we are approaching Scripture. This might be thought to be a strange question. Surely we go to Scripture for guidance, indeed for authoritative guidance? But this assumption both shortcuts a discussion about how God is heard through Scripture and also about the nature of Scripture itself.

As an Anglican, I am only too aware of the painful difficulties of hearing God speak in Scripture. In a communion where different modes of interpretation are leading to different ethical decisions and thus to potential schism, the question of how we interpret Scripture wisely is very pressing. One point on which Anglicans are, more or less, agreed is that we have to be self-aware and mature as we handle the Bible. As I have written elsewhere:

> Fundamentally, whilst the classic language of Anglicanism often refers to the Bible as the 'Word of God', this always sits over against the deeper assumption that the 'Word' is Christ. As *Windsor* reminds Anglicans, the phrase 'the authority of the Bible' should be understood as shorthand for 'the authority of the triune God, *exercised through* Scripture'.[1] It is a relational, dynamic and transformative not a fixed, restrictive and legalistic understanding of the nature of scriptural authority. God 'speaks' and 'does' as the Bible is 'heard' and 'lived', in keeping with his whole mission: people and situations being brought to new life.[2] *God is primary.*[3]

1. The Lambeth Commission on Communion (2004). *The Windsor Report* (London: Anglican Communion Office) paragraph 54, p. 27. (Author's italics.)
2. cf. Wright, N. T. (2005). *Scripture and the Authority of God* (London: SPCK), pp. 22, 23.
3. Bartlett, A. B. (2007). *A Passionate Balance* (London: Darton, Longman and Todd), p. 91. (Author's italics.)

This conviction about both the authority of Scripture, but also of the necessity of our self-awareness and modesty when we expound it, is closely connected to our understanding of the character of the Bible itself. This is not to return to the old arguments about 'inerrancy' – every word in the Bible is literally true – but rather to note the diverse and sophisticated way in which the Bible itself speaks, as well as the diverse and sophisticated ways in which we approach it. This has been explored in a very rich way by Professor David Ford.[1] He describes five different 'moods' of faith, which can also be read as five different moods in which Scripture speaks and within which we hear it speak:

Indicative mood or tense – 'it is or is not' – which affirms or denies. This is a theology of the blessing (and judgement) of God which affirms and confirms the identity of what is good, and denies and boundaries what is not true. I interpret this as Scripture helping us to clarify 'what is good and true and beautiful' in a situation. It is partly a theology which sees Scripture as helping us to make good judgements.

Imperative of command and obedience – 'do this or do not do this'. This is Scripture/Faith requiring (life-giving) obedience to divine command. This is often the mode in which Scripture is presented (and resented). I am sure Ford is right to make it only one mood of Scripture but I would also argue that it is a mode of Scripture which we cannot, and in fact do not, ever lose, whatever our theological perspective.

Interrogative that questions, probes, tests and suspects – 'why is it like this, does it have to be?' Ford sees this as a divine testing of the human. I would want to add to this the human interrogative of the divine; as is best exemplified in the biblical tradition of Lament. I read this as a dialogue, not one-way traffic.

Subjunctive, exploring the possibilities of what might be – 'what if?' This is the least definite and the most playful of the moods, best characterised by the parables. It opens up new insights but without an

1. Ford, D. (2007). *Christian Wisdom* (Cambridge: Cambridge University Press), p. 5 and pp. 45–51.

inappropriate definiteness. 'Perhaps?' 'What if?' Partly because so many of the areas explored in Practical Theology are so new and partly because of the hugely complex nature of the task itself, I think that Practical Theology is best conceived of as an 'is it?' rather than an 'it is' discipline. We conduct theological thought experiments. This mood is both essential for Practical Theology and meshes well with this discipline but it should be felt as a spur to further thinking and also a gentle goad to action, rather than navel-gazing!

The optative of desire – 'I wish'. This is the mood which expresses desire, longing, hope. Practical Theology is rooted in a desire to see human beings helped, healed, renewed. It is a discipline that grows out of the passion for change. This mood of Scripture incites this desire and gives it assurance that it meshes with divine desire.

These 'moods' relate closely to how we handle Scripture in Practical Theology.[1] Sometimes, as you will have noticed in the chapters, people are making *simple connections* between their real-life experience and Scripture. This is partly a way of affirming the relevance of faith to real life, of making connections between their own spiritual identity and this real-life experience, and partly the beginning of the journey of making conceptual sense of what is happening.

Some other chapters have tried to *extrapolate certain themes* from Scripture. So the chapter on alcohol addiction draws heavily on the Pauline sense of the divided self and how this encapsulates part of the human condition, as it is also understood by the human sciences. Here, both the human experience and also the biblical material have been systematised, conceptualised, and this makes it easier for them to converse with each other. In other words, we look to Scripture for a framework to shape our thinking and relate this to the framework we have developed through the human sciences so that together they say, 'This is how it is!'

Then there is another mode of approaching Scripture, which is to *look for authoritative judgements.* I used to be very sceptical about 'proof-

1. In this section I am drawing very heavily on a seminal article by my colleague Roger Walton, 'The Bible and Theology in Theological Reflection' in the *British Journal of Theological Education*, 2003, volume 13 no. 2. See also Ballard, P. and Holmes, S. (Eds) (2005). *The Bible in Pastoral Practice* (London: Darton, Longman and Todd).

texting' from the Bible (quoting a verse to prove a point), until I realised that I do it too! There are some issues of which I am so convinced that I rejoice that Scripture speaks with clear-cut authority: for example, the belief, widely found in Scripture, that God is especially on the side of the poor and weak and vulnerable. This is Scripture in imperative mood: 'Do it!'

In other chapters, *questions have been fired into Scripture*, trying to provoke an answer. This is my interpretation of the interrogative mood. Can we really find good news for abused women in the 'patriarchal' Bible? (We can, and will return to the finding of good news for such women in a moment.) But this poses the question: 'Where is God in this mess?' This is closely linked to the more subjunctive mood which asks, both of God and of human beings, 'But does it have to be this way?' It invites us to try experiments of seeing the situation differently, of conceiving of God's interaction with a situation differently.

But, above all, many of the chapters have *searched the Scripture for signs of hope*; both for models of how to access power for transformation and also for reassurance that it can be done. Think of the chapters which explored different aspects of addiction and how they portray where hope is to be found and trusted. Hence the frequent citing of Luke 4 where Jesus talks of his mission to bring liberation. This is Scripture as a means of bringing hope into a situation: both hope in the short term and a wider, eschatological (end of time) sense: 'It will be so.' This is Scripture enabling us, with faith, to connect with the action of God in the world. It is the mood of Scripture which drives us back into action.

Practical Theology and confidence in Christian theology

One of the reasons I am an enthusiast for Practical Theology, as opposed to other branches of theology, is that the results connect closely to real life and, indeed, they actively help real people. In this book, we have examples of Christian people wrestling with very difficult issues and finding resources in their Christian faith which help to *illuminate* the situation they are in and to *resource* them in facing these situations.

In this section of my chapter, which is part of our extended reflection on the place of theology in Practical Theology, I want to do two things: first, to note the areas where Christian theology gives us explanatory power and also personal, communal and spiritual resources to deal with difficult situations; and then to note briefly the theological areas which the chapters in this book have revealed as being in need of further attention.

In one sense it is not difficult for us, in the modern West, to feel a sense of the value of human beings or to be worried about the future of the planet. One of the joys of Practical Theology is to realise how often the Church 'got there first' – though it often did not recognise it! Without getting lost in the minutiae of debates about the 'how', the early chapters of Genesis provide us with a rich and imaginative account of the created order and of humanity's place within it. The nightmare has been the abuse of the concept of human 'dominion', but the good dream is the picture of the value and purpose of the created world alongside humankind, with humankind as its pinnacle. This gives Christians a very strong basis on which to do ecological theology. More, there is so much in the little phrase 'in the image of God'. It enables us to explore, subjunctively, what it is to be a human being. This has often been seen in purely spiritual or intellectual terms, but more recent thinking stresses the embodiedness, democracy and gender inclusivity of this phrase.[1] Of course, we have to be careful not to project on to Scripture our own contemporary desires – back to hermeneutics – but it is also the case that we may be able to see new things in Scripture, of which earlier generations, because of their different social patterns, were blind.

This rich mine of theological possibility is also present in another central Christian doctrine, the Incarnation. Again, the modern Church is enriching this doctrine as it stresses the valuing of *physicality* which is implicit in the Incarnation. God took 'flesh' and made it his own. This enormous valuing of humankind, in its embodiedness, is a weighty theological resource when struggling with social problems which tend to devalue human beings. This is theology in an indicative as well as an optative mood.

Conversely, even the doctrine of sin, which has been used to shortcut,

1. Bartlett, A. (2004). *Humane Christianity*, (London: Darton, Longman and Todd) pp. 12–23; and Middleton, J. R. (2005). *The Liberating Image* (Grand Rapids, Michigan: Brazos Press).

for example, so many Christian discussions of human behaviour – 'he is a sinful drunkard, lecher, bully, etc.' – in fact has the capacity to help us to illuminate human experiences.[1] The sense of trappedness which is such a deep part of human self-destructive behaviour, is also, of course, part of the doctrine of sin. 'For I do not understand my own actions. For I do not do what I want, but I do the very thing I hate.' (Romans 7:15) The studies in this book may make us cautious about throwing the word 'sin' too quickly, for example, at addictive problems, but they may also have reminded us of the addict's need for grace, for help, to enable them to break out of their trappedness. Further, the Christian understanding summed up in the word 'sin' may help us to be realistic about systemic failures, about the fallibility even of the good agencies, and about the sheer horror of some aspects of human behaviour. To answer an earlier question, an understanding of 'sin' is a concept and a reality which the Christian theologian does bring to the table, adding specific value to a discussion.

However, if Christian theology has much to contribute by way of insight into real human life, this aspect of theology remains relatively under-developed. In comparison with the shelves of books on the doctrine of the Trinity, serious and well-integrated theological discussion of what it is to be a human being (Christian theological anthropology) remains sparse.[2] Studies such as this book, which will enable, indeed force, theologians to face the reality of human life when thinking about humanness, are crucial for this work to be accomplished.

Practical Theology and Praxis

And so we turn at last to the green light. As Marx wrote, 'the philosophers have only interpreted the world, the point is to change it.'[3] The purpose of Practical Theology is to make a difference in real life. All of the chapters in this book are written by people who are involved in making a difference and you are reading this book, in part, because you too want to make a

1. See the very sophisticated exploration of this in McFadyen, A. (2000). *Bound to Sin* (Cambridge: Cambridge University Press).
2. An interesting counter-example is the latest work of the Church of England's Doctrine Commission, *Being Human* (London: Church House Publishing, 2003).
3. Marx, K. (1845). *Theses on Feuerbach*, thesis 11.

difference. Practical Theology is an engaged discipline. In the words of the old joke, the contribution you make to Practical Theology is more like the contribution of the pig than of the chicken to a full English breakfast. You are fully committed! This can make Practical Theology a little suspect. It appears to lack the detached objectivity of other theological disciplines. But as the Liberation Theologians have taught us, there are no neutral disciplines or detached studies in a world of unjust suffering. Practical Theology is refreshingly honest about the real contexts in which we study and think.

It is also refreshingly honest that we do not think and study as detached minds. The wrestling we do with the painful issues which we confront in this book does need to be done in a disciplined way. Emotive thinking and discussion is distracting and even dangerous. But conversely, we also know that real-life decisions are shaped by our processes of rumination, of deep inner reflection. We have noted several times that Practical Theology requires us to stop and look and that this is a spiritual activity. It was the slogan of the ancient Church that 'the one who prays is a theologian' (Evagrius). Thinking and talking about these issues in prayer and conscious of the presence of God does change how we approach them. Notice the role of a holistic theological approach to the human self which characterises the chapter on 'self-care'. This is not to say that prayer will always give us the 'right answers' . . .

Another way of discussing this is to use the language of 'wisdom'. Modern ethical discussion has moved away from a narrow focus on the rights and wrongs of individual issues, to discussion of how we become the sort of people who have been shaped to be wise people, who are likely to make good decisions in the midst of the muddle of real life.[1] Prayer and a disciplined spiritual life should help us to be the sort of people who can make wise decisions.

An apparently very different way of conceiving of the task of Practical Theology is to describe it as reflective *praxis*. In other words, it is value-shaped reflection on value-driven action.[2] While one of the temptations of

1. See, for example,Wells, S. (2004). *Improvisation: the drama of Christian ethics* (London: SPCK).
2. For a thorough exploration of the meaning of *praxis*, see Graham, E. (1996). *Transforming Practice* (London: Mowbray).

Christian ministry can be to try to impose conceptual convictions on to complex real-life situations, another is to slither into pragmatism. One of the ways to avoid this is consciously to ask the theological questions 'Why am I acting in this way and where is God in this situation?' Even if Christian insights and outcomes are not always so very different to those of a non-Christian (and we have already touched on why that may be the case and why that can be acceptable), they must nonetheless be held within a wider Christian theological framework if they are to make sense as Christian *praxis.* So as Christian practitioners we ask, 'Why is it right to continue to attempt to care for sex offenders?' as well as 'What understandings and practices need to be in place if this care is to be realistic?' These are both theological questions.

Practical Theology and Jesus

We all know that the answer to every Sunday school question is 'Jesus!' I want to finish this chapter with a final encouragement. Even if the Church has often had dirty hands, we can go back to the example of Jesus of Nazareth with confidence, because of our confidence in the doctrine of the Incarnation. And even if we still have to ask hard hermeneutical questions about how we translate the teaching and example of Jesus into our world, as Christians we have been captivated by the beauty of his life. For me, it is the heart of why I continue. And Jesus was a fine Practical Theologian: looking carefully at the experiences of those around him (he was enraged at the real hypocrisy of the religious elite); using language and concepts with which his listeners were deeply familiar (from agriculture or the home); and, above all, allowing his own experiences to re-shape his vision. It seems to be the case that Jesus initially conceived of his mission being to the People of Israel but was so taken by the faith of Gentiles that he came to see that his mission was to them too.[1] As St John said, Christians are called to '*do* the truth' (1 John 1:6). Jesus did it. So do we.

1. See, for example, the Syro-Phoenician woman in Mark 7:24-30, or the God-fearing Centurion (Matthew 8:5-13 and Luke 7:1-10).

Recommended reading

- Ballard, P. and Pritchard, J. (2006). *Practical Theology in Action* (2nd Edition) (London: SPCK).
- Bartlett, A., Hughes, C., and Walton, R. (forthcoming, 2009). *Real God, Real World* (London: SPCK).
- Graham, E., Ward, F. and Walton, H. *Theological Reflection* (vol. 1, 2005): *Methods* and (vol. 2, 2007): *Sources* (London: SCM).

- A very useful journal is *Contact,* soon to be re-launched as *Practical Theology.* Readers who wish to become involved in the further study and delivery of Practical Theology should consider joining the British and Irish Association for Practical Theology (BIAPT). www.biapt.org.uk. BIAPT membership includes subscription to *Contact.*

Concluding Reflections

Jocelyn Bryan and Brendan Geary

'Why do people behave the way that they do?' is a persistent question which underlies the behaviour patterns described in this book. Why do some people bully others, struggle with addiction, mismanage their aggression or their sexual desires and fantasies, while others manage and regulate their behaviour in ways which enable them to establish and sustain positive relationships which are supportive and fulfilling? There is no simple answer to this question. However, studies in developmental and personality psychology have begun to make significant contributions to our understanding of the factors which influence and shape our patterns of thinking, feeling and behaving, and to show how these factors contribute to the individual differences which we engage with daily in our relationships.

The nature/nurture debate

There is a genetic effect in all behaviour. Biology is a significant factor in determining behaviour, but genetic and non-genetic influences are not entirely separable. The chapters which have examined aggressive and violent behaviour have described the gender differences in these behaviour patterns and the relationship between aggression and the male hormone testosterone. However, these biological factors, though important, influence aggressive behaviour through an interplay between the genetic makeup of the person and the different environments and the nurturing the person experiences.

Several studies have supported the interaction between nature and environment – in particular, behaviour patterns. In both antisocial behaviour and depression the effect of adverse environments is most influential on those individuals who have been identified as genetically susceptible to these behaviours. Conversely these adverse environments have least impact on those who are not as genetically vulnerable.[1] We all respond to situations differently, even when we share a common environment such as the home. In families it is evident that the environment itself is experienced differently by each child, not only because of their different genetic make-up but also because of the way their parents relate to them due to gender differences, birth-order differences and the daily sequence of life events which are unique to that particular child. This goes some way to explaining why one member of a family may react violently when frustrated and another manage their anger in a different way, or why one child in the family copes better with a crisis than another.

The research in the development of personality has significance in helping to predict those who are at risk of developing psychopathologies (mental health problems) by identifying those features of environments which are associated with psychopathological outcomes when a child is developing. In a number of the chapters in this book the behaviour issues addressed are not categorised as psychopathological but they are psychological disorders which may be associated with some of the environmental factors below, which an adult experienced as a child:

- Persistent discord and conflict, particularly when it involves scapegoating or other forms of focused negativity directed toward an individual child. This has been identified as associated with some forms of passive-aggressive behaviour.
- Lack of individualised personal care-giving involving continuity over time. This is often associated with institutional upbringing and leads to difficulty in establishing and sustaining relationships because of its effect on developing secure attachments and self-esteem.
- A lack of reciprocal conversation and play, which is important for the development of social skills.

1. Rutter, M. (2002). 'Nature, nurture, and development: From evangelism through science toward policy and practice', *Child Development*, 73 (1) p. 3.

- A negative social ethos or social group that fosters maladaptive behaviour patterns.[1]

This area of research has significantly increased our knowledge of how human psychological development during childhood can predict behaviour patterns in adulthood. These predispositions have been seen in a number of areas such as early hyperactivity leading to later antisocial behaviour,[2] early conduct problems associated with a predisposition to substance use and abuse and this in turn leading to later depression.[3] However, the underlying processes and causes of these effects are not yet fully understood. The research indicates the importance of both our genetic make-up and environmental experience in shaping our behaviour. Understanding how these factors interact and the relative contribution of each in the formation of how we think, feel and behave and how our unique personalities develop is still a long way off. But when we encounter challenging behaviour in a person, the context of their development as a child and any genetic predispositions they carry must be recognised as having significance in our understanding of them.

Socialisation

One significant process which is part of the nurturing experience of children is socialisation. This is the process by which we acquire behaviour patterns that are acceptable in the society in which we live. The challenging and difficult behaviour patterns discussed in this book can be seen as problems of socialisation. Behaviours which others find difficult or problematic and are offensive or damaging to others are indicative of problems with socialisation. The main agents in this process during development are parents who teach their children the social and cultural

1. Rutter, M. (2002). 'Nature, nurture, and development: From evangelism through science toward policy and practice', *Child Development*, 73 (1), p. 8.
2. Rutter, M., Giller, H. and Hagell, A. (1998). *Antisocial Behaviour by Young People* (New York: Cambridge University Press).
3. Rutter, M. (In press). 'Substance use and abuse: Causal pathways considerations', in Rutter, M. and Taylor, E. (Eds) *Child and Adolescent Psychiatry* (4th edition) (Oxford: Blackwell Scientific), quoted in Rutter, M. (2002). 'Nature, nurture, and development: From evangelism through science toward policy and practice', *Child Development*, 73 (1) p. 12.

norms of behaviour. However, alongside the acquisition of behavioural norms, parents also engage in the process of the socialisation of emotions, and this is one of the most important aspects of family life.

The nurturing family context is the primary formational unit in which the child learns about social living. The effect on child development of the changing structure of family life and the increased complexity of the relationships within families has received a great deal of attention. However, it seems that, from a child's point of view, a family can take a variety of different forms and still function as a secure base for healthy development.

The relationship between the family context and aggression, conduct disturbance and delinquency is supported by a considerable body of evidence. The significant factors linked to these behaviour patterns are:

- Family discord and disruption
- Weak family relationships
- Criminality in other members of the family (parents and siblings)
- Ineffective discipline and supervision[1]

All these contribute to a weakening of the socialisation process. Patterson notes that four aspects are particularly significant:

- A lack of house rules so that there are no clear expectations of what is and is not acceptable.
- A lack of parental monitoring so parents are not adequately informed of the children's behaviour and emotions, and therefore are not able to respond appropriately.
- A lack of effective contingencies, which results in parents shouting and nagging. Praise and punishment are inconsistent and not adequately differentiated.
- A lack of techniques for dealing with crises or problems. Conflict leads to tension and dispute. Resolution is difficult to achieve or not attained.[2]

1. Rutter, M. and Rutter, M. (1993). *Developing Minds* (London: Penguin), p. 176.
2. Patterson, G. R. (1982). *Coercive Family Process* (Eugene, Oregon: Castalia) quoted in Rutter, M. and Rutter, M. (1993). *Developing Minds* (London: Penguin), p. 176.

It appears that problematic behaviour patterns associated with aggression may well be linked to the nurturing and social learning that was experienced by the adult in childhood. Models of aggressive behaviour as an appropriate and acceptable way of dealing with frustration, interpersonal difficulties or other relationship problems are learned and transferred to different contexts and situations. This is also associated with the finding that physical abuse predisposes an individual to aggressive violent behaviour. Hence, we can conclude that the effect of parental modelling and the parental role in the socialisation process are significant factors in our understanding of repeating patterns of violent and aggressive behaviour in adulthood.

Motivation and social cognition

Both our environment and our biology are aspects of life over which we have limited influence or control. The view of the person as a passive victim of unconscious impulses and responses, resulting from both biological processes and past experience, or the person as a passive respondent to changing environmental events, was called 'reciprocal determinism' by Bandura.[1] This was criticised for failing to take into account the role of our brains in interpreting the situation we are faced with and then making a conscious decision regarding our response. We select our behavioural responses from a vast range of possibilities. We decide what to do when faced with a particular situation. This decision is based upon a range of factors, including the memories we have of similar situations in the past, our motives and goals and our emotional state. Not all behaviour is processed in this way. There are occasions when we respond instinctively or impulsively. Learning to control and manage our impulses is a significant challenge, and in cases of abuse and violence the inability to do this leads to significant damage to others. However, it is undoubtedly true that people's behaviour patterns are influenced by their interpretation of the situation in which they find themselves and in which they choose how they will respond accordingly. People are responsive to situations, and also

1. Bandura, A. (1999). 'Social cognitive theory of personality', in Pervin, L. A. and John, O. P. (Eds), *Handbook of Personality: Theory and research* (New York: Guilford Press), pp. 154–196.

construct situations and influence them. They select the situations they engage with as well as being shaped and influenced by them. Likewise, they influence the behaviour of others as well as being influenced by the behaviour of others. Hence, we need to take into account how a person processes and interprets events, which includes their predictions of likely outcomes. This influences their choice of a course of action which will be determined by whatever goal they have in mind.

This represents a view of the person as someone who has expectancies and beliefs, competences and skills and who sets personal goals, and seeks to explain why people behave as they do in these terms. This is known as social cognitive theory and it offers an explanation of behaviour in terms of the different ways individuals perceive situations and how this influences their responses. So one person might be threatened by a situation and another excited by it simply because they interpret the situation in different ways. Behaviour is also influenced by the individual's perception of their ability to cope with a situation. If we feel insecure and uncomfortable, we behave in a very different way from a situation where we feel in control and are confident about the outcome. An important application of this theory is cognitive behaviour therapy which seeks to enable a person to change their interpretation of situations and other people's responses to them and so influence behaviour patterns and emotional responses. By controlling our mental processing of situations and events, we can change our behaviour.

Another significant factor in social cognitive theory is the effect of the goals we set for ourselves in situations. These depend on what is significant to a person at the time, what opportunities are available and their perceptions of what they can cope with and achieve. The chapters on addictions illustrate how a person's behaviour is directed by their desire or goal to change their emotional state or achieve a particular outcome. Hence, those who gamble set themselves the goal of the next win and this is accompanied by the incentive of the thrill which goes with the risk-taking involved. Likewise, the sex addicts seek to relieve negative feelings about themselves by engaging in the sexual acts which they find pleasurable. In instances of aggressive and violent behaviour, the goal of asserting power and superiority over another is achieved through bullying behaviour, and in some situations this manifests itself in physical violence. Achieving the goal one has set contributes to self-esteem, which is another recurrent theme in this book. The tendency to maintain, protect and enhance self-esteem by striving to achieve a sense of success and avoid failure is one of the defining characteristics of human nature and a significant motive in determining behaviour patterns, whether problematic or congenial to the person's well-being. Each of the issues discussed in this book is related in some way to self-esteem and a person's self-perception.

Self-esteem

Self-esteem concerns the self-evaluation or judgement about personal acceptability and worthiness to be loved, which carries with it pleasant or unpleasant feelings. It is related to the perceived views of the person by important others in his or her life.[1] It is a personal judgement of worthiness.[2] This sense of worthiness is developed through our relationships with others and by comparing ourselves with others. When we receive acceptance and praise, our sense of self-worth increases, and when we experience rejection and criticism, our sense of self-worth is diminished. Crocker and Park[3] suggest that we are selective in the things which we allow to affect our self-esteem. For one person being attractive, having lots of friends and being competent at a particular skill is significant for their self-esteem, but for another person it could be winning at sport, being in a stable marriage and gaining promotion in their job. They call these 'contingencies of self-worth.' The effects of events, circumstances and relationships on self-esteem are determined by a person's interpretation of the event and its relevance to the person's contingencies of self-worth. There is an obvious link between personal goals and these contingencies of self-worth. When we achieve one of our goals, our self-esteem increases, and when we fail or our attempts are thwarted, our self-esteem is lowered. Positive, high self-esteem is associated with good social relationships and personal fulfilment.

1. McGrath, J. and McGrath, A. (2001). *Self-Esteem: The cross and Christian confidence* (Leicester: IVP), p. 33.
2. Pervin, L. A. and John, O. P. (2001). *Personality: Theory and Research* (8th edition) (New York: Wiley), p. 184.
3. Crocker, J. and Park, L. E. (2003). 'Seeking: Construction, maintenance and protection of self-worth. in Leary, M. and Price Tangney, J. (Eds), *Handbook of Self and Identity* (New York/London: Guilford Press)

The way people respond to threats to their self-esteem or behave when their self-esteem is lowered is often associated with mental health issues, personality disorders and problematic behaviour. Both the avoidant personality disorder and the narcissistic personality disorder can be seen to be related to self-esteem issues.

The avoidant personality suffers from chronic extreme low self-esteem. Socially they are awkward and have difficulty forming social relationships. They find criticism and rejection very difficult to cope with and see others as superior and critical of them. Their thinking and interpretation of others is distorted, so that if someone is positive and accepting of them, they think that this person does not really know them. They avoid social situations and have a fear of rejection which they experience as anxiety in the few relationships they have. In contrast, the narcissistic personality feels special and superior and this affects the way they relate to others. This may be a strategy for defending a very fragile low self-esteem or evidence of an inflated level of self-esteem.[1]

The issues examined in this book reflect the ways in which people respond when they feel their self-esteem is threatened. One defence strategy is to avoid situations where failure is an anticipated outcome. In passive-aggressive behaviour patterns, the avoidance of conflict is a significant factor, especially if any expression of anger is seen as weakness, or conflict resolution is viewed in terms of a win/lose outcome. Another strategy, when the situation cannot be avoided, is to lower their expectations of the possible outcomes, thereby avoiding being disappointed by failure. This defensive pessimism is often a way of managing anxiety. However, this can be particularly difficult to manage in teams.

Baumeister[2] identifies self-handicapping as a strategy which may increase a person's chance of failure by deliberately taking alcohol, drugs or procrastinating and then attributing any poor performance to the self-induced handicap rather than personal ability. The excuses offered in passive-aggressive behaviour for failing to meet deadlines may be a manifestation

1. McGrath, J. and McGrath, A. (2001). *Self-Esteem: The cross and Christian confidence* (Leicester: IVP), pp. 54, 55.

2. Baumeister, R. F. (1998). 'The self', in Gilbert, D. T., Fiske, S. T. and Lindzey, G. (Eds) *Handbook of Social Psychology: Vol. 2* (4th edition) (New York: McGraw-Hill), pp. 680–740.

of this strategy, directing blame away from oneself and on to other external factors.

Of particular interest is the evidence which suggests that people respond to threats with anger and hostility and frequently lash out at others.[1] This is especially relevant in cases of domestic violence. The assumption that domestic violence is associated with low self-esteem in the perpetrators has been challenged by the lack of evidence to support this conclusively. Instead, the notion of threatened egotism provides a plausible explanation. We are used to hearing people speak of low self-esteem, with the implication that we should be working towards high self-esteem. However, it may be more helpful to think of self-esteem as a continuum, with mature self-esteem being situated between low self-esteem and inflated self-esteem. Inflated self-esteem, which is related to inflated egotism, is the source of a different set of problems, which often lead to violent behaviour. People like to think well of themselves, and generally react defensively to criticism.

If we take the case of domestic violence, for example, it is often suggested that male abusers must suffer from low self-esteem, and that the violence in some way restores their sense of maleness and power. It is perhaps more likely that men in violent relationships suffer from inflated self-esteem, and that perceived criticism from their female partner – nagging, silence, withdrawal of affection, refusal to provide whatever the man feels is necessary (for example, sexual contact) – can lead to the man's sense of himself being threatened. The man then has a choice: he either accepts the lower evaluation of himself or discredits the threat. Violence is often a way of discrediting the threat and re-establishing self-esteem.

This suggests that threatened high self-esteem is the cause of the violent aggressive behaviour rather than low self-esteem. In this case the man's belief in his superiority is threatened by his wife's superiority on some important dimension in their relationship. This makes him feel insecure, and he experiences threatened egotism which leads to him acting violently towards her. The cause of the violence is the threat posed to the man's belief in his own superiority. This can also explain the behaviour of hostile-

1. Baumeister, R. F., Smart, L. and Boden, J. M. (1996). 'Relation of threatened egotism to violence and aggression: The dark side of high self-esteem', *Psychological Review*, 103, 5–33.

aggressives whose threatened egos are expressed in anger and hostility when their plans are frustrated or challenged by others. Aggression is a response to fragile egotism which is characterised by a positive but vulnerable self-esteem. In spite of this behavioural response increasing the likelihood of rejection by others, the frustration experienced by the threat, particularly if it is experienced as unfair or unreasonable, triggers the aggressive response. Hostile-aggressives also adopt the strategy of focusing on the shortcomings of others when their self-esteem is threatened. They blame and ridicule others in order to inflate their own self-esteem by making comparisons with the negative evaluation they make of others.

Genuine, or mature, self-esteem is a true sense of self-worth, self-respect and an acceptance of one's strengths and weaknesses;[1] however, the findings indicate that instead of focusing on attaining this, people behave in ways that suggest they are naturally defensive and unwilling to acknowledge their weaknesses and shortcomings. It appears that the desire to maintain, enhance and protect self-esteem may lead to behaviours which detract from the ability to form and maintain caring relationships and may also damage physical and mental health.[2] The behaviours people adopt in response to threats to self-esteem – such as blame, anger, antagonism, aggression, avoidance and withdrawal[3] – reduce rather than enhance their chances of fulfilling their need for positive relationships. In addition, fluctuations in self-esteem are also associated with poor mental health, in particular depression and a number of personality disorders. There is also a relationship between self-esteem and the adoption of behaviours which have a negative impact on physical health, such as drinking alcohol, smoking and eating disorders.

To conclude, the idea that our sense of our self-worth is bound up with our appearance, achievements and what we do is a pervasive feature of our culture and environment. The goal of protecting, maintaining and increasing our levels of self-esteem is a major factor in our behaviour patterns. This

1. Rosenberg, M. (1979). *Conceiving the Self* (New York: Basic Books).
2. Crocker, J. and Park, L. E. (2003). 'Seeking: Construction, maintenance and protection of self-worth', in Leary, M. and Price Tangney, J. (Eds), *Handbook of Self and Identity* (New York/London: Guilford Press), pp. 304, 305.
3. Baumeister, R. F. (1998). 'The self', in Gilbert, D. T., Fiske, S. T. and Lindzey, G. (Eds), *Handbook of Social Psychology: Vol. 2* (4th edition) (New York: McGraw-Hill), pp. 680–740.

pursuit can have a damaging effect on relationships and on our physical and mental health, especially when self-esteem is threatened. This applies to those who have either a low or an inflated level of self-esteem, as shown above. In each of the issues addressed in this book, self-esteem is a significant factor in the explanation of the behaviour under examination.

Self-defeating behaviours

A number of the subjects dealt with in this book could be viewed as self-defeating behaviours. The cost to individuals of addictions, for example, often leads people to wonder why people begin to use drugs. The consequences of alcohol abuse or drug addiction can be devastating, leading to damage to health, broken relationships, significant financial loss if not poverty (which can lead to involvement in crime), with consequent damage. Other behaviours, such as bullying, may appear to benefit the perpetrator, but even here there are costs in terms of social relationships and self-worth, as society does not publicly condone bullying. Difficult people also suffer in various ways as a result of their behaviour. How do we account for these behaviours? Roy Baumeister, who has written extensively on this topic, identifies two key factors: threatened egotism and self-regulation failure. He adds that they are both related to emotional distress. Threatened egotism was discussed in the section on self-esteem. We will look now at self-regulation failure.

Self-regulation failure

Self-regulation (or self-control) is described as the ways in which we change our own responses, which can involve our thoughts, feelings and behaviours.[1] Many of the issues dealt with in this book relate to a failure of self-regulation – addictions, use of violence, sexual abuse, socially difficult behaviour, bullying. It has been suggested that success in life is a 'matter of being able to live with oneself and other people'.[2] From this perspective, these individuals are not making a success of their lives, which is one of

1. Baumeister, R. F. (1997). 'Esteem threat, self-regulatory breakdown, and emotional distress as factors in self-defeating behaviour', *Review of General Psychology*, 1 (2) 145–174.
2. Dolores Pushkar, quoted in Baumeister, R. F., Leith, K. P., Muraven, M. and Bratslavsky, E. (1998). 'Self-regulation as a key to success in life', in Pushkar, D., Bukowski, W. M., Schwartzman, A. E., Stack, D. M. and White, D. R. (Eds), *Improving Competence Across the Lifespan* (New York: Plenum).

the reasons that they demand our attention. What, then, does self-regulation involve? Baumeister outlines the following:[1]

- Affect regulation
- Control over our mental processes
- Managing our impulses
- Setting and reaching our goals
- Delay of gratification

The subject of addictions is vast and there has been considerable research into the causes of the various addictions, the characteristics of addictive behaviour and the personalities of addicts. However, one thing that all addictions appear to have in common is a desire in the person to change their emotional state. Alcohol relaxes people and disinhibits behaviour (even though it also acts as a depressant). Cigarettes stimulate, but, as a consequence of eliminating the craving that accompanies nicotine addiction, also lead to feelings of relaxation when the unpleasant feelings associated with withdrawal are removed. People who are addicted to internet pornography often use this to distract themselves from boredom, tiredness or loneliness, and become addicted to the excitement that internet sexual involvement provides. Some people can spend hours surfing sites to find more stimulating images, connect with more attractive partners or find other dates. Sex addicts use sex partly to change negative feelings into pleasurable ones, and child abusers pursue sexual contact with children for a range of reasons, one of which is emotional satisfaction. Gamblers appear to become involved in gambling partly as it distracts them from problems they face in their lives, as well as the thrill involved in hoping for the next big win. Bullies, presumably, feel a sense of superiority when they belittle, humiliate or exclude their victims, and violent men experience release of tension when they assault their partner. In all of these cases the behaviour has a mood-altering effect which is rewarding in the short term, even though it may result in poor consequences in the long term.

Another aspect of self-regulation is our ability to control our mental

1. Baumeister, R. F. and Heatherton, T. F. (1996). 'Self-regulation failure: An overview', *Psychological Inquiry*, 7, (1) 1–15.

processes. This is the foundation of cognitive-behavioural therapy, which is the therapeutic approach favoured with most of the behaviours outlined in this book. Sex offenders and addicts, for example, are taught in group therapy how to identify the triggers that lead to their abusive or addictive behaviour. These include negative mood states. Rather than seek the substances or behaviours that lead to loss of control or damage to another person, the individuals are taught how to identify the trigger and to take evasive action. This is the foundation of the approach known as Relapse Prevention.[1] Clearly, the earlier in the relapse chain that thinking and behaviour are changed, the more effective the outcome. The same is also true of violent behaviour in general, as the ability to stop and think and deliberately change our thinking can lead to more socially acceptable and self-beneficial behaviour.

There is little we can do to change our impulses, and attempting to control them can often lead to internal stress and tension which is not always healthy or helpful. Self-regulation involves acknowledging our impulses but refusing to give in to them. For example, a man may feel angry with his partner but that does not have to lead to violence. He can walk away, talk himself down or attempt to listen to his partner. This involves awareness of the impulse with a decision to behave in a different way. The same is true of addictions.

Self-regulation can fail because of underregulation or misregulation. Underregulation happens when we fail to make the effort to change a response that will lead to a more positive outcome. So, for example, a person who is dependent on alcohol may know from experience that regulating how much alcohol they drink feels outside their control. Walking into a pub thinking, 'I'll just have one drink', may be an example of underregulation, since the person is unlikely to be able to limit the amount of alcohol consumed and walk out of the pub sober. Similarly, if a person who is addicted to internet pornography switches on his computer late at night, he is setting himself up to fail as it only takes three clicks to find stimulating images. Misregulation involves efforts at changing which do not bring about the desired result – for example, using alcohol to

1. Marlatt, G. and Gordon, J. R. (Eds) (1985) *Relapse Prevention* (New York: Guilford Press).

change how we feel, leading to a hangover and social, relational, financial and health problems. There are healthier ways to change how we feel, and part of life is learning how to tolerate uncomfortable feelings.

Our goals are also related to self-regulation. If we want to live in harmony with others while respecting ourselves, then this precludes behaviours that will lead to alienation from others or feelings of shame, embarrassment or guilt. It is important to set goals that are appropriate and manageable, so that we are not setting ourselves up for failure.

Lastly it has been noted that people who can delay gratification are often more successful in life. Those who cannot tolerate frustration are more likely to react precipitously or give in to temptations. Baumeister describes self-control as a 'moral muscle' which gets depleted if over-used. It is interesting to note, for example, that more violent and impulsive crimes, or sexual acts that people later regret, happen more often in the very early hours of the morning than at other times.[1] It is suggested that after spending all day regulating our lives in various ways our supply of self-control may be used up. This is often compounded by the use of alcohol, which both relaxes and also disinhibits behaviours we might avoid when not under its influence. It would also appear to be the case, however, that this 'moral muscle' can be strengthened with practice and regular use, so, for example, attempting to give up alcohol, gambling, cigarettes or other addictive substances or behaviours may be more successful after several attempts, as the person learns from each attempt until success is finally achieved. This is reflected in the Motivational Interviewing approach to changing health behaviours, where it is accepted that relapse is part of recovery.[2] If people could accept that a lapse is a single mistake and not a catastrophe, then they could return to their attempted change of behaviour. Unfortunately, the combination of pleasure, relief from the stress of abstaining and the feelings of failure involved often leads to complete collapse rather than picking themselves up and starting again.

1. Baumeister, R. F. and Heatherton, T. F. (1996). 'Self-regulation failure: An overview', *Psychological Inquiry*, 7 (1) 3.
2. Miller, W. R. and Rollnick, S. (2002). *Motivational Interviewing: Preparing people for change* (London: Guilford Press), p. 213.

Negative moods

Negative moods are often involved in the various behaviours discussed in this book. Research has shown that when people experience negative mood states, especially when they are aroused as a result of feeling angry, embarrassed or frustrated, they are prone to making high-risk decisions. When people are not aroused and feel well, they are inclined to take low risks. In a sense, it is when people have little or nothing to lose (or feel that way) that the high risk with the promise of a big (emotional or financial) pay-off is more attractive. Inevitably this leads to self-defeating outcomes, and, with gamblers, substance abusers or sex offenders, outcomes that can jeopardise the well-being of others.

Men and women can be addicted to sex, gambling, alcohol, nicotine or any other substance, in order to help change their mood. It is also well known that part of the addictive process is the withdrawal effects of not having the substance (or experience). In order to maintain the same level of satisfaction, more of the drug is required. Biologically, addictions activate two different systems in the brain: the pleasure system and the reinforcement system. The pleasure system ceases to function while the reinforcement system continues to demand the substance or behaviour that leads to the neural changes to which the body has become accustomed.[1] Usually, this involves increases in the neurotransmitters of serotonin and dopamine, which lead to feelings of happiness and well-being. Once the body has learned that a behaviour or substance provides a shortcut to increased pleasure, it is difficult to change without experiencing the unpleasant sensations and feelings that are described as withdrawal symptoms.

Gender

Another important issue reflected in the topics dealt with in this book is the differences between men and women. Addictions can affect men and women, and there are female sex offenders and women who bully. However, there are important differences in these areas,[2] and in the area

1. Carlson, N. R. (2005). *Foundations of Biological Psychology* (London: Pearson).
2. Ciarrocchi, J. W. (2002). *Counselling Problem Gamblers* (London: Academic Press), p. 16; Center for Substance Abuse Treatment (1994). *Practical Approaches in the Treatment of Women who Abuse Alcohol and Other Drugs* (Rockville, Maryland: Department of Health and Human Services, Public Health Service).

of violence, as Lesley Orr has pointed out in her chapter on domestic violence. For example, men are 40 times more likely to kill another man than a woman is likely to kill another woman.[1] Anthony Clare noted that in domestic violence disputes women were twice more likely to be injured than men and much more likely to be victims of repeated attacks than men.[2]

Some people have argued that aggression is innate in men and that speed, courage and aggression were useful in the evolution of men to ensure the provision of food and in the competition for mates to guarantee reproduction. However, Clare argues that while aggression may be innate, malice is not. He quotes a researcher who examined the issue of male violence and concluded that biology is clearly important, but is not the sole factor. Social issues, such as deprivation, inequality, injustice, overcrowding, poverty and cultural attitudes, also play their part, as well as psychological factors, especially lack of affection, inconsistent or absent parenting, severely dysfunctional families and gender stereotypes. This is discussed in the chapter on adult bullying. It also helps to explain the kind of people who resort to violence that are described by Michael Fitzsimons in his chapter on violence in the workplace.

In the chapter on child abuse it was noted that not all sex offenders are men. Research on female offenders identifies three types:[3]

1. Women who abuse with a male
2. Women who sexually abuse teenage boys
3. Women who sexually abuse pre-pubescent children

Women who abuse with men are often in emotionally dependent relationships and act partly out of fear. The second group are often involved in unsatisfactory marriages and believe they have fallen in love. It appears that they can benefit from therapy as they are helped to work through their own emotional issues and confront the reality of the emotional and power imbalance in the abusive relationship. As with male offenders, they

1. Daly, M. and Wilson, M. (1988). *Homicide* (New York: Aldine de Gruyter).
2. Clare, A. (2000). *On Men* (London: Chatto and Windus).
3. Hunter, J. A. and Matthews, R. (1997). 'Sexual deviance in females', in Richard Laws, D. and O'Donohue, W. (Eds) *Sexual Deviance: Theory, assessment, and treatment* (New York: Guilford Press), pp. 465–480.

often become involved with emotionally needy adolescent males. The third category often comprises adolescent girls or women who were victims of abuse or emotional deprivation themselves. The gender issue is clearly important when dealing with this group as it is not appropriate to generalise from the experience of male offenders.

The same is true of bullying. It was suggested in the chapter on adult bullying that men tend to use direct aggression and women use indirect aggression. It has been suggested that one of the significant differences between men and women is that men tend to be better at constructing and dealing with systems (a system is anything that takes inputs and delivers outputs, such as a computer, a machine or weather patterns). Women tend to be better at empathising, which involves an ability to read the mind of another person and to predict a range of possible outcomes rather than only one possible outcome.[1] This is important, for bullying as direct aggression usually involves an unpleasant consequence that relates to the behaviour. Indirect aggression, on the other hand, requires an ability to read the mind of the other. A policy of exclusion, for example, or removal from an email list, is a more strategic behaviour, where the consequences may not be immediate or even visible, than a straightforward insult, harangue or sexual approach.[2]

One of the other significant differences between men and women relates to verbal ability, particularly in the area of articulating and expressing emotions. Men often feel ill-equipped to explain how they feel and this may be particularly galling if a female partner is belittling or critical. This involves a threat to the man's power and status. Lacking an ability to express their feelings, many men will resort to violence. Anthony Clare suggests that men's comparative inarticulacy compared to women's, particularly when trying to express their feelings, is a factor that contributes to male violence. Men often feel frustrated and resort to violence because they claim they cannot express their feelings in any other way. At the same time, men can also be verbally aggressive and intimidating.[3]

1. Baron-Cohen, S. (2003). *The Essential Difference* (UK: Penguin).
2. Baron-Cohen, S. (2003). *The Essential Difference* (UK: Penguin).
3. Clare, A. (2000). *On Men* (London: Chatto and Windus), p. 47.

Women's speech is more cooperative and focused on establishing relationships. Men's speech, however, is more competitive. Women are better at negotiating and articulating the perspective of the other and at taking turns. Men, on the other hand, want to dominate to make sure that their perspective is heard. It can be more difficult, in work situations, to deal with a man who is aggressive, as he may lack the skills to listen, see the perspective of others or negotiate.[1] High-status men often have better language skills as well as access to levers of power and influence, which they can use to achieve their goals.

Boundaries

Another important issue that emerges in the subjects dealt with in this book is that of boundaries. People with healthy boundaries know where their world ends and the world of the other begins. Bullies and people who resort to violence intrude on the personal boundaries of others in ways that cause fear, and possibly damage, to the victim or their reputation. People with problems of addictions often trespass on the boundaries of others, in terms of finance, relationships or contractual obligations. But they also cross personal boundaries in terms of self-worth or morality. Part of the wisdom of the Twelve Step tradition, which emerged out of Alcoholics Anonymous and has since been copied or adapted by other self-help groups, is the need to take a fearless self-inventory and to make amends to people who have been hurt or offended by the actions of the addict.

Healthy living requires an ability to know one's personal limits and how to respect the lives of other people. The various issues that are dealt with in this book all involve problems in terms of boundaries. Child abusers do not respect the physical, emotional, sexual and legal boundaries of the child. They allow their own needs to take precedence. Addicts in the grip of their addiction will sacrifice significant relationships and self-respect in pursuit of the 'fix', be it emotional or sexual. Bullies push uninvited into the living and work spaces of others to humiliate or belittle for personal satisfaction, or to appear powerful or clever in the eyes of others. Part of the responsibility of managers or clergy is to ensure that the rights of

1. Baron-Cohen, S. (2003). *The Essential Difference* (UK: Penguin).

others are respected and that difficult people do not trespass on or interfere with the work of others.

Religion and well-being

The subjects in this book relate to mental health and violent or difficult behaviours. People who exhibit these problems or behaviours are unlikely to be satisfied with their lives, even if some of their behaviours bring them momentary feelings of pleasure or happiness. There has been considerable research in recent years into the relationship between religiousness and life satisfaction. Diener and Myers cite research from the United States and across 14 Western nations which suggests that 'Happiness and life satisfaction rise with strength of religious affiliation and frequency of worship attendance'.[1] They note that religious people are less likely to become delinquent or indulge in other non-social behaviours. They are more likely to be happily married, be physically healthier and live longer. They are slightly less vulnerable to depression and report higher levels of well-being. They also note that highly spiritual people were twice as likely as other people to say they were 'very happy'. They report that the best predictors of well-being in the elderly were good health and participation in religion. They also report that those with a strong faith returned to positive levels of well-being more quickly after suffering a major loss.

One area of religiousness that has been the subject of reasonably thorough investigation is Gordon Allport's distinction between intrinsic and extrinsic religiousness.[2] Intrinsic religiousness is 'religion as a meaning-endowing framework', whereas extrinsic religiousness is defined as the 'religion of comfort and social convention'.[3] When extrinsics[4] and intrinsics are compared, intrinsics appear healthier on measures of well-being, internal locus of control and anxiety. Intrinsics also scored lower on factors

1. Diener, E. and Myers, D. G. (1995). 'Who is happy?', *Psychological Science*, 6, 10–19, p. 16.
2. Allport, G. W. (1954). *The Individual and His Religion: A psychological interpretation* (New York: Macmillan).
3. Donohue, M. J. (1985). 'Intrinsic and extrinsic religiousness: Review and meta-analysis', *Journal of Personality and Social Psychology*, 48, 400–419.
4. Alker, H. A. and Gawin, F. (1978). 'On the intrapsychic specificity of happiness', *Journal of Personality*, 46, 311–322.

labelled egocentric sexuality and restlessness, which could be related to use of sex as a coping mechanism and poor impulse control in people with addictions or those who have difficulty managing anger.

This research suggests that there are benefits for people who hold a sincerely held faith and level of church attendance, and numerous studies have linked spirituality to well-being. The sense of being connected to something larger than oneself, which is labelled transcendence, is also seen as life-enhancing. Spirituality has long been considered an important part of recovery for people caught in addictions. Similar research has also been done with sex offenders and pathological gamblers.[1]

The authors of the various chapters in this book have offered a section entitled 'A Christian response', in order to offer insights from the perspective of Christian faith. The research that has been presented in this section also suggests that religious faith, religious practices and spirituality can also help those whose behaviour is problematic, self-defeating or difficult, to manage their lives better, be more respectful of others and live with more personal satisfaction.

1. Ciarrocchi, J. W. and Deneke, E. (2004). 'Happiness and the varieties of religious experience: Religious support, practices, and spirituality as predictors of well-being', *Research in the Social Scientific Study of Religion*, 15, 235–262.

Conclusion

Why do people behave as they do? This book has attempted to analyse some complex, difficult and challenging behaviour patterns. Each human being is unique in both biology and experience. The interaction between our nature and our nurture and the underlying processes involved in determining how we think, feel and behave continue to be the focus of significant research which has far-reaching implications for applications in genetics and in finding effective intervention and treatment programmes, which it is hoped enhance psychosocial development for those who are at risk. Our unique personalities develop throughout our lifespan and are characterised by our emotional and behavioural responses. Emotion management and self-regulation have important implications for our own behaviour and well-being. Developments in psychology and counselling offer approaches to treatment that can help those who are motivated to manage negative emotions better, improving the quality of their lives and resulting in less distress and potential damage to the lives of others.

Appendices

Appendix 1

Gamblers Anonymous '20 Questions'

1. Did you ever lose time from work or school due to gambling?
2. Has gambling ever made your home life unhappy?
3. Did gambling affect your reputation?
4. Have you ever felt remorse after gambling?
5. Did you ever gamble to get money with which to pay debts or otherwise solve financial difficulties?
6. Did gambling cause a decrease in your ambition or efficiency?
7. After losing did you feel you must return as soon as possible and win back your losses?
8. After a win did you have a strong urge to return and win more?
9. Did you often gamble until your last dollar was gone?
10. Did you ever borrow to finance your gambling?
11. Have you ever sold anything to finance gambling?
12. Were you reluctant to use 'gambling money' for normal expenditures?
13. Did gambling make you careless of the welfare of yourself or your family?
14. Did you ever gamble longer than you had planned?
15. Have you ever gambled to escape worry or trouble?
16. Have you ever committed, or considered committing, an illegal act to finance gambling?
17. Did gambling cause you to have difficulty in sleeping?
18. Do arguments, disappointments or frustrations create within you an urge to gamble?
19. Did you ever have an urge to celebrate any good fortune by a few hours of gambling?
20. Have you ever considered self-destruction or suicide as a result of your gambling?

Most compulsive gamblers will answer 'Yes' to at least seven of these questions.

CAGE: A Screen for Alcohol Problems

1. Have you ever felt you should **C**ut down on your drinking? ('C')
2. Have people **A**nnoyed you by criticising your drinking? ('A')
3. Have you ever felt bad or **G**uilty about your drinking? ('G')
4. Have you ever had a drink first thing in the morning to steady your nerves or to get rid of a hangover? (**E**ye opener; 'E')

CAGE can identify alcohol problems over the lifetime. Two positive responses are considered a positive test.

DAST (Drug Abuse Screening Test)

1. Have you used drugs other than those required for medical reasons?
2. Do you abuse more than one drug at a time?
3. Are you always able to stop using drugs when you want to?
4. Have you had 'blackouts' or 'flashbacks' as a result of drug use?
5. Do you ever feel bad or guilty because of your use of drugs?
6. Does your spouse or a parent ever complain about your involvement with drugs?
7. Have you neglected your family because of your use of drugs?
8. Have you engaged in illegal activities in order to obtain drugs?
9. Have you ever experienced withdrawal symptoms (felt sick) when you stopped taking drugs?
10. Have you had medical problems as a result of your drug use (e.g. memory loss, hepatitis)?

Answering 'Yes' to five or more of these questions indicates a possible problem with drugs.

Appendix 2

USHAW COLLEGE
BULLYING AND HARASSMENT POLICY

1.0 BULLYING AND HARASSMENT

Ushaw College is committed to developing a working environment in which bullying and harassment are known to be unacceptable and are not tolerated at any level of the organisation. The College seeks to ensure that every individual can work effectively in comfort and dignity. The College will provide any employee who suffers bullying or harassment with an appropriate form of redress and seeks to guarantee that complainants will not encounter any form of reprisal or victimisation as a result of their complaint.

2.0 OBJECTIVES

The objectives of this policy are to:

- Create a supportive working environment free from all forms of bullying and harassment
- Prevent the harassment and victimisation of employees in the workplace
- Make explicit those behaviours which will not be tolerated.
- Provide practical guidance to all employees on how to deal with harassment and bullying
- Deal with any allegation of harassment seriously, confidentially and with the utmost discretion
- Encourage all employees to behave in an appropriate manner at all times
- Communicate the procedures relating to harassment and ensure that they are implemented

3.0 DEFINITIONS

3.1 Harassment

Harassment is defined as unreciprocated and unwelcome comments or actions, which are considered objectionable by the recipient. The policy encompasses harassment with regard to gender, race, sexuality, disability, religion, age or political views. The three main forms of harassment are sexual, racial and disability. Types of behaviour the policy seeks to prevent include:

- unwelcome sexual remarks, jokes or verbal abuse
- unwanted physical contact
- the display of pornographic pictures
- behaviour which ridicules an individual because of their sexuality
- racially derogatory remarks or racist jokes
- the display of racially offensive material

3.2 Bullying

Bullying is defined as persistent actions, criticism or personal abuse, which humiliates, intimidates or undermines the individual involved. Bullying can involve a person in authority abusing their power and bullying subordinates or an individual bullying a peer or a group of people picking on one individual. Bullying can take varying forms including:

- severe verbal abuse
- intimidating or aggressive behaviour
- excessive teasing or humiliation
- imposing unrealistic targets
- unfair and excessive criticism, possibly in front of colleagues
- isolating or openly ignoring someone
- physical assault
- taking credit for others' initiatives and achievements
- sending abusive or intimidating messages by email

As with harassment, bullying is defined largely by the *impact* of the behaviour on the recipient, *not* its intention.

4.0 EFFECTS OF HARASSMENT

Harassment carries with it a high price for both the College and its employees. Ushaw College recognises that harassment can cause employees to be subject to fear, stress and anxiety, which can put great strains on personal and family life. It can lead to illness, increased absenteeism, an apparent lack of commitment, poor performance and even resignation. All these have a direct impact on organisational effectiveness.

The damage, tension and conflict within the workplace which harassment creates not only results in poor morale but higher labour turnover, reduced productivity, lower efficiency and divided teams. Although the effects may be difficult to quantify, they will eventually show through in the performance of the Company.

Certain types of harassment may constitute unlawful discrimination under the Sex Discrimination Act 1975, the Race Relations Act 1976 and the Disability Discrimination Act 1995.

5.0 RESPONSIBILITIES

All employees are responsible for their individual compliance with the terms of this policy and for the development of a working environment in which the dignity of all employees is respected.

All Managers have a duty to ensure that harassment does not occur in work areas for which they are responsible. Managers have a further responsibility to explain the College's policy to their staff and to take steps to positively promote the policy.

All Managers/Supervisors must be responsive and supportive to any member of staff who complains about harassment; provide advice on the procedure to be adopted and maintain confidentiality.

It is the responsibility of the Senior Management Team to regularly review complaints of harassment and bullying and how they have been resolved, in order to ensure that the College's policy is working effectively.

The complainant should be contacted following the formal resolution of the problem to establish whether the solution has been effective. Where it has not, further action may be necessary.

All employees and in particular Supervisors/Managers, etc. have responsibilities to ensure the continuing success of the implementation of the policy by:

- refraining from harassment and bullying
- bringing to the attention of the Management any suspected practices in breach of this policy
- working together to promote a harmonious working environment free from all forms of bullying and harassment

No Manager shall threaten or insinuate, either explicitly or implicitly, that an employee's rejection of sexual advances will be used as a basis for an employment decision affecting that employee. Such conduct by a manager will be treated as a serious offence.

Disciplinary action, up to and including dismissal, will be taken against those failing to fulfil their responsibilities under this policy.

6.0 BULLYING AND HARASSMENT COMPLAINTS PROCEDURE

An employee subjected to bullying or harassment has two options in seeking a resolution: an informal and formal approach. (These options are not mutually exclusive.)

6.1 Informal Approach

An employee can seek confidential informal advice and support from their Manager or the President.

In certain instances it may be appropriate for the complainant to approach the alleged perpetrator personally indicating that a particular action is regarded as offensive. The complainant should warn the alleged perpetrator that should the behaviour continue a formal complaint will be made to the alleged perpetrator's line manager. The threat of a formal complaint will often be sufficient to dissuade the alleged perpetrator from repeating the behaviour. Alternatively the complainant can request a colleague or Manager to speak to the alleged perpetrator informally.

If the informal approach has proved ineffective or the alleged offence is of a serious nature it may be necessary to adopt a formal approach.

6.2 Formal Approach

At all times, whether or not informal steps have been taken, any employee who feels that they have been harassed or bullied may make a formal complaint.

Because of the sensitivity of such complaints and the need to resolve them speedily, the complaint should be made in writing and sent to the complainant's Manager as soon as possible.

Should the allegation be made against the Manager, the written complaint should be sent to a more senior level of Management, i.e. the President.

Every effort should be made to address the issue within five working days from the receipt of the complaint.

6.3 Investigation Procedure – Formal Approach Only

The President will ensure that a full investigation is made into any allegation of bullying or harassment.

The complainant and the person against whom the allegations are made will be interviewed separately and the proceedings will be confidential.

Both the complainant and the person against whom the allegations are made may be accompanied or represented at all stages of the procedure by a fellow employee. The individual under investigation and the complainant must understand that no victimisation, as a result of the complaint, is to occur.

Any witnesses will be interviewed and will be required to respect the need for confidentiality. Any breach of this confidentiality may result in disciplinary action.

An accurate record will be made of the investigation and its conclusion. Both the complainant and the person against whom the allegations are made will be informed in writing of the findings of the investigation and the action to be taken within five working days after the conclusion of the investigation.

6.4 Outcome

If, following investigation, it is found that bullying/harassment has taken place, appropriate use should be made of the College's Disciplinary Procedure. **Disciplinary action up to and including the possibility of dismissal may be taken**.

If it is considered appropriate to issue a disciplinary warning, it may be necessary to consider an alternative post or reallocation of work for the offender in order that they and the complainant do not continue to work together should they work in close proximity.

If an employee is dissatisfied with any disciplinary decision an appeal can be made in accordance with the company's Appeals Procedure.

If, following investigation, it is considered that no bullying or harassment has taken place, any record of the accusation will be removed from the accused's personal file.

Employees shall be protected from intimidation, victimisation or discrimination for filing a complaint or assisting in an investigation. Retaliating against an employee for complaining about harassment is a disciplinary offence.

It must also be advised that any employee who raises a complaint, which upon investigation is proven to be deliberately vexatious, then that employee will themselves become the subject of disciplinary proceedings.

If the complainant is not satisfied with the outcome then they may ask to have the case reviewed by the Senior Management Team.

Any allegation of harassment or bullying which is found to be malicious will also be treated as a serious disciplinary offence.

About the Contributors

Alan Bartlett is an Anglican priest. He is currently the St John's College Director of the Durham Doctor of Ministry programme, involved in the teaching and supervision of Practical Theology. Previously he was a curate in West Newcastle and a youth worker in Bermondsey. He is married with two teenage children. He has published *Humane Christianity* (Darton, Longman and Todd, 2004) and *A Passionate Balance: The Anglican Tradition* (Darton, Longman and Todd, 2007).

Mark Brouwer is an ordained pastor in the Christian Reformed Church, and serves full-time as a trainer and recovery coach in the field of sex addiction. He has been the founding pastor of two new churches, serving as senior pastor for 15 years. He now coordinates workshops and training events for Faithful and True Ministries (a counselling and recovery ministry), teaches seminars about sexuality and healthy leadership, and coaches people in recovery from sex addiction. He is married and has two teenage children.

Jocelyn Bryan is a tutor at the Wesley Study Centre, Durham, and a Methodist local preacher. She teaches Psychology and Christian Ministry, Sexuality, Gender and Christian Ministry and some Practical Theology. Her PhD is in psychology, where she studied ageing and memory. Her research interest is in the interface between psychology, theology and Christian ministry, and she has published on adolescence. She is married and has three teenage children.

Christopher C. H. Cook is a Professorial Research Fellow in the Department of Theology and Religion at Durham University. He trained at St George's Hospital Medical School, London, and has worked in the psychiatry of substance misuse for 22 years. He worked as Professor of the Psychiatry of Alcohol Misuse at the University of Kent from 1997 to 2003. He was ordained as an Anglican priest in Canterbury Cathedral in 2001. He is interested in spirituality, theology and mental health, and has published a book on *Alcohol, Addiction and Christian Ethics* (Cambridge University Press, 2006).

Michael Fitzsimons is a Catholic priest. He is currently assistant priest at the parish of Christ the King and Our Lady in Liverpool. Prior to entering the priesthood Michael trained as a youth and community worker and has experience of working with young people and adults in a wide variety of settings, including projects working with homeless people, detached youth work, community projects and prisons.

Brendan Geary is a Marist brother, and Director of Human Formation at Ushaw College, the Catholic seminary for the North of England. He has worked as a teacher, spiritual director and psychotherapist, and specialised in work with victims and perpetrators of sexual abuse. He has worked in the United Kingdom, Africa and the United States, and has published papers on sex offenders, counselling and spirituality.

Mark Laaser is the founder of Faithful and True Ministries, a counselling and recovery ministry focused on sex addiction. He is the author of numerous books, including *Healing the Wounds of Sexual Addiction* (Zondervan, 2004), *The Pornography Trap* (Beacon Hill Press of Kansas City, 2002) and *The LIFE Guide for Men* (Xulon Press, 2002). He is a frequent guest on radio and television shows that deal with recovery from sex addiction, and has been a lecturer, workshop leader, seminar designer and presenter for the last 20 years. He is married and has three adult children.

Edmund Montgomery is a seminarian at Ushaw College, Durham, preparing for ordination to the Catholic priesthood. Before beginning his formation at seminary he read Law at the University of Derby, graduating in 2005, and completed the BA in Theology and Ministry, accredited by the University of Durham, in June 2008.

Alison Moore currently works as Adviser in Pastoral Care and Counselling for the Diocese of Durham, Church of England. She trained in counselling in the 1980s, for many years specialising in work with conflicted relationships. She is now responsible for running the diocesan counselling service in Durham. Training and consultancy in pastoral care for parish groups and ministers also make up a large part of her role. She is committed to being a good 'translator' of technical language, whether therapeutic or theological, which can be both incomprehensible and disempowering to those who encounter it.

Lesley Orr is a historian, writer and activist, previously at Glasgow University and currently based at Scottish Women's Aid to develop the Scottish Government's national strategy to address violence against women. She has degrees in philosophy, politics, theology and ecclesiastical history, and has researched, published and taught practical theology, religious and social history. She was consultant to the World Council of Churches project 'Overcoming Violence Against Women,' and coordinated an action-research project at Edinburgh University entitled *Out of the Shadows: Christianity and violence against women in Scotland*. Her roots are in the Church of Scotland and she has a lifelong involvement in the ecumenical Iona Community.

James Walsh is a Catholic layman. He is a licensed pastoral counsellor working in private practice in Newark, Delaware, USA. He is also Assistant Professor of Community Counselling at Wilmington University, where he teaches on a variety of topics, including Psychopathology and Addiction, and provides supervision of clinical interns. He has been working to help compulsive gamblers and their families for over ten years as a national certified gambling counsellor, and has published research on gambling and spirituality. He is married and has two adult children.

Index of Subjects

Index of Authors